BORN S̶ ̶N̶G̶

From Surviving the Great Famine to Teaching Tai Chi to Millions

To Maria
May you tie flowers

Paul L

DR. PAUL LAM

with Julie Bawden-Davis

Tai Chi Productions

Copyright © 2015 Paul Lam
Published by Tai Chi Productions
6 Fisher Place
Narwee, NSW 2209 Australia

ISBN: 978-0-9925128-2-8 Print version
ISBN: 978-0-9925128-3-5 Ebook version
Library of Congress Control Number: 2015902554

Printed in South Korea
by Four Colour Print Group, Louisville, Kentucky

Cover design by Cathy Klein
Book design by Andrea Leljak
Cover photo by Hazel Thompson
Publishing services by eFrog Press (www.efrogpress.com)

To Aunt, whose unconditional love gave me strength.

FOREWORD AND ACKNOWLEDGEMENTS

In 2009, I took a group of my tai chi family to meet my family in China. When the two families met and emotions ran high, I became so moved by the experience that it sparked a burning desire to share my life story. The fact that many members of my Tai Chi for Health family urged me to write this book proved that it was time to share my life journey.

For more than five years, I expended much time and energy writing this book. I found the task enormously challenging. At times the pain and pleasure of revisiting my often tumultuous past weighed heavily on me and felt almost unbearable.

My intention with this book is to share through my life experience my belief that no matter how desperate things are, there is always hope. With hard work and love you can overcome almost anything. Tai chi transformed my life, and I want to share how effective the Tai Chi for Health program is at improving health and wellness. Whatever you seek with tai chi, I am sure you'll gain much more in return for your efforts. Whether you wish increased mobility, pain relief, development of inner strength and serenity, or life fulfillment; tai chi will bring you more benefits than I can begin to describe.

Tai chi helped me to engage and overcome my challenges so that I could enjoy my life more fully, as well as develop my personal growth and harmony. The transformational practice empowered me to turn the emotional turmoil invoked by writing this memoir into a healing process.

There are numerous people I would like to thank for helping to make this book a reality. There are really too many individuals to list, but I will mention a few. Thanks to my publisher, Linda Scott, who encouraged and assisted me at every stage with her heart and passion; and my editor, Julie Bawden-Davis, whose magical writing made my voice clear and audible. My story could not be told as truly without her amazing skill.

Thanks also to my family: Eunice, Matthew, Andrea, and my brothers and sisters. A special mention for my nephew, Dr. Vincent Lam, whose advice as a world-renowned writer was most valuable. Also, thank you to members of my school, especially Pat Webber, Sybil Wong, Dr. Janet Cromb, Fiona Black, Marta Venegas, and Philo and Mati Kaarma. Many people have assisted in varying and very valuable ways, including Dr. Pam Kircher, Caroline Demoise, Elizabeth Mitchell, Dr. Rhayun Song, Dr. Tang Ching Lau, Marty Kidder, Bob Casey, Anne Bower, John and Sandy Walter, Robin and Doug Malby, Anna Bennett, Shelia Rae, Carmen Murray, Jennifer Chung, Simon Yuen, and Nuala Perrin.

I am most grateful to Hazel Thompson, who converted my dictation to readable text. Enthusiastic and empathetic to my story and intention, Hazel created a safe place in my heart that helped stimulate my thinking and brought forth my past without rekindling feelings of insecurity. Without Hazel's help, this book would not have been possible.

CONTENTS

PART THREE: *Australia*

PART FOUR: *The World*

INTRODUCTION

May 15, 2010: Wellness Day, People's Association Headquarters, Singapore

In the deep of the night, I huddled with Aunt in the cramped storeroom four of us called home since being evicted from the family estate. I tried to close my ears to the jeers and shouts in the courtyard while Aunt anchored me by pulling me even tighter to her skeletal chest. Yet again the Communists had come, bursting into the room after dark and dragging my frail grandmother out into the courtyard for another savage beating. Trapped and powerless in the time of the Midnight Terrors, fear besieged us.

My heart pounded and my palms sweated as the shouting became even louder. With a shock, I snapped back to the present as I realized that time in China occurred long ago. I stood onstage in Singapore at a huge public event. The shouting came from an excited audience waiting to learn tai chi from me.

I stood on the stage built especially for this Wellness Day occasion as the grand field in front of me brimmed with participants, official photographers, videographers, and TV and newspaper crews. Regaining composure, I welcomed a thunderous cheer from the audience. Two thousand people traveled here to this field in Singapore in the early morning hours to learn from me about the life-altering possibilities of tai chi.

Taking a deep breath, I straightened my posture and put my mind into "upright" awareness, expanding my joints from within, and welcoming the energy that coursed through my body. This balancing calmed my mind, putting me in a *jing* state—mindful, serene, in the present. I gestured with my arms to introduce the two CEOs of the People's Association flanking me and Professor Lau—my colleague, assistant, and translator. This action sparked another giant cheer.

Then I led the audience in my warm-up exercises, first walking in place to loosen joints and then standing with feet shoulder width apart. Extending my arms in front of me with palms facing toward me, I brought my hands inches from my face, then turned the palms outward and slowly extended my arms while stretching my neck and shoulders.

As we continued, I shared the moves from my Tai Chi for Arthritis program, always attuned to the crowd, thanks to a skill Aunt taught me as a child. "When you enter a room, Bon Trong," she told me, using my given name, "you must stop and absorb the mood before you act or react. Only then should you proceed." Unlike the Communist crowd brainwashed by Chairman Mao to beat Grandmother all those years ago, this crowd emanated a palatable positive energy that I gladly embraced. My grandmother and aunt would be so proud!

Focusing on tai chi, I cleared my mind, banishing my childhood fears. While my tumultuous early life was a past reality, I remained mindful that for thirty-eight years I had introduced people all over the globe to the wonders of tai chi and its ability to improve health and wellness in a wide variety of ways. For many, those improvements proved transformational.

My life journey that started with a harrowing childhood in Communist China surviving the Great Famine, though fraught with pain and suffering, brought me to that stage on that particular day. As I looked out at the sea of smiling faces, I knew I had finally reached a place of peace from where I could spread more precious peace. My calling to share tai chi with the world empowered me to conquer my traumatic past. This was a true miracle, because on many occasions during my young life, it did not appear that I would live very long at all.

PART ONE

China

CHAPTER 1

LEFT BEHIND IN CHINA

Fortune and flowers do not last forever.
— Chinese proverb

My father had to be mistaken the day he named me Bon Trong. Meaning "born to be strong" in Chinese, my given name taunted me for many years.

Born in 1948 in Vietnam, the fourth child of Chinese parents, I entered the world happy; but several illnesses lay in wait to claim me during my infancy, including the potentially fatal tentacles of diphtheria.

My father said that I used to laugh happily when he carried me, but then the leading baby killer in that part of the world came to call on my little body, and everything changed.

No treatment existed back then. They banished babies with diphtheria to an isolation hospital to eventually perish. But my father refused to give up on me. Instead, he kept me home, locating a French doctor who claimed to be able to cure the childhood scourge with a radical new treatment involving administering large injections directly into the lower abdomen.

Despite his meager wages as an English teacher, my father managed to scrape together enough money for one week of the exorbitantly priced treatment. Right before the money ran out, my fever broke, and I recovered quickly.

My father had no way of knowing at the time, but the "doctor's" sham of a treatment had nothing to do with my recovery. As a matter of fact, I learned years later after my medical training that the injections directly into my abdomen could have perforated my bowel and threatened my life with peritonitis. I am convinced that my father's love and faith saved me.

Sadly for my father, after that week of holding me down while the French doctor administered the injections, I no longer laughed and smiled when he approached. Instead, I screamed every time he came near me.

My time with my father would be limited. When I was ten months old, my mother brought me on a fateful trip to visit my paternal and maternal grandmothers in Southern China. My older brothers and sister also went on the trip and returned to Saigon after the visit finished, but I did not make the return flight.

According to Chinese tradition, in order to ascend to heaven, a direct male relative must see you off at your death ceremony. My father was an only child and lived too far away to take on this responsibility, so my paternal grandmother wanted one of her son's children to see her off to her celestial home. Upon hearing of the request by letter, my father instructed my mother to comply. In the tradition of fealty to your parents, he told her, it was their cultural obligation.

Though they told me later that Grandmother requested that my mother leave behind my next-oldest brother, Bon Quoc ("born to be solid"), to see her off into heaven, Mother didn't want to part with her cute and happy four-year-old, so she had the idea to leave me, her infant son. At first she felt torn over the decision, but the conflict resolved itself when she came to think of my near-death from diphtheria as an omen from the gods that I did not belong to her. Destiny meant for me to belong instead to my grandmother. On the practical side, mother also realized that a ten-month-old baby required a lot more care than a four-year-old. Mother took my siblings and returned to Vietnam without me. I would never live with them again.

Since I was less than a year old when she gave me to my grandmother, I don't consciously remember being left behind, though in later years I wondered why I ended up living with Grandmother. For a long time, I struggled greatly with feelings of abandonment. In true Chinese fashion, I believed the abandonment was my fault. As a baby, though, I lived a princely life in Grandmother's house.

A dignified lady of few words, Grandmother carried herself in the style befitting a well-respected Chinese matriarch. She wore her jet-black hair in a classical bun at the nape of her neck; her skin was lustrous porcelain; and she possessed slender, delicately curved eyebrows. Normally stern with others, around me she appeared gentle, smiling, and indulgent. Grandmother often prayed to her gods to direct the mosquitoes to bite her instead of me, and her prayers worked. Throughout my life, mosquitoes have avoided me, preferring to feast on others. My children are allergic to mosquito bites and are bitten when I am spared. Unfortunately, no matter how vigorously I appealed to the gods to keep the mosquitos away from my kids and to bite me instead—it didn't work!

I could and did try Grandmother's patience, however, like the Chinese New Year when I was two years old. On this most important day of the year, Grandmother had Aunt scrub the eleven-room house for the occasion. In order to guarantee that the interior remained spotless and ready for the many visitors to soon come calling, Grandmother sent me and a playmate outside to keep ourselves occupied. What fun we experienced when we had the inspired idea to relieve ourselves in the soft, clay earth. After we finished urinating, we noticed that the moist soil had formed yellow mud cakes. They seemed a splendid contribution to the New Year celebration, so we separated them from the dry soil and carried our offerings into the house, placing them in the center of the lounge room on the gleaming terra-cotta tile floor.

Chinese New Year is an auspicious occasion when even the poorest families gather to share the most elaborate meals they can manage. Because it is an optimistic time considered to set the tone for the rest of the year, it is bad luck to exchange harsh words or scold children on the first day of the New Year. For this reason, though Grandmother's eyes filled with flames, she held her tongue when she saw the yellow cakes on her freshly scrubbed floor. Instead, to comfort and reassure herself, she muttered, "Just wait until tomorrow." Although I don't remember anything monumental happening the next day.

Every day of the year, Grandmother took great pride in keeping her treasured house as spotless as possible. The building was constructed at the rear of the original family house that dated back to about the time that Captain Cook first set eyes on Australia nearly two hundred and fifty years prior. Our ancestor, an important national government minister, built the old house for his retirement years. His position of power and respect was rare for a person from that part of China because the ruling Northerners considered Southerners like my ancestors less cultured and even "barbarians."

Built in classical Chinese style, the old house was incredibly grand for that period in that part of China. A huge front door flanked by stone lions opened into a forecourt paved with stone slabs. Rooms lined both sides, and a doorway led through to the central courtyard, beyond which lay the elegant formal lounge. There was located the spiritual center of the compound, where the family held ancestor-worship ceremonies, greeted the most honored guests, and held major household meetings. Two smaller side entrances led to more rooms and opened into a large backyard. The entire structure stood thanks to the support of solid granite pillars and carved wooden beams magnificently painted with figures and scenes. (These pillars remain today, but the beams and their artwork were destroyed or taken by Red Guards in the 1960s during China's Cultural Revolution.)

Though the old house remained grand, the family coffers had become depleted by the time my paternal great-grandfather reached adulthood. In their turn, my grandfather and his elder brother ventured overseas to seek a new family fortune. They landed in Vietnam, worked long and hard and eventually established a large store—six shops joined together—selling fishing supplies in Cholon, the Chinatown of Saigon. The buildings still stand today, but the store, Lam Har San, was divided into six different shops. The family business eventually went broke, about thirty years following the death of both brothers.

Around 1930, my grandfather sent money back home to build the new house in the backyard of the grand old house. Though it took months to travel between China and Vietnam by ship, and the journey proved treacherous, the Lams kept two family homes and lived divided. Most of the family lived in Vietnam where they made the money, but they always had a base in China. So when my grandfather lived in Vietnam, he sent money to care for his wife in China and to build her a new home. By the time I arrived, however, my grandfather had died ten years earlier. According to Chinese tradition, upon his death, his elder brother should take over care of his brother's family. That meant that during the Japanese invasion in China, my widowed grandmother fled to Vietnam to live with her brother-in-law in 1938, but went back to China as soon as the country defeated Japan in 1946.

Grandmother returned to reign over her new, eleven-room home. As for the old house, the family sold much of the structure. They managed to keep the central lounge and a few rooms. In the lounge lay an altar that held ancestral tablets carved with the names of ancestors. There during festive seasons, the family honored ancestors and made offerings to the gods. Grandmother also used part of the building for storage, including the tiny room off the central lounge that contained a stockpile of rice. No one gave much thought to the room at the time, but it would one day become my universe.

In 1950, our household consisted of my paternal grandmother; Aunt (Ma Xiang); Aunt's adopted son, Ben Zheng; and the young manservant whom we called Little Uncle.

At the age of fourteen, my aunt married my father's cousin. The Lam family, like many Chinese families, was very inclusive. My grandfather and his brother treated both families as one. All cousins were ranked and treated as siblings, and the extended family lived in the same house (families in both countries had big houses).

Aunt's husband was a gambler and an opium addict before marriage. The parents arranged the marriage hoping the union would transform him, but it did not. As a result, Aunt became the scapegoat for his transgressions, despite the fact that she was still a child and unequipped to control an adult male with two addictions, particularly in an era when women had no rights. Everyone treated her badly, except Grandmother and my father, and things got much worse when her husband died from an overdose at the age of thirty. After his death when the opportunity came along, Aunt gladly opted for the chance to live with Grandmother in China.

A small, delicate lady with gentle features, Aunt spoke softly, moved quietly, and absorbed the mood of others. All those years of living at the bottom of the family taught her survival skills. She learned to anticipate everyone's feelings and desires because she had to please everyone. This responsibility came naturally to Aunt, who epitomized pure kindness. Even at our lowest, most desperate times, she still worried about anyone in trouble, like the beggars on the street, despite the fact that we weren't far removed from them.

Young children possess a sixth sense like animals. They know if people like and care for them. The moment we met, I immediately gravitated to Aunt. Whenever she came near me, I stopped crying, and she lulled me into contentment when she carried me around like her joey (a baby kangaroo inside its mother's pouch). Cousin Zheng, who Aunt adopted at three years old, was fifteen years older than me. He enjoyed hoisting me onto his shoulders and walking me around the village to show off my perpetual smile.

Grandmother treated me like a prince, Aunt gave me unconditional love, Zheng showed me off, and we lived in a beautiful house.

For a moment, life was sweet.

CHAPTER 2

THE END OF GRANDMOTHER'S WALK ON EARTH

*A child's life is like a piece of paper
on which every person leaves a mark.*
— Chinese proverb

Like the traditional matriarch that she was, Grandmother believed that if you were a good person—charitable and respectful of your elders and authority—you would be treated justly by the gods and the emperor and government. By following that time-honored rule, she had always gained the respect of everyone around her. And she held her head high because of that respect.

But traditional China was coming undone.

After decisive victories against Chiang Kai-shek's nationalist Kuomintang in the decades-long Chinese civil war, Mao Zedong proclaimed the formation of the People's Republic of China on October 1, 1949, and became chairman. Information traveled slowly in those days, and Chairman Mao's Communist Party of China (CPC) had yet to take control of our part of China. Two months later, when my mother left me with Grandmother and returned to Vietnam, life appeared to be moving along as usual. Mother sailed off with my siblings, content in the knowledge that she had fulfilled my grandmother's request for me to see her into the next life. She had no idea that I would fulfill that obligation much sooner than anyone would expect and that she had consigned me to a life of hell.

From 1950 through 1951, the CPC implemented the Land Reform Law aimed at redistributing property and wealth amongst the people. Disguised as a high-minded ideal that would deliver

Chinese peasants (the vast majority of the country's population) from exploitation by landowners, the land reform resulted in bloodshed. This bloodshed fulfilled Chairman Mao's documented behind-the-scenes desire to destroy millions of people in order to facilitate agrarian reform. The process of seizing land from one class of society and giving control of it to another resulted in violence, millions of deaths, coercion, reverse exploitation, and base opportunism—all government sanctioned.

CPC officials traveled to each city, town, and village in the vast country and worked with the locals to identify the so-called "rich" people they believed were exploiting the poor who worked for them. They seized everything from the more well-to-do residents— including homes, money, livestock, tools, and land—and gave it all to the villagers. The officials encouraged public humiliations and executions. The more people denounced, according to Chairman Mao's plan, the more secure would be the Communists' rule.

Just a few days after I made the mud cakes, Grandmother was trampled in this stampede of greed.

Our ancestral house had been passed down through the generations and the new house was built with overseas money. My grandfather had also purchased a small plot of land with that same money. According to the strict definitions laid out by the CPC, because Grandfather spent overseas money, our family didn't exploit the people. But foxes like Ah Noh (a childhood nickname meaning "little boy") lay in wait, ready to pounce on any opportunity. A farmer who worked the land along with his own, Ah Noh paid us whatever he felt appropriate in rent, which usually amounted to nothing. His demands weren't disputed by two powerless widowed ladies, a teenager, and a two-year-old. With no man to defend Grandmother's house, Ah Noh saw his chance and accused her of exploiting him. Other former friends and neighbors cast their allegiance to her aside for their own prosperity and also rushed in to denounce Grandmother. The CPC then classified us as landlords, and as a result, they seized our plot of land and the houses and their contents and divided our estate among many families, who took possession of our former home.

As "enemies of the people," landlords endured unrelenting persecution and discrimination, and the label would never be removed. We were relegated to live in the rice storage room of the old house. As the head of the family, Grandmother bore the brunt of the punishment.

If only it had stopped at eviction. For more than four years, CPC officials forced Grandmother to visit the local Communist office during the day for interrogations, and on many nights the wolves visited our meager living quarters. Fists pounding on the storeroom door jolted us awake, and they dragged Grandmother into the courtyard outside our room and beat her. When it rained, they commanded her to stand under the junction of the gutters where the water pounded on her back and head until she collapsed. Other times they pushed Grandmother down to kneel on broken shells. On too many occasions to count, her tormenters, which included former acquaintances, returned her to us badly injured. Aunt, Cousin Zheng and I had no choice but to huddle in the little storage room, helpless against the animals that relentlessly tortured a defenseless old lady. During those times of the Midnight Terrors, overwhelming fear seized me. To this day the terror still surfaces on rare occasions, such as when I hear a sudden, unexpected loud noise or I'm wakened from a sound sleep.

Grandmother mourned the loss of our house and belongings, the loss of respect and dignity, but worst of all the humiliation and repeated physical abuse. She prayed to her gods for rescue, but the gods did not respond to her prayers. Twisted in torment physically, emotionally, and spiritually, Grandmother's face grew dark and sullen. We tiptoed around her, our hearts filled with sadness and dread of a worst fate about to spring its ugly head on all of us at any time. Living with the oppressive weight of worry and fear, we seldom went outside, except for food and supplies.

I know now that Aunt transported me through those dark days. At the worst of times, I rested my head on her chest and hugged her body, feeling her warmth and love, which made me feel safe and comfortable. She always hugged me during times of stress—like the Midnight Terrors. During those moments in her arms, Aunt was my world—only love and comfort. Nothing else mattered.

About two years after the Land Reform began, the CPC gave Aunt permission to work, so she became a street vendor. Carrying two baskets of needles and threads and other light household items, she rose early each day and went to the market, selling for miniscule profit. Four years old at the time, I remember excitedly awaiting her return from the market. Every day she brought me something, such as a tiny piece of candy or a preserved olive. I loved my treat, but Aunt's return was the true sunshine of my day.

Though it should have filled Grandmother with pride, what occurred when I started school may have triggered her death. Soon after I turned six, Zheng took me to my first day of school. I remember it being very busy. The school seemed large, with many children running around chasing each other, at least for the first few days. Born early in the year, I was the youngest in my class.

I loved reading even at preschool age, so by the time I entered school, I could read around the third grade level. One day my teacher praised me on my reading skills. By then the other kids knew of my "black label" as a landlord, so they reacted negatively to the praise I received. After class, a couple of kids pushed me to the ground and spat on me, yelling, "You pig! You dirty landlord's kid. You think you are so clever. We will show human garbage who's the boss."

According to Chinese tradition at that time, when one kid bullied another, the parents of the two children would talk, and the bully would be chastised. I went home in tears to tell Grandmother about my altercation.

"Ah B, you must pretend to be dumb. Just stay home," said Grandmother, choking back tears. My parents were rare Chinese who understood English, which is how I came to be called Ah B. In their Chinese way of pronunciation, B was short for baby, and all children are referred to by their birth order. For instance, my eldest brother is number one B and I am fourth B. Ah is the common beginning of the affectionate way of addressing someone you know well. For example, I addressed my childhood friend De "Ah De."

I learned to play dumb very quickly. Within seconds I could look like the village idiot, and I mastered various skills to escape notice. Like a wisp of smoke in a windstorm, when necessary

I could fade away as if almost never there. I attended school, which was compulsory at the time, but I always went straight home and hid away in our tiny storeroom. I avoided all group activities and sports.

Years later I realized that because Grandmother asked my parents to leave me behind, she felt the trajectory of my life was her responsibility. While she endured the mental and physical torture, she clung to hope for me and my future. Just about every Chinese parent believes in learning and will do anything for their children to get a good education. The famous proverb in Chinese culture, "In studying books, there is endless gold," was often on Grandmother's mind when I first went to school before I was pushed down by the black label. This ancient proverb gives hope to Chinese parents, no matter how down and out they are.

Over many centuries, the Chinese government had been manned with scholars selected from the annual National Scholastic Examination. Like our Lam ancestor, who scored among the top ten nationally and eventually became the national minister, the all-important first step to high position and power came from the national examination. What I encountered in school told Grandmother I had no chance of getting a good education or experiencing any future prospects in China. She knew from everything the new government had implemented, that we'd be doomed forever. The black label would plague us for life, and we were destined to be among the country's many national scapegoats. This extinguished her last hopes.

At my young age of seven, I didn't understand life and death. Aunt told me that the gods took Grandmother to a faraway place way up in heaven where she would be happy and peaceful. I had heard her beaten since the Land Reform and watched with a heavy heart as her once regal face appeared perpetually ashen and sullen. I felt relief that she would seek refuge with her gods, although I missed her very much.

I carried the memorial post with Grandmother's name at the funeral ceremony. Undernourished and small, my biggest challenge proved what to wear. Unlike Westerners, Chinese don white for funerals and red for weddings. The only white clothing I could get belonged to my older cousin Moo, ten years my senior. His pants were so long I had to pull them up as high as possible and tie them with a string, folding up the legs several times. His shirttail hung down the length of my small body, the shirtsleeves covering my hands as I struggled to keep the pants from falling off while carrying the post that ushered Grandmother to the next world.

Aunt often told me that the grief about losing her belongings caused Grandmother's death, and I believed her. The explanation seemed plausible, as Grandmother often talked with profound sadness about the new house, including its contents, like the shiny cutlery and intricately carved furniture.

Never would Aunt dare tell me that the Communist persecution was the real reason she believed Grandmother died. In later years, I realized that Aunt once again protected me from the truth. The material goods didn't matter. One slip from me about Communist persecution killing Grandmother and we would all be much worse off. Being persecuted, tortured, and humiliated ground Grandmother down, but the prospect of my entire life being doomed put the nail in her coffin. When she realized I had no future because of the Communist system, she felt so devastated for me that she took all of the blame on herself, and the weight of that blame killed her. The way they practiced Communism in China was so severe that countless millions of people perished directly from it. Grandmother ended up as one of those casualties. Being a lady with rich experience in life, she saw clearly that no matter how hard I studied or how clever I was, there would be no "endless gold" for me in China.

CHAPTER 3

AUNT AND COUSIN ZHENG

Flowers leave some of their fragrance
in the hand that bestows them.
— Chinese proverb

After Grandmother's departure, Aunt, Cousin Zheng, and I lived under constant threat in the small storage room—so close we read each other's thoughts. Any unexpected noise outside or raised voices caused us to jump simultaneously. When one of us felt unwell or uneasy, we all absorbed the discomfort. As a result, we didn't talk much. Aunt would simply glance to one side, intending to get something, like our lone rice bowl. Without saying a word, I would retrieve it, setting it in her hands. And when we needed something outside of the storeroom, such as wood or coal for cooking, Zheng silently slipped out the door, easing it shut behind him.

No sewage system existed in the storage room. We had a toilet potty near the bed in the corner of the room. This consisted of a wooden bucket with a cover and two handles for carrying. Only ladies used indoor potties, except in an emergency. Zheng and I relieved ourselves in the public toilet at the far corner of our small street. This consisted of a large hole made of two pieces of stone slabs with a crack in the middle to pass your excretions. The farmers had the odious job of collecting the contents of the potties and the public toilets and treating the sewage to convert it to fertilizer. Apart from the potty and a small bed where Aunt and I slept, hardly any space remained in the room, so Cousin Zheng put two planks of wood together every night and slept on them.

Except for the government building, the village had no electricity. A torch was a luxury we couldn't afford, so in the dark of night our only means of light came from a small kerosene lamp. The cheap but useful contraption consisted of a glass bottle for holding the kerosene, a thin roll of cotton immersed inside, and a thread that came out of the top and connected to a glass cover by a metal ring. A dial allowed us to roll the cotton up or down to control the flame and the glass cover had an opening on top for air circulation.

In addition to providing light, the lamp served as a powerful weapon against mosquitoes. Aunt and I slept on the same bed with a mosquito net over it to form a tent. In the daytime, we rolled up the net's front curtain and lowered it again at night to seal up the bed. Mosquitoes got into our sleeping area during the day, though, so when we closed the net at night, even Grandmother's prayers to the gods didn't work in the little space we shared with the hungry insects. Aunt taught me how to eliminate them with the kerosene lamp, however.

Taking the lamp into our bed, we sat in silence, our ears tuned for the unmistakable whirr of mosquitoes. Spotting the winged pest, I held my breath and eased the lamp close to the insect, which flew straight for the flame and death by incineration. I quickly became proficient at zapping mosquitoes, my heart leaping in delight at each singed insect.

Years later, my Buddhist friend Jef Morris exclaimed when he saw me swat a mosquito, "Paul, it could have been your brother in a previous life." I did not dare tell him how many I had eliminated in my childhood. Since then, I've avoided killing insects as much as possible.

Aunt always appeared weak and meek, perhaps because she pushed herself to care for me and Cousin Zheng. Though she rarely complained, I knew she suffered from a wide variety of aches and pains, like headaches and backaches. I responded by doing all that I could at my young age to anticipate her needs and give her some rest, such as cleaning up to save her work. Unconsciously, I longed to find the magic powers to cure her illnesses, which may have planted the seeds for my work helping people through tai chi and medicine. Although in my wildest dreams I never thought about becoming a doctor back then. That would have been like seeing a pig fly. Black labeled and holed up in the miniscule storeroom, we were too low to think of any job, let alone a position of high authority such as a physician, and certainly not in another country.

Aunt taught me many life skills, including housework chores like food preparation and cooking. On very rare occasions, we bought a tiny dish of special duck meat cooked with herbs and spices—a unique recipe from our village. I would savor one or two minute pieces of duck, reveling in the most delicious food I had ever tasted. Years later when I returned to China after an absence of thirteen years, I gave my cousin some money to buy me a plate of this special duck meat from the same vendor. When I bit into the dish expecting an incredible taste sensation, I found it shocking that the meat I once feasted on tasted ordinary and tough.

In addition to keeping house, my Aunt taught me to use my hands to create. Skilled in handicrafts, she made items from bamboo, wove baskets, crocheted, and knitted. When I reached six years old, I began helping her at the market stall. Sometimes she left me in charge while she went to the toilet. If I sold an item like a bamboo basket during her absence, she would beam at me upon her return and exclaim, "You are so clever, Ah B." My chest would fill with pride, because I had contributed to dinner that day.

Excellent at analyzing people despite illiteracy, Aunt worked out if they were friend or foe, what they wanted from her, and how to avoid antagonism, as a lowly person would. I learned this survival skill from her. On many occasions, she explained the world to me so that I wouldn't make any potentially fatal mistakes. This happened when I was eight years old and saw Ah Noh beating his own mother because she wouldn't give him her last possession—a gold ring from his late father. Shocked to see the lady kneeling on the floor begging her son to stop and leave the ring, I ran to Aunt hoping she could help.

"We cannot interfere, Ah B," she whispered, a mixture of worry, fear, and pity in her eyes. To get her point across about how we were in no position to help, she told me that Ah Noh had been one of the people who beat Grandmother before her death. "We are lucky that Ah Noh doesn't come to beat us as well," she told me, ending the conversation.

At the time, I didn't know that Ah Noh was just one of many people fueled to behave barbarically by the Chinese government's encouragement of immoral acts. The landlord label fabricated by Mao Zedong carried a life sentence for entire families down through generations. The government ensured that just about everything we did—schooling, jobs, travel, marriage—received the black label seal of disapproval. The label brought us persecution, discrimination, and an unimaginable handicap. We were often openly called names, like dog, rat, and poison element. The Communists told the peasants who the landlords formerly "oppressed" that they were responsible for correcting and killing us when necessary. If a crime occurred, everyone immediately suspected black label people, who were guilty until proven innocent—although the latter seldom occurred. Newspapers and official documents stated that black label families were all human garbage.

In contrast to Ah Noh and his mother, Aunt had the support of me and Cousin Zheng. My cousin was a tall, good-looking man. Athletic and strong and an excellent bike rider and swimmer, Zheng spoke well and exuded a natural charm and charisma. He looked so much like Paul Newman that after I escaped China, the first time I saw the American actor in a movie, I thought, *That's Zheng!*

Zheng's biological parents were poor farmers who lived about three miles (five kilometers) away from us. He visited them regularly and took me there many times. They were very kind people, and Zheng could have, like many others, denounced us to give himself political points. Determined to stay with Aunt and support her, Zheng refused to leave, while just about anyone else in the same position would have.

During an official meeting when a local bureaucrat decided to show off just how cruel he could be amidst the mass hysteria that Mao so painstakingly encouraged and cultivated, Zheng received a sledgehammer blow to his skull that nearly killed him. Despite suffering, sacrificing, and nearly dying, Cousin Zheng never wavered in his devotion to Aunt. He lived his entire life treated as a lowly being without any opportunity. What a brave man.

CHAPTER 4

MOMENTS OF REFUGE

A smile can erase a million worries.
— Chinese proverb

Around the same time Mother left me in China, my uncle (my mother's oldest brother) also left two of his daughters to live with our two maternal grandmothers while he went to Indonesia with his wife and other kids. Both close in age to me, my cousins Tang Gui Li and Tang Gui Zhi became like sisters. Visiting them at the home of my grandmothers provided a welcome respite. So much did I enjoy my time at their house that from the age of eight, when given permission, I walked two hours to their home in Shantou, which was about six miles (ten kilometers) from the village where I lived with Aunt and Cousin Zheng.

My two maternal grandmothers were wives number three and four of my mother's father, who died many years earlier under suspicious circumstances. Like my paternal grandfather, my maternal grandfather ventured to a foreign country to seek his fortune, and he found it in Indonesia. He made it into the mega-rich league in Pontianak, one of the biggest cities in the country. Grandfather owned a host of different businesses, one of which happened to be the first-ever movie house in Indonesia. They played silent movies starring Charlie Chaplin, which are still megahits in the country today. At the time, Chinese custom dictated that the rich have many wives, so my grandfather had eight. My grandmother (wife number three) became good friends with wife number four, and after my grandfather's death, the two women lived together in complete harmony.

We called my mother's mother Big Grandmother and the sister grandmother Little Grandmother, because the big grandmother was older and much taller and the little grandmother was younger and petite. Outspoken and loud, Big Grandmother proved well suited to the Chinese husband role of head of the family. She loved to socialize and bargain and possessed a quick temper, but settled down fast.

Little Grandmother prized cleanliness. She scrubbed the home often, including the toilet, which she cleaned daily. On one occasion, I made the mistake of forgetting to wash my hands after a pee. She scolded me severely about cleanliness, and I've never forgotten to wash my hands since. Besides admonishing us about cleanliness, Little Grandmother generally remained quiet, except for rare occasions when she became firm about an idea and refused to waiver. When she got upset, everyone—including Big Grandmother—tiptoed around her and did as she wanted.

Before my grandfather married my grandmothers, his number one and number two wives bore him no children, so he adopted five sons. Later, Big Grandmother gave birth to two boys and one girl (my mother, the number two child). Little Grandmother gave birth to a boy. The four other wives didn't have any children, so nine kids existed—five older adopted sons and four blood children.

As they grew up, it didn't take long for the adopted sons to notice differences between themselves and the younger children. Blood is much thicker than water. The adopted sons felt threatened regarding their inheritance. They worried that all of the money would go to the blood children—especially when Grandfather began sending money back home to Shantou where he bought a whole street and named it after his eldest blood son, my uncle Ye Zhen. At that point, it seemed likely to the adopted sons that Grandfather's vast fortune might be slipping from their hands.

Grandfather gave one of the adopted sons a business in Singapore to manage. Feeling threatened by the younger brothers, the son started to plan a future for himself. He borrowed large sums of money from Grandfather's contacts to start his own business, and when Grandfather found out, he became very angry. In the middle of another project at the time, the unexpected debt put Grandfather in a tight spot financially, so he set off to Singapore in one of his international liners (he owned several) to sort out the son. Two days later the ship returned. The captain said that Grandfather, in his midfifties at the time, committed suicide because of the debts. The explanation seemed implausible because the debt was minute compared to his vast fortune. Many people speculated about a murder conspiracy. They surmised that the murderer buried his body at sea so authorities had no evidence to investigate.

At the time of my grandfather's death, my grandmothers were in their thirties, and they had very young children. The five older brothers planned to divide the fortune amongst themselves, accusing the grandmothers of being too young to care for money. The matter went to court and the judge divided grandfather's fortune into six equal portions. Each of the older sons received one portion, and the two grandmothers and the blood children together received just one portion. It seemed unfair, but that's what happened. A sixth of the fortune was still a considerable amount. The two grandmothers felt unhappy in Indonesia, so they sold their property and relocated to China to live in the biggest house on their own street in Shantou.

Shantou was the second-largest city after Guangzhou in the Guangdong province. Because it was a major city, the CPC officials there acted more civilized during the Land Reform. As a result, Big Grandmother, who ran the household, received better treatment than my paternal grandmother. She never experienced physical torture, but they did give her a bill of "people's debts" to pay after the CPC took her valuables. A very clever woman, Big Grandmother rented out all her spare rooms to pay for the debt so that people believed her penniless. Meanwhile, she hid some of her jewelry and diamonds in secret corners of the house, and those jewels helped her family survive for many years. The quality of life she and her family experienced after the Land Reform paled in comparison to prior, but it was hugely better than ours.

I loved visiting my maternal grandmothers, because of the better quality of life they experienced and the attention they gave me. I also greatly enjoyed my friendship with my cousins and seeing my mother's youngest brother, Younger Uncle, who also lived with the grandmothers. There in Shantou no one kicked me, and

I could walk down the street unrecognized. I couldn't live with the grandmothers on a fulltime basis, because it would be impossible to get permission from the government to do so. Absolutely no freedom existed in China. Even moving next door required that you obtain many official permissions. We got our food through ration tickets. I brought mine with me when I stayed with the grandmothers for more than one meal.

I spent much of the summer holidays with the grandmothers. I enjoyed the long walk to their home and learning from them both. They taught me about Chinese culture and gave me great wisdom and love. I also loved playing with Gui Li and Gui Zhi, with whom I became very close during our formative years. We shared some common ground since we hadn't met our parents and siblings and grew up with grandmothers.

According to the custom of family in higher Chinese society, the two grandmothers were very strict and did not allow my cousins to go outside to play with friends, so the girls welcomed having me as a playmate. They envied me my freedom to wander anywhere, and I envied their upper-class lifestyle, culture, finesse, and intelligence.

My cousins and I learned from one another. I showed them how to make bamboo baskets, and they appeared impressed by my country-boy ability. They showed me how to crochet, and I enjoyed that, too. I did, however, keep those skills to myself because other boys would have made fun of me. Occasionally my cousins showed me their toys, which I viewed with envy. Their possessions, such as a simple blue-and-white streaked marble, appeared stunningly beautiful to me—like a priceless treasure. I'd never owned beautiful marbles, or even plain ones. As a country kid, I made my own toys from mud, stones, and bamboo, like my gun for shooting targets. I created it from an empty bamboo cylinder and another piece of bamboo for a spring, which I bent and inserted into the cylinder. I'd place a small pebble in the tube and push the lever, which made the spring work and propelled the stone.

Years later on my first visit to New York, I bought each of my children a large bag of marbles featuring a wide assortment of colors and shapes. I always spared no expense buying my kids toys, especially if they even remotely encouraged learning. On this occasion, however, Matthew and Andrea were teenagers and found the marbles to be a little unexpected.

"D [both kids call me D], they are beautiful," said Andrea. "But aren't we a little too old to play marbles?"

I didn't tell Andrea then, but I can tell her now. The gorgeous marbles fulfilled the wish of the deprived little boy I'd once been.

Sometimes when my cousins argued, they each campaigned for me to side with one or the other. I greatly enjoyed those occasions, because it made me feel important enough to be sought after. Li is like Big Grandmother, who cared for her. Tall with large, curvy eyebrows, she was beautiful and sweet when happy. Smaller and petite like Little Grandmother, who took charge of her, Zhi was clever and hardworking and always at the top of her class. When I asked her once, "How do you get full marks for all of your tests?" she just smiled in her cute way and responded, "I don't know."

Perhaps because of her intelligence, when Zhi knew she was right about something, she never gave in. As the older sibling, Li often tried to exert her authority during such instances, but she came up against a stone mountain with Zhi, who always knew more than both of us and persisted in being right. When they argued, both turned to me, the country bumpkin, to settle the argument. "Well, who is right?" Zhi would ask me, with her hands on her hips, "Is the earth round or flat, Big Brother B?"

During those years, I also found solace walking amongst the rice paddies that surrounded the village where I lived with Aunt. The area was located in China's rice belt amidst plentiful water and fertile soil. Most of the local residents farmed, planting acres and acres of paddies. Tranquil and stunningly beautiful, the rice paddies featured neatly divided squares of water-filled areas lined with borders of green grass. Rice grows from tiny green shoots into tall leafy plants, and the mature rice has golden tassels that flutter in the wind. At various times throughout the day, the sunlight caught the green and gold of the growing rice, creating a moving tapestry on the water.

For most of its growing life, rice needs much water, and for that reason farmers planted the fields next to the river. Every day they transferred water from the river to the paddies with an ingenious "water cart." The contraption consisted of a large, wide ladder lined with drawers. The pump lay next to the river and leaned over a ditch leading to the paddy. The drawer at the riverside scooped up water; then the farmer stepped on a pedal and the action moved the drawers up the slope, delivering water from the river to the rice paddies. The empty drawers then rotated to the bottom to collect more water. It looked like so much fun and effortless as the farmers worked the water carts while talking to their friends. One day when I was nine years old, a friendly farmer let me try to work the cart. Much to his amusement, the steps were so heavy I could hardly move the paddle.

Sometimes enterprising farmers put small fishes in the paddies so that they'd grow and the farmers gained double harvests from the same land. As I walked the paddies, the faint gurgling sound of the little fishes coming up to the surface always put a smile on my face. Little did I know at the time that smiles would soon disappear from the land, along with the fishes and rice paddies.

CHAPTER 5

THE GREAT FAMINE

Like weather,
one's fortune may change by the evening.
— Chinese proverb

Certainly Chairman Mao Zedong couldn't hear the rumbling in my stomach, and he must not have known that someone stole our rice. Otherwise, he would have come to our rescue. I had, after all, squeezed my eyes tight and prayed—his kind face in my mind's eye, asking him for an overflowing bowl of rice and not the mere handful of tiny grains Aunt always made into congee. But even the thin, tasteless porridge seemed like a royal feast now that our ration had been stolen a full five days before we would receive more rice.

Once verdant and lush, the land around us stood consumed. The sky no longer home to birds, the rice paddies and river no longer a haven for the small fish I once walked past, and the land no longer bursting forth with vegetation. As I lay in the still void of the tiny storeroom, my twelve-year-old heart cried as I watched Aunt's skeletal hands check and recheck the bowl where the grains of rice once were. Her eyes darted back and forth from the bowl to my face, as if to weigh the physical toll yet another five days without sustenance would inflict on my body and soul. I could feel her fear and desperation for my life.

By the third day without food, my stomach stopped rumbling. I heard only silence as my spirit slipped from my body and began to float. And then Cousin Zheng, who had been out scavenging for food, appeared at the door. "Come, Ah B," he said, putting out a hand to pull me to my feet. "I just found out that Little Uncle works as a cook at a match factory nearby. Remember how he carried you around when you were a small child? Maybe he can help us."

A distant relative sent to Grandmother's household as a young boy to be a servant, Little Uncle became like a member of our family. We called him Little Uncle, because he was the youngest of his family. When the Communists took over in 1951 and confiscated our house, they sent Little Uncle back to his parents. Like all of our friends and relatives, he stayed away, but he did care what happened to us. Once in a blue moon, I ran across Little Uncle waiting for me in quiet corners. He'd ask about everyone, and then obviously terrified about being discovered, he would furtively slip me a few dollars (a significant sum, especially for us). Each time he did this, Little Uncle risked getting himself in serious trouble with the Communist government. Despite the terrifying potential consequences, the money he gave us felt like a gift from Heaven. What an angel. Our hearts remained warmed for months at his brave generosity.

It had been some time since we'd seen Little Uncle. The CPC moved him to a factory away from our hometown. We didn't know he had returned to the area until Zheng stumbled upon him in the match factory.

On our way to see if Little Uncle could help us, we traveled the dusty streets in silence, knocking quietly on the door of the match factory when we arrived. A kind man with an almost feminine way of moving, Little Uncle greeted us affectionately and ushered us inside, his eyes clouding at the sight of our skeletal appearances. Despite putting himself in danger for helping us, he slipped Zheng a small bag of rice for Aunt. Little Uncle kept me with him, laying my nearly weightless body in a small room next to the kitchen where he resided. I stayed with him for three days while he slipped me spoonfuls of congee until my spirit no longer hovered over my body, but took up residence once again.

At the time, most Chinese suffered from starvation, and rice was more precious than gold. I discovered that like other workplaces, everyone in the match factory brought their own bowls of rice. The cooks added water and steamed the rice bowls in huge factory pans. Like most cooks, Little Uncle took a few grains from each bowl and hid them, which enabled him to save up the little bag of rice he gave to Zheng. He took a huge risk stealing those grains and giving them to us—not to mention how much money he could have gotten for the bag of edible gold on the black market.

I'd been saved from death, after all, but by Little Uncle, not Chairman Mao. A brainwashed young boy at the time, I had no idea that as I prayed for salvation, China's dictator led me and millions of his own people to death's door, pushing many through it. Beginning in 1958, the Great Leap Forward period devised by Mao became his disastrous and deadly dream to modernize China and hasten the development of agriculture and industry so the country would surpass Britain in an impossible time frame—just fifteen years. A genius at military and political strategy, the country's leader with little knowledge of the national economy pushed his way despite expert advice to the contrary and clear evidence of impending catastrophe. His plan killed between fifty and seventy million people over a three-year period through starvation and malnutrition.

In his grand plan, Mao divided the whole of China into a series of communes, each containing about five thousand families. People worked for the commune and not for themselves. The communes provided schools and nurseries to take care of children so all adults could work. Mao's scheme sent all of the country's farmers to work in the factories and to build dams and large industrial projects, while he left the women and children to mind the land and gather the harvest. I was eleven years old when the Great Leap Forward began in 1958. I worked in the rice paddies, and like most of the other children and women, in our ignorance we made a mess of the once masterfully managed system, wasting crops and failing to prepare the land for the following year. The hard labor also challenged my malnourished body and underdeveloped bones and joints, later leading to arthritis in my early teens.

Naturally with the unskilled in charge, food production plummeted. Despite the excellent growing weather of 1959, many of the fields became barren, and the land failed to bear crops. Poor weather came in 1960 and combined with Mao's policy led to total crop collapse. Some parts of China experienced floods, while in other growing areas drought became a major problem. Even though we lived in a rice belt, in my village adults and children starved to death—some children because their desperate guardians or parents took their rations. Hunger can drive people to do almost anything. The air hung gray with desperation and no one smiled, except for the few privileged Communist officials and their families. The CPC severely punished numerous people for stealing food. According to Frank Dikotter's book, *Mao's Great Famine*, in a county near where we lived, officials beat a six-year-old child to death for stealing a small amount of rice, and they forced another father to bury his five-year-old boy alive for taking a handful of food. A few days later the father died of grief. Many people became so desperate for food that they ate soil and died of bowel blockage.

While the women and children worked the fields, the CPC—which controlled everything including land, tools, animals, and people—ordered those men who farmed for decades to work in factories and undertake enormous, impractical projects that ended in disasters and contributed to the collapse of the country's industry. The CPC set unrealistic goals and immediately suppressed any professional and technical knowledge that would refute those goals. To please Mao and not face execution, the Communist bosses set goals knowing they had no chance of meeting them. This meant taking on impossible projects, such as producing steel and industrial products without any knowledge or equipment. When they couldn't meet the goals, the bosses faced prison and death.

Our school distilled steel. We took pots and pans from our homes and melted them together with any other scraps we could find in a homemade furnace. This resulted in a grand total of three tiny black metal pieces that we called steel. Fearsomely powerful, the Chinese propaganda machine whipped people into a frenzy. The whole school dressed up, beating drums and dancing around in celebration at our "success." We paraded noisily all the way to the local commune headquarters to report the "good news" to the commune boss. Schools all over the country wasted good utensils and immense amounts of time and energy to produce rubbish.

To put it in perspective, many people contributed the only cookware they owned to create the useless black metal.

During the famine, those with the black label were treated worse than everyone else. Our monthly rations were much less than others. We got just enough rice to keep us from quick starvation, but to ensure a slow death. When we ate our rice congee, we wiped the bowls until not a trace of food remained. What a naïve hope I clung to for Mao to save us. While I starved and prayed for food, at a secret meeting with his top officials in the Jinjiang Hotel in Shanghai on March 25, 1959, Mao announced: "There is not enough to eat, people starve to death. It is better to let half of the people die so that the other half can eat their fill." The half who Mao planned to "let" die by giving them the lowest ration of food were the black label individuals, whom he referred to as "enemies of the people." According to Jasper Becker in his book, *Hungry Ghosts, Mao's Secret Famine*, these enemies who died in the greatest numbers consisted of landlords (us), rich peasants, former members of the nationalist regime, religious leaders, rightists, counterrevolutionaries, and the families of such individuals.

Though hunger weakened Cousin Zheng, Aunt, and I, we scouted like vultures for anything edible. One night Aunt awakened me, warning me to be silent. She had a small pot in which she boiled some water and put in pieces of beef. So that no one could smell the food, she closed the one small window of the storeroom and stuffed the door cracks with clothes. Cousin Zheng told us he picked the meat up after it fell off a truck, but years later I realized the impossibility of this occurring during the famine. Zheng knowingly staked his life and stole that piece of meat. The CPC tortured and killed many for less—especially black label people. That meat tasted so heavenly!

Fortunately, people became more preoccupied with starvation during the famine, so the bullying subsided. We remained black labeled and discriminated against, but experienced no physical abuse, as chronic malnutrition eroded everyone's strength. In the midst of the famine, life seemed so slow and time became irrelevant. We enjoyed no weekends or special days—just unrelenting hunger, exhaustion, and lassitude.

My father did send money to us every three months. It proved a difficult task because Vietnam was a capitalist country then and, therefore, an enemy of the CPC. No diplomatic ties existed, so money went through a black market. Father would write to tell us he sent thirty vitamin pills, which meant he sent thirty dollars (about five US dollars). We wrote back using a ghostwriter (until I learned to write) to say:

"Thanks very much, my dearest, respected father. Your vitamin pills are very helpful. They saved our lives."

Under the circumstances, we couldn't convey our true situation to Father. Even if I could write, they screened all overseas mail. Though most of China starved, government notices and big slogans touted the enormous success of the Great Leap Forward with its "incredible harvests" and praised the magnificent leadership of Chairman Mao. Despite the fact that we had no food, the literature generated by Mao's propaganda mill announced news of areas that yielded incredible harvests thanks to the grand leader's ingenuity. One flyer I read said that we yielded ten thousand catty (the catty is the Chinese traditional mass measurement equivalent to around $1\frac{1}{3}$ pounds) in a mu (a unit measurement for land equivalent to 666 square meters or 0.16 acre). That meant, according to the flyer, that an acre of land produced eighty-three thousand pounds of rice. For a starving boy like me and millions of others, that constituted a rice dream in hell. Considering the slick power of Mao's propaganda machine, it's easy to understand why most people outside China didn't realize the truth, unless they became motivated to dig up the facts. For that reason, I couldn't blame my parents for not sending more money because they did not know how close we were to dying from starvation. Like most of the world, they were blind to our dire situation.

Years later in 1972, while studying medicine at the University of New South Wales in Sydney, Australia, I attended a public lecture by the famous author Dr. Han Suyin. Her presentation showed me how the mighty Chinese propaganda machine did a thorough job of turning black into total white. Dr. Han wrote many books about China and visited regularly, painting a beautiful picture of the country and saying how much better the new China was and praising the wonders of the country's Communist system. She described a completely different China than the one I knew and in which my family still suffered. I wondered if she realized that the government sets up special show villages for foreign visitors. When someone asked her questions about the truth behind the pictures she painted, Dr. Han replied: "I am a physician. I am trained to call a spade a spade, and that is what I saw in China. The modern China is wonderful." Angry and in tears, but too shy to speak out against her, I walked out.

To this day, I still wonder how we did survive the famine. Aunt, Cousin Zheng, and I hovered on the precipice of death by starvation for so long that I believe sheer refusal to give in and our love for one another kept us alive. Aunt knew that if she died, with no one to care for me, I would soon follow, and I knew she wouldn't live if I died. Aunt loved me so deeply that she never even thought about eating my rations, as many parents did. Instead, she quietly gave me some of her food, pushing herself even closer to death. She would and nearly did give her life for me. The bond of love that we clung to kept us both alive.

The disastrous Great Leap Forward seemed to have no end for us, China's powerless and ignorant masses. By 1960, the situation became so desperate that Mao had no choice but to officially resign as chairman. He remained the country's honorary chair, moving away from the capital of Beijing to Shanghai and stepping down from running the country. Liu Shaoqi took over as the executive chairman. With his moderate colleagues Zhou Enlai and Deng Xiaoping, Liu Shaoqi instituted more pragmatic policies.

By 1961, things began to turn around with the new, more realistic and sane management. We noticed a little more food in our rations, and imminent death no longer choked the air that we breathed. As my stomach rumbled a little less often, my mind became even more aware of an unquenched thirst for nourishment.

CHAPTER 6

THE EMPTY PERIOD

A book tightly shut is but a block of paper.
— Chinese proverb

In 1960, I finished primary school, but because of the cursed black label I was denied entrance to high school.

Nowadays we are bombarded with information and almost overwhelming stimulation every waking moment. We possess so many excess material objects and are faced with too many choices. Just try to choose cereal from the many boxes offered in the supermarket. We have too much to eat; too much temptation and too many choices when it comes to career paths, holiday locations, and what car and house to buy. In half a day today, I experience more stimulation than I did from 1960 to 1962. I have so much interesting material to read, I wish I had more hours in a day for reading.

But in China in 1960, we had nothing to do and nowhere to go. No newspaper for us and very little for me to read. When I found a scrap of paper, no matter how worn and dirty, I always spread it out and gingerly wiped away dust or dirt so that I could read and reread the words.

We had no plan, no hope, no excitement, no phone, and hardly any friends. Most people turned away from us because they risked being labeled as conspirators. I did have one friend, De, a classmate whose father served as an undercover Communist agent prior to the CPC victory over China. Before the takeover by the CPC, De's father realized that his work might not be recognized by the new regime, so he took his family to Hong Kong. He was right to flee, as some of his colleagues were executed by the new government when no one came forward to vouch for their undercover mission. Imagine how they felt. They risked their lives to bring the CPC to power, only to end up losing their lives to that very same CPC. Just like Mao's closest colleague, Liu Shaoqi, the national chairman who led the country out of the Great Famine. He died along with millions of other faithful Mao followers during the Cultural Revolution. Liu passed away in jail, and Mao suppressed the news of his death for ten years.

De would have been safe in Hong Kong, but after an argument with her husband, De's mother returned home to China, taking her number two son, De, and leaving the number one son with her husband. The CPC treated De as the same landlord class as me (proof they didn't recognize his father's work). We shared a similar fate, and the friendship at least gave me someone to talk to and made the time a little less lonely.

Short and thin, with small eyes and high cheekbones, De loved to talk in a lecturing tone and enjoyed sharing his knowledge. In addition to undergoing the same hardships as I did with starvation, he nearly died during the Cultural Revolution that occurred later. The CPC sent him to a farm where he lived in solitary confinement and nearly perished. Fortunately, he survived and started a small printing business. His love for the written word caused him to save something I wrote him many years ago. When I reconnected with De forty years after I left China, he showed me something I had forgotten about that brought back the immense void I felt in my life back then. When I went to visit him as a boy one day all those years ago and he wasn't home, I picked up a piece of paper and wrote something on it, leaving it for him. When we met four decades later, he pulled out of his pocket the note I had left in his house. On the scrap of paper, I had written the words of a famous Chinese poem titled, "Song of Tomorrow."

Tomorrow after tomorrow
How many tomorrows are there?
If I spend my life waiting for tomorrow
My whole life will be a waste.

Like the physical starvation, the mental desert in which I aimlessly wandered back in 1960–62 gnawed at my mind and soul. The human brain needs stimulation. Extreme mental, social, and sensory deprivation can lead to severe mental disorders. The social isolation and discrimination we underwent in China felt in many ways worse than the starvation. Studies of primitive tribes show that socially isolated individuals often die or go mad. We experienced all three—social, mental, and physical deprivation. The only thing that kept us hanging on was each other. Especially my aunt and me. Her unconditional love gave me my self-worth, and I wouldn't have survived physically or mentally without it.

As the food situation improved and rations increased little by little, the air of death and desperation faded. I felt almost like a prisoner waiting for the jury to decide on a death sentence. Once that sentence went in favor of me, the prisoner, the stress and desperation left, but great emptiness lingered as I became aware of my hunger for knowledge. Total nothingness is like a giant void. It is not peaceful, but creates a great thirst for something to happen. I asked myself questions like: "Why am I here? What is life?" The feeling of wasting my life knowing I'd never have a chance in China threatened to drown me. From that long, deep void, something like a seed emerged from nowhere and started to germinate, growing into a burning desire to learn and do something worthwhile. In my subconscious came a fierce outcry. I wanted to live a meaningful life—not just exist. I wanted to bring my beloved aunt a better and healthier life. And I wanted a purpose for my life.

For a long time, I felt bad about those two wasted years, especially later on when I became one of the oldest students in high school and university. Then one day some twenty years later, I suddenly realized that the Empty Period wasn't a waste, but my awakening, and that it changed my life forever. That time without intellectual stimulation helped me appreciate the pleasure of learning and the prestige of being useful, and it started me searching for a fulfilling life. I came to love working hard, learning, and making use of every opportunity that came my way. The great void prepared me for the great fulfillment in life.

One day in 1962, as I walked aimlessly, I overheard two boys talking about a new high school located in Chaozhou, a city sixty-two miles (100 kilometers) from home. I caught the gist that the school was funded by contributions from overseas Chinese and was open to everyone, especially children with overseas parents like me. I felt like a drowning person suddenly handed a life jacket. With excitement raging within me, I turned around and quizzed the boys about the school, my mind and body suddenly waking up from the stupor into which I had fallen during those two empty years.

I raced back to talk to Aunt, the words spilling out of me in an excited rush as I explained the school the boys described.

"Education is so very important, Ah B. Your father would want you to do this!" she said, catching my excitement. "I will find the money to send you to the school."

Too young and eager to wonder how she would find the money while we still struggled in the very deep waters of debt, I focused my attention on the entrance exam just two weeks away. I borrowed books and studied every waking hour possible— hoping and praying that I would succeed and pass the exam, despite my two empty years.

Chapter 7

MY NEW SCHOOL

A book holds a house of gold.

— Chinese proverb

I couldn't believe that I passed the entrance examination.

Soon after, I found myself in boarding school away from Aunt for the first time. Though thrilled to finally have a chance to do something with my life and wanting to make the most out of the opportunity, I missed Aunt terribly. Little did I know that the experience was a precursor to the more permanent separation that would come later.

The newly constructed school consisted of a few small, shabby wooden buildings that included cramped classrooms containing wooden benches, tables where we took notes, and blackboards for the teachers. The other students wore tattered clothing like me, and we each received a small lockable box that measured about two feet (60 cm) high and one foot (30 cm) wide and deep. We stored all of our possessions inside the boxes, which sat on the corner of our beds. To fit as many students as possible into the small living quarters, we slept on bunk beds so narrow that turning over in your sleep often sent you toppling to the floor—a rude awakening for those in the top bunks.

Washing proved a Spartan affair. We carried a bucket of warm (if we were lucky) water from the straw-roofed kitchen to the tin "shower" shed and rinsed ourselves off with a cup. In winter, if we had no hot water, some of us washed quickly in icy cold water. I inherited my father's obsessive compulsive cleaning gene, so I chose to freeze rather than go unwashed. Summertime made bathing much more pleasant. We washed ourselves and swam in a creek that wound its way around the perimeter of the school. I learned to clean my own clothes in the creek, organize my time, and get along with an entire school of strangers.

As new leaders succeeded Mao Zedong, conditions in the country rapidly improved. (The Chinese people are resilient when they have a chance.) The food supply continued to improve— meager, but no longer starvation rations. We brought our own food to school, delivering our bowls containing rice to the cook, who steamed them for us. By that time, he most likely didn't need to pinch a few grains for himself. Aunt gave me a small jar with dry, preserved meat when I came home once a month. On special days, I extracted a small piece of the meat from the treasure jar to top my rice. Most of the kids were boarders with relatives overseas, and many brought more food than me. I knew Aunt did her best, so I tried not to show that I had less.

These conditions may sound harsh now, but except for living without Aunt, my life was heavenly compared to before. Most of my classmates came from similar backgrounds, so I rarely experienced discrimination and was assessed fairly. Best of all, I truly appreciated learning. I studied every available minute, reveling in the opportunity to exercise my mind. I always loved discovering how things work and hadn't been as interested in remembering facts, but at that time even the most boring and mundane topics excited me. At home with Aunt, I squinted to read by the dim light of the smelly kerosene lamp, but at school I experienced the luxury of studying after dinner in our classroom under the light from an electric bulb. Looking back, I now see what a blessing the Empty Period was for me. From those years deprived of the opportunity to learn came a consuming yet empowering hunger for knowledge.

I gained top marks for all subjects in school, except physical education. Somehow I believed myself poorly coordinated and really disliked any exercises, especially in groups. Most likely my avoidance of sports came from the black label abuse of kids at my primary school. If you are anxious about mixing with others, you cannot excel at group sports. The ridicule I experienced as a child made me feel clumsy and unable to perform well with any exercise.

Before the end of my first year at the boarding school, Teacher Yen, who taught physical education, summoned me. He said that Teacher Liu, who was in charge of my class and liked me very much, said I would be the top student of the year if I passed physical education. Previously displaying a somewhat disdainful attitude toward me, Teacher Yen was impressed with my academic achievement and, as a result, made a special effort to help me get through his physical education class.

Due to my lack of practice at physical education, Teacher Yen found the task of helping me somewhat challenging. One day I heard him chuckling to himself and muttering, "Bon Trong [meaning 'born to be strong']? What a weakling. How could your father give you such a name?"

At the end of the first year, I achieved top of my class and they awarded me the special prize for excellence. Despite my excitement and Aunt's great pride in me, I didn't attribute the accomplishment to my ability. Instead I assumed I was first in my class because I had worked hard and was older than the other students. This feeling of inferiority that had its roots in the black label has followed me throughout my life. Even after I won a gold medal in the Third International Tai Chi Competition in Beijing in 1992, I believed I won because of how hard I worked. Looking back on those days at boarding school, I know that never in my wildest dreams would I have thought that one day I would travel around the world teaching exercise to millions of people. Teacher Yen would be so proud of me!

Despite the "premium" living conditions at the school, I missed Aunt. As I went about my days, I often found myself suddenly in a spot, lonely and lost at the overwhelming ache in my heart. When I could afford the bus fare, I looked forward to visiting her, although when I did get home I felt sad to see her weakening and looking sicker and more worried. Aunt refrained from telling me, but I later worked out that my school fees and living expenses must have been a nearly impossible burden for her. How do you borrow more money when you are up to your eyebrows in debt? My guess is that she got most of the funds from a friendly loan shark woman in the neighborhood, but I was away from home and still immature at fourteen, so it's hard to know for sure.

I also looked forward to visiting my maternal grandmothers and cousins. With the threat of starvation gone, I began noticing human needs and felt attracted to my lovely, feminine cousins. I admired the girls and wanted to be friendly to them, but I felt silly and awkward. They were like princesses, and I was a Chinese hillbilly.

Li had a lovely face and a delicate curve in her eyebrows, so when she laughed her eyes squeezed into a cute curve. She had a dimple on the right side of her mouth that came out when she became upset and made her look even more attractive. Relatively spoiled and picky about her diet, she threw a tantrum when things didn't go her way. My top secret was that I loved seeing her throw a tantrum just to see her dimple. Though I felt tempted on occasions to intentionally upset her, I never dared.

Zhi was petite, and I greatly admired her intellectual ability. Meticulous and obsessive, she produced schoolwork of the highest quality. Up to year nine, she earned full marks for every subject, every exam, and every assignment. That had never happened at her school, so they held a celebration just for her. It was hard to imagine she could not gain entrance into a university. Damn the black label!

I had no idea about the birds and the bees, as sex was an absolute taboo subject in China. I wondered how the male penis worked apart from peeing. I'd never seen a picture of a vagina, let alone seen one in person, and I certainly didn't know back then that they're made to interact with each other. I found it fascinating to be around my cousins as they began to blossom into young women, and I could vaguely sense the growing sexual energy that emanated from them. I liked them very much before, but something else seemed to make me like them immeasurably more.

When I stayed with the grandmothers, I usually slept in the same double bed as Big Grandmother and Li. Grandmother lay on the outside so we kids wouldn't fall out of the bed. Li lay in the middle, and I stretched out on the far end against the wall in the opposite direction with my head by their feet, so we didn't face each other. One hot summer night we slept on a thin straw mat on the floor. That time Li lay right next to me, not head against foot, but alongside. I sensed an intangible feeling—or was it my imagination? She lay in the dark next to me, and I couldn't help myself. I heard her sweet, quiet breathing as though she sent me a message, so I put out my finger and slowly, slowly touched the edge of her pillow. That gave me an amazing satisfaction. I felt I'd communicated with her at a closer level, and that was as far as it went. We did actually touch each other in our younger days when we went out to see Chinese operas and the grandmothers made us hold hands so we wouldn't get lost. I enjoyed the hand-holding. The girls had soft hands, whereas mine were rough. When we grew older, all hand-holding stopped, however. China features a very prohibitive culture, and we responded by being very inhibited.

Consanguinity is different in China than many parts of the Western world. As long as you don't have the same surname, you can marry. This is not unusual. Worldwide, ten percent of marriages are amongst cousins, and in the Middle East something like fifty percent of the marriages are. This is not surprising given that in inhibited cultures, cousins have the advantage of interacting. I never dreamed that I could be good enough for my princess-like cousins, but I felt something special for both girls.

After I left China, the CPC sent Li to a small, isolated tea farm 372 miles (600 km) from her home. She lived and worked there for eighteen years, and they only permitted her to leave the farm for two weeks each year for Chinese New Year. During one of those two-week periods, she married a man from Guangzhou, but they only saw each other once a year. They ended up having two children, whom they had to leave with a farmer's family to look after, and they would only see the children once a year. What a contrast from Li's protected upbringing.

After finishing high school, not only could Zhi not enter a university, but she found it impossible to find a job—also because of the black label. They planned to send her away like Li, but one of the grandmothers became ill, so the CPC let her stay to care for her—what a lucky escape. After two years and lots of bribery, Zhi got a job as a factory cleaner. A brilliant scholar like her working as a cleaner. She got the job in the city of Shantou where discrimination against the black label was much less than in our country town. More proof that I would have had no chance of any job if I had stayed in China.

In 1981, during one of my visits to China, I stopped in Guangzhou overnight. They granted Li special leave to come visit me, because in those days, they considered having a foreign relative visit a significant event. I stayed in a four-star hotel (a Chinese rating comparable to two stars in places like the US), but it was sheer luxury compared to Li's poor, country tea farm. Before she could come to my room, Li had to register and show her IDs, and I went down to the desk to prove she was my cousin by filling out a long detailed form that declared our relationship. That was the normal routine in China at the time.

Tired from her hot and dusty journey, Li looked around in awe at the hotel. She stood a foot shorter than me and was dressed in a dark shirt covered in patches and darker, shabby pants. After her shower, she looked so fresh and beautiful like I remembered her. When we talked during that visit, she told me how she and her husband hardly saw each other, and they experienced relationship problems as a result. Once again overwhelmed by her physical presence, I felt close to her and wanted to take her into my arms to comfort her, but my Chinese side prevented me. Li and I shared a deep emotional connection that might have been more than sibling love. I do have a sweet feeling whenever I think of her.

A few years after we met in the hotel, Li wrote to me asking for money to bribe officials so that she could leave the tea farm to join her family. I felt so happy to be able to help. The bribe proved successful. She went to live with her husband in Guangzhou, retiring around the age of forty-eight. Li lived a happy, contented life, learning tai chi in the park and becoming a Christian, until she died in an accident in 2007. At the time, I was in Seoul doing a series of tai chi workshops. Teaching usually energizes me and makes me feel great, but that day I felt strange and out of sorts with a nagging headache. That night I received an e-mail from my cousin's son that Li had had an accident. A motorbike backed into her and knocked her into a post. She had a brain hemorrhage and fell into a coma around the time I felt strange; she passed away the next day. My friend and medical colleague, Dr. Pam Kircher, is an expert on near-death experiences. Her book, *Love is the Link*, describes her own near death experience as a child and the various ways people communicate with their loved ones when death is near. I often wonder if Li tried to say good-bye to me.

Whenever I visited Aunt, I always stayed at Shantou where Zhi lived, so she and I met more often. We really enjoyed talking about the old times, the grandmothers, and our outlooks on life. After the Cultural Revolution ended, Zhi worked as a secretary and later a clerk until her retirement, although she never did have the opportunity to use her talent. She still holds my admiration for her intellectual ability, and I also enjoy how we share experiences and thoughts. It is challenging to find people with whom I have mutual trust and a complementary level of intellect that inspires in-depth communication. I count myself extremely fortunate to be able to interact and share with Zhi and other intellectually stimulating individuals.

This was the case my second year in high school when my friend De also came to the school. Familiar with how things worked, I guided him around. Chaozhou is a pretty place. The West Lake (though of the same name, it is much smaller than the famous West Lake in Hangzhou) is beautiful. De and I often walked around it at nighttime talking, debating, and arguing. Stimulating and fulfilling—life was wonderful at that time.

Then one morning in the middle of the term, a peculiar feeling told me that something was about to happen. Feeling strangely anxious, I calmed myself by putting my last small piece of salted meat on top of my rice before I took the bowl for steaming. My mouth watered in anticipation of the treat, but I never got to enjoy that meal.

CHAPTER 8

THE QUIET ESCAPE

A mountain of knives and a sea of fire.
— Chinese proverb

After first period, Cousin Zheng surprised me by appearing outside of my classroom. Because of the long distance and bus fare, he'd never visited me at school before. As soon as Zheng saw me, he grabbed my arm and pulled me into a quiet corner. "Your father sent someone to fetch you to Vietnam," he whispered. "Pack your stuff and don't tell anyone. We are leaving right now. I will tell your teacher there is an urgent matter at home and you have to leave right away."

With all of my possessions located inside the two-by-one-foot storage box, it took only minutes to gather them. I left my blanket and pillow as Zheng instructed, so that people would think I planned to return. He said he'd take care of it later. As we caught the bus, it felt like a dream. Deep in my heart I didn't believe I would be leaving home and school. Up to that point at the age of sixteen, my whole world consisted of Aunt, the village, and school. I'd never known anyone to have left China, the notorious, inescapable Bamboo Curtain.

The trip home seemed to drag on forever, but it only took four hours. After we got off the bus and headed toward the storeroom, it hit me. I would be leaving Aunt. The landscape blurred as my tears began to flow at the thought. Zheng strode ahead at a brisk pace. The palatable excitement he left in his wake soon energized me, so I wiped the tears away and caught up with him.

The idea of leaving China to join my family had always been in the background but never seemed a possibility. In 1961, during the Great Famine, Big Grandmother sent us a message that Aunt Lotus from Vietnam had come to Shantou and wanted to see me. The news shocked us. The CPC could, and often did, retain, imprison, or persecute visitors from overseas since the days of the Land Reform. No one from overseas ever visited China from Vietnam because Vietnam was under capitalist American control. That made Vietnam an enemy of China. They would suspect anyone from there of being a spy, so no one ever took the risk. The CPC could sentence to death anyone suspected of spying. Most overseas Chinese regarded it as a fate worse than death to return and be detained in China. Every day countless numbers of people swam across the sea to Hong Kong to escape China. Many drowned, and officials caught others and sent them back to face a jail sentence. It would be madness to return to China of your own free will, but Aunt Lotus did. What an incredibly brave lady.

Over the years, I had heard about my father's cousin Aunt Lotus. A family legend, she had the reputation of being a kind lady with good business acumen, who went out of her way to help others. When her employees were sick, Aunt Lotus nursed them back to health personally. Most wealthy Chinese ladies never dreamed of doing such a thing. When I met her, I immediately noticed her broad face, prominent chin, and kind smile.

"Fourth B, your mum is my best friend," said Aunt Lotus, her eyes twinkling with kindness. "I will treat you like my son." Then she hugged me and kissed my cheek. Her display of affection shocked me, as it clashed with the no-touching, inhibited Chinese way. I recovered quickly, however, letting her warmth and love embrace my heart, where it has stayed. Aunt Lotus asked how we were doing. Given that my aunt and I thought still being alive was doing well, I refrained from revealing the full extent of how bad things were. Aunt Lotus already knew the truth regarding the Great Famine, which is why she risked her life to come to China. She visited to take care of her mother and sister in Shantou. Aunt Lotus gave us food and three hundred dollars—a huge sum. I suspected Aunt had incurred an impossible debt surviving the Great Famine.

As a woman of honor, she would slave to pay the debtors back, but it proved an impossible task. The burden of not being able to repay her financial obligations most likely consumed her, so when Aunt Lotus gave her the money, she felt overwhelming relief and gratitude. Aunt even started to kneel down to Aunt Lotus to thank her, but Aunt Lotus held my aunt's hands to stop her from doing so and assured her that it was all right.

A rarity in her era, Aunt Lotus displayed vision, an adventurous spirit, and a deep respect for Chinese traditions. She was truly one of the most amazing ladies I have ever met. Contrary to the Chinese culture of emphasizing the negative, Aunt Lotus lived a positive life. She always focused on the best in people and events and expressed appreciation for everything that people did for her. For example, when she migrated to Canada in the 1970s to live near her children just before Vietnam fell to the Viet Cong, I visited her whenever I could. If I bought her a present, no matter how small, she always expressed her appreciation. On one occasion, I forgot to bring her a gift, so my sister-in-law, Rosalie, Aunt Lotus's daughter, gave me a box of tea as my present. After I left, Aunt Lotus called to tell me how much she enjoyed the tea and asked me where I bought it. I felt so embarrassed that the next time I saw her I bought my own present. By then I knew she liked tea, so I bought the very best tea I could buy. She was ninety-two years old in 2011 when I last saw her in a retirement village. Although her memory had started to fail, she remained dignified and positive. Rosalie brought her coffee, and she commented that it tasted wonderful. Whomever Aunt Lotus talked about, she emphasized their good points. What a lady.

I always wondered how Aunt Lotus managed to travel into China. She told Big Grandmother that she heard about the famine and decided she must come to care for her mother and sister. The Chinese propaganda machine painted a beautiful picture for the rest of the world, but many caring Chinese, such as Aunt Lotus, knew better. At the time of her arrival, the Chinese official outreach magazine, *China Reconstruction*, showcased glossy photos of well-fed people dancing on top of burgeoning rice fields. China even gave away millions of tons of rice as aid to other countries to show the world that it was well off, despite the fact that countless millions of Chinese were dying of starvation. Today Chinese official documents show that many Chinese starved to death right outside of the governmental rice storage buildings, which still had plenty in storage. It took years for the information to come out about the immensity of the Great Famine. Today's reliable estimates are based on the recent release of governmental archives. Many top-secret records remain inaccessible. As a result, no one knows the exact number of people who died of starvation, but scholars agree that the numbers are staggering.

Aunt Lotus managed to get in and out of China because she went to Cambodia and got a false passport as a Cambodian citizen. At the time, Cambodia was a neutral country with China. She probably obtained the passport through one of the powerful underworld organizations prevalent throughout Southeast Asia. She must have paid a fortune to the organization, because of the high risk of cutting through the thick and treacherous Bamboo Curtain. Aunt Lotus arrived with a mountain of luggage containing food, clothing, and medicine, creating quite a stir among the locals. To this day, I have yet to meet someone as outrageously courageous. She managed to get safely out of China and went back to advise Father to increase our allowance of "medicine pills." He started sending more money, which improved our conditions and carried us off the precipice of starvation.

Before Aunt Lotus departed, she planted the seeds for my escape—instructions with Aunt to apply for permission for me to leave China to join my parents. Aunt took the necessary steps, but things moved slowly. It took government officials more than a year to reply that since my parents resided overseas, the Chinese government would grant me permission to join them when I turned twenty-one. I could only leave prior to that if one of my parents did the unthinkable and came to China to personally escort me out of the country. If one of my parents came to China, like Aunt Lotus had, he or she risked detainment. Like my aunt, I thought very little of myself. I never dreamed that anyone would take such a risk for me.

When Aunt Lotus heard about the government's decision regarding my inability to leave China, she approached Father again to remind him of my desperate situation.

"You have to get Fourth B out of China now, not when he reaches twenty-one years old, if he survives that long," she told him. "There is no hope or future for him there."

Father offered to pay any amount he could afford, but admitted that he didn't know how to go about extracting me. Headmaster of the most famous English school in Vietnam at the time, he made big money. Aunt Lotus responded by digging deep into her connections and went back to the organization that helped her make the journey to China. They agreed to take on the assignment—a true *Mission: Impossible*. In those days, the Chinese government was secretive; it only had diplomatic relationships with a handful of countries outside of the Communist bloc. Traffic in and out of the Bamboo Curtain involved many hazards, and connecting with the Chinese government at any level proved a difficult task.

The underworld organization devised an ingenious, daring plan. At that time, smuggling was the only way to get out of China. Doing so risked the lives of all involved. Their emissary, a Mr. Wu, originally came from China. He had gone to Hong Kong, but left behind a wife and child in China and wanted to take them to Hong Kong to live. Mr. Wu needed the money and means to get them out of China, so he worked with the organization. They bought a passport from a Cambodian Chinese man, took a page out, and replaced it with a false page with Mr. Wu's photo. They gave him a signed letter from my father appointing him as my guardian to take me to Cambodia through Hong Kong. The whole operation was fraught with danger and uncertainty. We had no way of knowing ahead of time if the CPC would accept a written letter from Father, and Mr. Wu's true identity could be discovered at any point during the process. China didn't, and to a lesser degree still doesn't, value human life. In addition to the millions of people who perished during the Great Famine, the Land Reform and the Cultural Revolution took countless millions more lives. When it came to illegal activities like using a false passport to escape the country, the CPC executed people for far less serious infractions. I had a patient who was a sailor from Hong Kong working on a Hong Kong-owned ship. The Secret Police arrested him while on shore leave and said that someone identified him as a spy. They tortured him for a confession and then jailed him for ten years. No one, including his family, had any idea what happened to him until the CPC released him a decade later, an absolutely innocent man. Today, though conditions have much improved in China, the people still have no real choice of their political representatives or freedom of the press. The police have absolute power and bureaucracy rules. While China is currently stable, without a set system that works like a democracy as in countries like Australia, the UK, and the USA, there is the possibility that at any time a different leadership could destroy millions of lives.

Fortunately, I was still young and didn't fully understand the danger Mr. Wu, myself, and his family would soon face. My most difficult task proved to be saying good-bye—especially to Aunt. When I got home from school, I had two days to get ready. I could see the profound sadness in my aunt's eyes. I knew it would break her heart to part with me, and my own heart ached with an intense pain I had never experienced. When Aunt and I talked during that final time, we discussed everything but our pain. She tried hard to show her happiness for my opportunity, and we never discussed the subject of my returning because we knew it would be impossible. To leave China was like life and death in those days; no one ever returned to visit.

Back then we never used the words "love" or even "care," but Aunt and I experienced a bond so strong and so deep that no words existed to describe it adequately anyway. Aunt always thought about my well-being. Before I left, she kept telling me to make sure I wore warm clothes on cold days and to have an egg on my birthday. An egg was considered a delicacy, and to this day I have an egg on my birthday, which I celebrate by the Chinese (Lunar) calendar in memory of my aunt. My kids complain to me just about every year when they exclaim, "Dad, we can never remember your birthday. It changes every year."

During my final days in China, I also visited the grandmothers, who were saddened to lose me. They gave me money and a pair of pants to replace my tatty ones and took me to buy new shoes. I was short and small for my sixteen years from malnutrition, but my feet were broad because I had hardly ever worn shoes, so they had free range to grow. They seemed to get swallowed up in my new shoes, which felt uncomfortable and strange. I did feel important wearing them along with my new pants, though.

Thoroughly brainwashed like me, my female cousins expressed concern. Despite being persecuted, we remained totally committed to Communism, believing Mao to be the savior of the world. The CPC painted the picture of Hong Kong as a dangerous place full of money-hungry people, criminals, and prostitutes. Zhi and Li warned me to be careful and to remain faithful to Communism. I promised them that I would be like a lotus. In Chinese literature, the lotus is admired for being clean inside despite growing from the mud. I vowed to remain a clean, innocent, and faithful Communist, despite living in muddy Hong Kong.

I also felt great sadness about saying good-bye to Younger Uncle. Big Grandmother's son had a speech problem and learning difficulties. Because his disability made him appear mentally and physically small with a downtrodden appearance, Grandmother felt ashamed and hit him with her shoe when she felt upset with him. A grown man and physically strong enough to overcome Grandmother, he remained submissive and just cried like a helpless child. Because of his limited abilities, Younger Uncle couldn't work at a proper job, but he managed to do small jobs for people and buy and sell items, such as tiny porcelain dogs. On my final trip there, feeling depressed about leaving and never returning, I took one of those dogs and hid it under a potted plant. Doing that made me feel a little better because it gave me hope that one day I would return by some miracle to retrieve the hidden treasure. I did return thirteen years later, but the plant pot and porcelain dog were long gone. Sadly, Younger Uncle and both the grandmothers had passed away by then.

After I packed, I waited for Mr. Wu on the planned day, my eyes puffy from crying and my heart aching. But he didn't show up. The following day, Mr. Wu's wife said that the CPC had jailed him because the police discovered his plan to take me out of the country illegally. She told me to do nothing and wait. After waiting four days, which seemed like ages, Mrs. Wu sent a message to say that Mr. Wu was released from jail and to be ready again the next day. No one who went to jail ever came out easily. Most sentences consisted of years or ended in death—that much I knew. How could someone who just got out of jail be ready to do the very thing for which the CPC jailed him? The whole experience felt unreal and frightening. Was I really going to leave China, and how safe would the passage be?

As promised, the next day Mr. and Mrs. Wu came with their young daughter and took me. To prevent the word leaking out about my departure, I could only say good-bye to Aunt and the grandmothers. I had no idea what to feel in those final hours. Mostly I felt numb from the pain of leaving Aunt behind and fear about my future. Aunt kept saying that leaving would be good for me, and she knew I would have a better life overseas.

"You have no future here at home with the most useless person in the world (meaning herself)," she said. She also expressed relief at passing the responsibility for me back to my parents. I knew she only wanted the best for me. Ever since I could remember, I felt angry with the gods for dishing out such a harsh fate to my dear aunt. Powerless as we were, I always dreamed about giving her a better life.

"I will come back with a big bag of money for you, Aunt," I proclaimed to her, but none of us believed it.

The CPC had absolute power over the people and never acted with kindness. Being in jail was like condemnation to hell; getting out alive rarely happened. Mr. Wu had to have an incredibly powerful organization backing him to still get the permit to take me out of China. It turned out that the organization had bribed related officials but missed one, so he had arrested Mr. Wu to get his share.

Mr. Wu seemed to be a smart and calm man. Without becoming flustered, he took his wife, child, and me to Shenzhen, a tiny fishing village near the Hong Kong border. Shantou is about three hundred and ten miles (500 km) from Hong Kong, so it took a full day bus trip to arrive at Shenzhen. When we got to the border, I thought we'd simply cross, since the government officially approved our leaving, but it wasn't that easy. We were required to wait in a tiny hotel prior to crossing because the Hong Kong authority only allowed a few persons a day to cross. I discovered that many people, in fact almost the whole community there, had waited for months, eventually becoming so desperate once their money ran out that they tried to swim to Hong Kong. Escapees caught by Hong Kong police were sent back to China and imprisoned. Those who gave up and returned home to China moved to the bottom of the black label list.

Young and sad about leaving my home, I didn't notice the air of desperation in Shenzhen. Instead, I enjoyed playing with Mr. Wu's daughter and caring for her while Mr. and Mrs. Wu spent time with each other. I also enjoyed the luxury of sleeping on the floor on a foam mattress and using a real toilet. More importantly, we ate great food. Every day the meals contained some meat. My mouth waters when I remember a dish with sweet-and-sour pork ribs.

As the time wore on and Mr. Wu tried each day to find a way to get us across the border, his face grew darker with worry. He must have finally received instructions from the organization because one day he came back to our room looking relieved. He took us by bus to Zhuhai and then to Macau by ferry. Macau was a Portuguese colony at the time and less strict than Hong Kong about allowing in immigrants. The organization made arrangements so that we could uneventfully pass the ferry customs there.

During my journey to Hong Kong, my school found out about my escape. My teacher, Teacher Liu, who really liked me, took a risk to tell my friend De to notify me that after I left, the school declared me a number one enemy of the people. They described me as an undercover spy just like a rotten apple—rosy outside but black on the inside. They said I pretended to be loyal to the Communists while undermining them. Everyone in the school stood ready to accuse me of crimes against the state. I shudder to think if my (legally sanctioned) journey had been unsuccessful and I had ended up back at school. I could have been stoned to death! Fortunately, I did not know how close I came to that fate. Instead, I enjoyed the food and the hotel—albeit missing Aunt badly.

From Macau we crossed to Hong Kong on the ferry, and I got seasick as I stepped on a ship for the first time in my life. I didn't want to attract attention to our party, so I forced myself to control the nausea. Mr. Wu saw my ashen face and told me to go out on deck to get some fresh air. It was dark, and I felt better and stayed there. As we approached Hong Kong, I saw millions of lights in the distance that grew larger as we drew closer. The stunning beauty of the city overwhelmed me. We seemed to be sailing into heaven. At that moment what I'd been taught about Hong Kong being the center of sin and greed slipped from my mind.

Upon landing, we joined a long queue. Mr. Wu told us to appear nonchalant, but I saw his normally calm face pale and sweating. Perhaps he felt seasick, too? We seemed to wait in line for ages. When our turn came, an officer grabbed our passports and asked Mr. Wu many questions. He examined our documents for a long time and then escorted us to an enclosed room where we waited as Mr. Wu became more and more nervous. By then, I realized the gravity of the situation and became scared. Were we about to be sent back to China and thrown in jail? My stomach churned and I felt almost unable to hold down my vomit when the door opened and in walked an immigration officer. I didn't know Cantonese, the local dialect then, so I didn't understand what they said. All of a sudden, the officer smiled and handed back our passports. We were free to enter Hong Kong.

The color rushed back into Mr. Wu's face. He looked like a man previously awaiting a hanging suddenly pardoned. We headed to my uncle's house on the electric tram. I felt weak and nauseous, so we went to ride on the top deck. As we traveled through the city, the unfamiliar motion proved the last straw. I felt ashamed to make a mess, but vomited onto the floor.

I've spent many years wondering how much my father paid to get me out of China and how much power and bribery the organization that made it possible wielded. I now understand my incredible luck. It's been fifty years since I left China and entered Hong Kong. I have met many people and read widely about China, but I have not heard of anyone experiencing a similar *Mission: Impossible* escape.

Mr. Wu handed me over to my fourth uncle—no doubt with considerable relief on his part. He had been my guardian through the most dangerous time of my life, but I never saw him again.

As Mr. Wu left me with my uncle, it hit me that I'd entered another world. Leaving China was like the difference between life and death. At the time, returning to see Aunt seemed impossible, and that realization devastated me. Aunt's sweet, kind face filled my mind, and I could see her weeping for me as I wept for her. How could life be so cruel? For many months, the sadness hung like a dark cloud, threatening to overwhelm me. Gradually, the clouds parted and I glimpsed light. The more I learned about my new surroundings, the more I wondered what the next world had in store for me.

PART TWO

Hong Kong

CHAPTER 9

BEING A LOTUS

The tree that does not bend with the wind
will be broken by the wind.
— Chinese proverb

A slightly plump, jovial man, my uncle appeared happy to see me, which made me feel better. He took me to his home—a crowded little apartment filled with life in North Point, Hong Kong, where he lived with his wife and four children. My cousins adapted to me quickly, although the eldest, Boon, initially found the situation awkward. According to Chinese custom, Boon, who is two years younger than me, would have to pay respect to his shorter and less educated cousin, who didn't even know the dialect. Once Boon discovered that I admired him and required his help, he gladly assumed big brotherhood. I also got along well with the other children—the oldest girl, Yan, the next sister, Sun, and the youngest boy, Hao—who were all separated by about two years.

Boon and I slept in the lounge. We spent our nights in a little canvas bed that we opened and spread out every evening after everyone had settled down. The lounge was so small that the bed reached wall to wall. We slept side by side and had to be careful turning over in the narrow space, as one stray arm could mean punching the other person.

Every day when the kids returned from school, the house filled with laughter and conversation. I greatly enjoyed playing and interacting with my cousins, who found it entertaining to teach me the local dialect. How wonderful to have plenty of delicious food. In retrospect, they had the normal quantity of food for an upper middle-class family, but a feast compared to our pauper meals in China. How do you compare the diet of a poor beggar to a multiple millionaire? One of my favorite foods was the delicious, preserved sausages that Fourth Aunt steamed. Luckily, at sixteen, my bones hadn't yet become set, so with adequate nutrition, within six months I towered over Boon by half a head and my trouser hems barely covered my knees.

Next in rank among my father's cousins, my uncle was number four, so I called him Fourth Uncle and referred to his wife as Fourth Aunt. A short, good-looking lady, Fourth Aunt exuded kindness, as well as great intellect. She graduated from university—a rare feat in those days for anyone, let alone a woman. Always patient and kind with me and her children, Fourth Aunt talked in a pleasant, positive manner. Everything she said made excellent sense to me. I kept thinking what a lucky man Fourth Uncle was to have her as his wife.

Fourth Aunt helped me through some difficult times as I adjusted to the polar opposite way of life in Hong Kong. Her kindness and understanding allowed me to gain some confidence and comfort. She showed me many skills, such as how to address people, how to relate to others, how to do my homework, and even how to tie a tie (I still do it her way). She was intelligent yet most unassuming. One day Fourth Aunt proudly told me how my cousin Sun came home from school and quietly handed my aunt her report card, then went to play with her siblings. Fourth Aunt noted that she earned the top marks in every subject in her class. My aunt felt great pride about Sun's modesty. In a Chinese family from Hong Kong where academic achievement is highly prized, most kids would announce their achievement, but not brilliant and humble Sun, who was just like her mother. Before she became a full-time housewife, Fourth Aunt edited a magazine. When I read things she had written, I was in awe. Her beautiful handwriting showed so much character and her words were magical.

When I arrived in Hong Kong, I could only speak the Chaozhounese dialect, not the Cantonese dialect used there. Even though Chaozhounese and Cantonese are spoken within the same province of Guangdong, they are totally different. I couldn't understand a single word of Cantonese. Fourth Uncle spoke both dialects fluently, but he worked long hours and kept busy with his four kids when he got home. Fourth Aunt had more time, but she spoke Cantonese and could only understand some of the basic words I used in Chaozhounese. Thanks to patient tutoring from her, I learned the basics of the new dialect. Everyone in school made fun of my strong accent as I struggled to learn, but Fourth Aunt encouraged me to keep trying and to ignore the taunts. It took a year before I could speak Cantonese and communicate adequately with the locals. I found the experience especially frustrating and felt so left out until I finally began to understand what people said.

During the rare times when Fourth Aunt wasn't too busy and surrounded by her own children, I shadowed her. Fourth Aunt's kindness reminded me of my beloved aunt, and this brought up the impossible pain and sadness I felt at leaving her behind in China.

My second day in Hong Kong, Fourth Uncle took me for my first ride in a private car, his Triumph. I felt so privileged as he drove me around Hong Kong. To my knowledge, no one in China owned a private car, and only the very top government officials could ride in one. My uncle stopped at the top of a hill and showed me a school. Ling Nan Middle School lay nestled near the summit of a mountain and featured a beautiful view. A grand archway to the school announced the name in magnificent Chinese calligraphy. Ling Nan once held the distinction as the most famous university in Southern China. When the CPC took over China, some of the staff went to Hong Kong and set up the middle school, which became one of the best Chinese schools in Hong Kong. My uncle said to me as we sat in the car looking at the school, "I hope you get in there one day." I didn't reply, but I thought to myself, *No way. I would never be good enough. But I sure wish I could.*

At that time, Hong Kong was the most densely populated city in the world. If you walked the streets, you'd see millions of Chinese rushing around. When I arrived in 1964, to an outsider I looked like all of the other local Chinese kids, which makes it difficult to understand what a challenge I experienced assimilating.

After growing up in a small village in Communist China, moving to this bustling capitalist city sent me into culture shock. I dressed and talked differently and appeared awkward and slow compared to the busy, fast-moving, and efficient Hong Kong people. A strong discrimination existed among many Hong Kong people against late arrivals from China, even though most residents originally came from China. They looked down on anyone under the influence of Communism. Because I stuck out, the locals treated me badly, especially because of my inability to communicate verbally. Chinese is a complex language that evolved over thousands of years. The written language remained the same throughout China, but there are hundreds of dissimilar dialects and local slang. This worked in the old days, because most people were born and died in the same village and only a privileged few could read and write—but it makes it difficult in modern times.

In an attempt to make the language easier to grasp, the CPC simplified the written characters. A Chinese character, each of which represents an entire word, can be quite elaborate. Some have more than twenty strokes. The CPC knew it would be much easier to write with fewer strokes, so they made changes. For example, book was once 書, but they created the simplified version 书. Those new symbols made writing Chinese easier, but unfortunately for me, Hong Kong people hated the simplified forms, most likely because they represented Communism. In an entire test paper in Hong Kong, if the teacher found one simplified character, you'd be penalized by getting zero for the whole paper. So initially I couldn't even communicate with the written word, because the Hong Kong people didn't recognize the simplified characters or felt too ashamed to admit it.

That meant I had to relearn how to write the entire Chinese vocabulary (all words). Prior to learning how to write them, in school I collected many eggs (the Hong Kong expression referring to zero marks on tests). If these were real eggs, my aunt would have been happy that I had so many.

The local attitude toward the Chinese from China proved a worse problem for me than the language barrier. I arrived in Hong Kong with a giant handicap consisting of the picture of Hong Kong painted by the CPC's propaganda machine that brainwashed me to remain a loyal Communist.

Thinking back now, I realize the absurdity. The CPC deprived us of human rights, our possessions, and our house, and my grandmother died from persecution. We narrowly escaped starvation. Yet as a successfully brainwashed loyal Mao follower, I proved a slow learner and persisted in feverishly supporting the Communists and adhered to my belief in Communism. My efforts to defend Communism certainly did not endear me to the people of Hong Kong.

My blind belief back then helped me understand now how people can be manipulated. Many examples exist of brainwashing, such as what occurs in cults and with battered women. People being manipulated may even defend their abusers. Once I developed my awareness of how I'd been manipulated in China, I became acutely adverse to any propaganda and mass educational techniques. I've also learned not to make snap judgments without thorough research.

People often fail to see the distinction between the citizens of a country and their government. Leaders on dangerous power trips, like Mao, who caused the death of millions and brought a country to its knees, and Hitler, will always exist. After arriving in Hong Kong, it took two long years for me to realize I'd been brainwashed. Once I realized that I'd been duped, I tried to tell people the harsh truth about China and Communism, but then I met with angry "patriotic" Chinese, who even perceived me as a traitor. While many people know consciously that the ruling party does not represent the country—the CPC didn't represent the Chinese people any more than the Nazis represented the Germans—they often interpret criticism of the Chinese government as being against China. The most disturbing incident occurred when I told a group of my classmates during medical school about the cruelty of the CPC. A girl from Malaysia with Chinese ancestors became angry and hit the table with her fist, yelling, "How can you say that about China? Aren't you Chinese? You are a traitor!"

In recent years with more freedom in China, the government has allowed the release of some information about Mao's reign of terror, and a number of good books about China and its politicians have surfaced, including *The Private Life of Chairman Mao* written by his personal physician Li Zhisui (this book is still banned in China); *Life and Death in Shanghai* by Nien Cheng, which chronicles the author's harrowing ordeal as a target; and the book *Mao's Great Famine* by Frank Dikotter. These authors made great efforts to uncover the truth for our benefit. Only through knowing and facing the truth can we as a human race find better systems to live as communities in harmony and prosperity. Mao and Hitler would never have caused such catastrophic damage to the human race if there had not been others to support them.

While escaping Communism gave me a better, more hopeful life in Hong Kong, I most enjoyed the opportunity to meet my family. Going to Vietnam proved infeasible, because the country was at war, and I would have been automatically conscripted into military service. I have always wondered if I would have been as close to my family if we'd grown up together. In Hong Kong, I soon found out.

Chapter 10

MEETING FAMILY

The lotus root may be severed,
but its fibered threads are still connected.

— Chinese proverb

I found the prospect of finally meeting my family exciting and overwhelming. Aunt told me so many wonderful stories about my father that I built him up as a godlike figure in my imagination. I couldn't wait to meet him, though I feared that my god might not approve of me.

Father lived an exciting life that deserves a book of its own. His surname was Lin林. In Chinese, the surname comes first. His name is the same as mine, but spelled differently. Lin is based on the Pinyin system, like all Chinese currently from China. My name is Lam and is based on the Cantonese phonetic system, like many people from Hong Kong. Lam means forest in Chinese. His Christian name was Hon Tuyen. Hon means "Chinese" and Tuyen means "a spring." This meant he was the spring to China. Later Father adopted the name William and called his school William Lin Middle School. It became a household name in Vietnam as the most famous English school in the country.

Father was a very handsome and charismatic man. At the age of eighteen, while a high school student in Shantou, father met Bao (her name means "jewel"), a beautiful classmate from a rich family, who fell in love with him. Circumstances prevented them from doing more than exchanging a few notes. As soon as the school's headmaster found out about the notes, he called my father into his office and expelled him on the spot, because Bao was the local warlord's mistress.

At the time, China consisted of many regions. An army general or a warlord, who possessed absolute power, commanded each region. If warlords decided they didn't like someone, executing the person would be no more serious than swatting a fly. So it was considered a minor matter when the much older local warlord, who had heard about Bao's beauty, instructed the family to bring her to him. He liked the look of her, so he raped her and deemed her his possession. Despite the fact that she came from a rich and well-respected family, she had no choice but to comply. If she were to object in a classical Chinese manner by committing suicide, her family would be in deep water. It may be difficult to imagine nowadays that the actions of one girl could lead to the execution of an entire family, but that frequently occurred back then in China.

If the friendship between my father and Bao had been discovered, my father and the headmaster would have probably been shot. The terrified headmaster told my father to get out of the country immediately. The prospect infuriated Father, but he knew he had no choice. It had been ten years since his father (my grandfather) had died, so his mother (Grandmother) had to scrape together the fare for my father to take the boat to Vietnam, and then he left straightaway. The boat journey from Shantou to Vietnam took a month in those days. When he arrived in Vietnam, Foreign Grandmother (the second wife Grandfather married—called "foreign" because she was of Vietnamese origin) was head of the family, as all the male elders had died. Bao had already written ahead to Father in Vietnam, and Foreign Grandmother had read the letters. (Privacy is a rare commodity in Chinese culture, and the head of the family possesses immense power over all other members.) Father landed in Vietnam and received a good scolding regarding the letters, but nothing compared to the alternative if he had stayed in China. Then I wouldn't be here to tell the tale!

By the time he reached twenty-one, Father had thoroughly charmed Foreign Grandmother. He talked her into paying his fare to Hong Kong so he could learn English. A true visionary, Father saw the potential of mastering English years before anyone around him did. In those days, studying overseas proved a huge task. Foreign Grandmother gave him the fare, plus one hundred dollars, but made it clear that from then on he must take care of himself. Despite knowing no English, he got into one of the best schools in Hong Kong—King's College. Within months he became so good at grammar that he began tutoring his classmates privately and earned enough money to cover his own fees and living expenses. From the beginning, he showed ingenuity when it came to teaching.

One of his students admired him so much that he took Father home to introduce him to his beautiful younger sister, who became my mother. According to my mother, Big Grandmother (her mother) fell in love with Father straightaway. I can believe that because, although my parents divorced before I reunited with them, whenever I talked to Big Grandmother about my father, her eyes lit up and she almost always took his side.

Father went back to Vietnam after his marriage to my mother and started working in the family store, the fishermen supply wholesale business. Gradually business declined, however. Father saw the end coming and decided to leave and start his own company selling wholesale seafood, but that business also quickly failed due to lack of capital, so he ended up declaring bankruptcy.

It is not surprising that Father then turned to teaching, which he had found he liked immensely while tutoring fellow students in Hong Kong. He possessed a gift for teaching and also knew English, which soon made him a sought after teacher. One day a pretty student named Huong said to Father, "Mister Lin, you are a wonderful teacher. You should start your own school." Being logical, Father said to her in his typical way, "I cannot start my own school because number one, I don't have the money; and number two, I don't have any connections to get a license." As is the case in many countries, in Vietnam you got nowhere without connections and money.

Huong replied, "Oh, that's all right. I will take care of that." She proceeded to loan him the money and got him a license. Huong turned out to be an extremely well-connected lady from a very wealthy family, and like many ladies she found my father attractive. After he migrated to Australia years later, I grilled him to get material for the reconstruction of my life. I wanted to know all about him, especially his romantic life, because he was well known as a womanizer.

Looking him straight in the eyes and using my most professional interrogative manner, I asked him, "Father, was Huong good-looking?"

"Many Vietnamese ladies are slim and beautiful; Huong was exceptionally so," he replied.

"Did you go to bed with Huong?"

He looked into my eyes and said, "I have an absolute unbroken rule. Never sleep with my students."

He answered me with pride in his eyes, but I thought I caught a glimpse of regret.

After the help from Huong, entirely through his own efforts, Father's William Lin Middle School began to thrive. Admittedly, the American presence proved helpful. During the time of the Vietnam War, the US sent many soldiers there, so English proved a useful tool for the locals to have in order to get well-paying jobs. Father was a genius at teaching as well as organizing and conducting educational business. Soon his school became famous and had a long waiting list, despite the fact that he charged several times more than other schools. Even now his school has alumni all over the world. His graduation certificate was worth its weight in gold.

After the Communist takeover of Vietnam, many Vietnamese fled the country, creating a refugee crisis in the world. Various countries took in Vietnamese refugees, and even immigration officials knew about my father's school. Mr. Du, a teacher who worked for Father, came to Australia as a refugee and as soon as government officials discovered that he taught at Father's school, they offered him citizenship and a job to interpret for the refugees.

Father's American connection landed him in trouble with the Communists when they took over Vietnam. They threw him into jail straightaway, but just as quickly released him. Later on he discovered that Huong possessed Communist connections and wielded considerable influence. Remembering him even after all of those years, she sent a message to the prison telling them to release him.

Father had a reputation as a womanizer, but not because of a lack of well-groomed, highly educated, and beautiful ladies knocking on his door after his divorce. He knew he could become emotionally dependent too easily, and he saw that as a weakness. He didn't want to fall in love with and "damage" the life of a lady from a well-respected background, so he kept his distance from them. In the Chinese culture, it is considered that a married woman or a woman who has lost her virginity is a withered (damaged) flower. Father did not want to hurt anyone, so he thought if he got involved with ladies who sold themselves, he wouldn't get emotionally involved, and they had nothing to lose since they were already "damaged." In any case, Father often paid for his women, but he became emotionally involved with them soon enough.

Not that I condone what he did, but it is also Chinese culture that children don't criticize their parents. I didn't know the full circumstances of his situation, so I feel I have no right to judge anyone, especially my own father. I sensed that Father was a caring, loving, kind man who especially felt responsible for his ladies. Perhaps he wanted to make up for not being able to take care of Bao. His definition of responsibility proved different from our present day idea, but he truly cared.

I was sixteen when we reunited, and Father totally charmed me. For me, he turned out to indeed be a loving god and the perfect father of my dreams. Father came to Hong Kong to meet me four months after I arrived and we spent a week together. When we saw each other, he hugged me, and I really loved that sensation and the contact. He ruffled my hair, and it made me feel comforted and cherished.

We stayed in the Southern Nation Hotel for the week; a much nicer hotel than the little one in Shenzhen where I stayed with Mr. Wu and his wife and daughter during my escape from China. At that time, Hong Kong also rationed water, so in the apartment where Fourth Uncle lived we had no bath. We filled up many containers once a week and used a bucket of hot water for cleaning. This didn't bother me, as it was much better than what I grew up with back in China. But I had never seen a bath until I stayed in the hotel with Father. He showed me how to fill up the bathtub and how to bathe. Soaking in the warm water felt so heavenly that I didn't want to get out. Finally an hour later, Father knocked on the door to see if I was all right.

Each night I dined with Father and a group of his friends. After dinner he went out with them and I returned to the hotel to study. He didn't spend much time alone with me. On one rare occasion, we had half an hour alone, so he gave me an English grammar lesson. I still have the piece of paper he wrote on during the mini lecture. Father was a magical teacher—so clear, so precise, so logical, and so easy to understand. I learned more in that mini lesson than in weeks of school.

Not surprisingly, Father also loved to learn. In 1998 at eighty-two years old, a few months before he passed away from kidney cancer, he sat on his hospital bed and pointed to a spool of Micropore (the white sticky tape used in hospitals). He asked me to bring it to him and inquired about its name, requesting that I write it down, which I did. Then he took the paper and started sounding out the word. The next day, Father asked me to pass him the Micropore. No wonder I admired him.

During that week together in Hong Kong, I wanted to tell Father about the sixteen years I lived in China. I started to share the experience, but the ability to read people's feelings that I learned from Aunt soon told me he didn't want to hear about my tumultuous childhood, so I stopped. How I wish he would have been interested. Father hid his disappointment in me well. At the time, the rest of my siblings were smart and well educated, while I felt awkward and very dumb, yet at the same time very proud to have such a brilliant, well-respected father. As I got to know him better later, I realized he was indeed very disappointed in me. It was a blessing that he did hide that feeling well. Imagine the first time you meet your god and find out you're a disappointment.

I admired my father greatly for his kind heart, his achievements, his brilliance, and the fact that he educated many thousands of people. Consciously and unconsciously, I tried to copy him and make him proud of me. Now I am in my sixties. If my father could hear me, I would love to say to him, "Hey, Dad, I am one up on you. I managed to give up gambling and smoking (Yes, I did become addicted to both; I will tell you later.) And I have students all over the world, too." I probably wouldn't want to upset him by telling him I that have taught more people than he did.

Soon after Father's visit to Hong Kong, Mother came. After the divorce with my father, she found a job as a teacher and cared for my younger sister, Julia. She married a different man, a headmaster and one of the most respected academics in Saigon. I was told that he was a very nice man, who would do anything for Mother and took good care of her and Julia, as well as my other siblings when they needed help.

My parents' divorce was a complicated matter that I only heard about after the fact. Both strong-minded individuals, they possessed very different personalities and rather than complement one another, they seemed to live in disharmony. Mother came from an extremely wealthy family and may have felt that Father wasn't good enough for her. And Father had a gambling problem that he blamed on Mother. As a child of Chinese origin, I don't want to judge them. I don't think it was anyone's fault—sometimes marriages just don't work out.

My encounter with my mother proved a very different story than with my father. She didn't hide her disappointment in me at all. The minute she looked at me, she saw a piece of "rough wood" (a Chinese expression for being dumb) and felt ashamed. Right from the very first day, she dressed me down, telling me all of my faults: I was extravagant; I spent too much money, and on and on about my hopelessness. I always believed I was ignorant, uneducated, and dumb. Whatever bad things Mother could think of, that was me. She confirmed all of my suspicions. I felt so ashamed that if the ground split open, I would have gladly dived into it.

As an example of my extravagance, Mother said someone told her that I would only wear Arrow brand shirts. At that time, Arrow was a top shirt brand, although coming from brandless China I didn't even know what brand names were. I felt lucky to own a pair of baggy pants and some shirts—never mind the name on the shirts. After Mother said this to me, I asked around about brand names. Then I thought, *Even a "rough wood" like me knows it's silly to pay more just for a name.* To this day, I've never worn an Arrow shirt.

In China growing up, I imagined my mother to be as loving as Aunt, if not more so. After all, blood is thicker than water. Everyone told me about Mother's beauty and clever mind. When

I finally met her, I didn't feel disappointment. Instead I felt overwhelmed about being an embarrassment to her. At the time, I didn't realize the importance of self-esteem, and whatever little of it I had, Mother squashed. I know now that without Aunt's deep and unconditional love, I wouldn't have been able to repair my self-esteem and develop it at all.

I never forgot my dream to bring a better life to Aunt back home, so I saved every penny. I walked thirty minutes to school to save a twenty-cent train fare and then sent whatever money I could scrape together to Aunt. Despite this extreme frugality, I still believed what Mother said about me being extravagant. I never questioned how she knew that. So eager was I to live up to her expectations that I dutifully promised her to be frugal, study hard, and behave well. After we met, each week I sent her an account of every cent I spent. (Come to think of it, that's probably why I hate listing my expenses for my tax return. I did the list for months and months for Mother.) One day she wrote me and said, "I don't have time to read them, so don't send me any more."

As the years went by, I met Mother again. She left her second husband before Vietnam fell to the Viet Cong and immigrated to the US. She lived in New York City. She was an amazing lady, full of life and vigor. At seventy she still taught full time as a kindergarten teacher. Despite her limited English, when she landed in the US in 1968—the same year I started medical school—she managed to get a green card, went to college, and worked until well past seventy. Mother also managed to find a way to get into a government subsidized, three-bedroom apartment that even the locals found difficult to obtain.

What a great joy it was to meet my two sisters. I met my elder sister, Celia, the year after meeting my parents when she was heading to study in the US and stopped for a few days in Hong Kong. The beautiful daughter of a famous headmaster, she displayed a confident, almost regal bearing. Men rushed to open doors for her, and one of our distant cousins, Lo, became instantly infatuated with her. I admired and fell in love with my big sister, and she treated me kindly. She realized that my country upbringing had not prepared me for city social life, so she taught me all kinds of proper mannerisms in the Western world, such as how to introduce acquaintances to new friends when you bump into each other.

Eight years later when we met again while I visited the US on scholarship and we were taking a walk and talking, I commented to Celia, "Wouldn't it be really cool to live one's life with a respectable job and wear formal clothes, and then have another life as a hippy and let it all hang out?" I love the freedom of sloppy clothes and creative thinking. The idea of two different jobs—unknown to me then—really appealed to me.

At that comment, Celia stopped suddenly and said, "Hey, Paul, it's a good thing I did not grow up with you, because you could be a bad influence."

Me? An influence on my sophisticated sister? That comment made me feel so good. As I learned more about my sister, I noticed that Celia possessed strong self-control and always made a big effort with her tidy and formal appearance. Maybe deep down she longed to let her hair down sometimes.

Soon after Celia's visit, my younger sister, Julia, a talented pianist, also passed through on her way to study overseas. She heard about Celia and me having a good time and demanded the same attention, except better. It made me feel so proud to be an older brother.

Mother warned me about Julia's brilliance and unpredictable artist's temperament and told me to treat her with great care and respect. I was pleasantly surprised to find Julia a perfect younger sister. Pretty and well behaved, she showed no signs of an artistic temperament. We get along very well, and she has trust in me. Many years later during pregnancy, she experienced gestational diabetes (a temporary form of diabetes during pregnancy that usually disappears after the birth of the child but does increase the chance of getting diabetes later in life). I advised her to avoid eating sugar. As an experienced family physician, I know how few people follow and adhere to medical advice regarding diet, but I felt pleased to see that she took my advice for more than thirty years and didn't develop diabetes.

During her trip to Hong Kong, Julia and I enjoyed a wonderful time. I tried to take her to more places than Celia. Well, that was what I told her anyway. What good would a big brother be if he can't take his younger sister to more fun places than anyone else? It still amazes me that despite growing up separately, we share many commonalities as siblings. We all possess big eyes like Father, and there is a tone we use when talking that sounds like him. All of us like working hard and enjoy sharing ideas and skills. Julia is a well-respected, award-winning piano teacher today, and my brothers both love teaching.

I also enjoyed meeting my nieces and nephew, especially Vincent, the son of my elder brother Andrew. I first met Vincent when he was five and a bright but naughty boy. If I stood near a puddle, Vincent could not resist throwing a pebble in to splash my trousers. We had a game going: he would try to get away with calling me Paul instead of Uncle. Being Chinese, I taught my kids to address their uncles as uncle; even my friends are uncles. My kids would never call my brother Andrew, even in jest. When Vincent called me Paul, I would pretend not to hear him, even when he shouted. When he really wanted to play, he gave in and called me Uncle Paul, and then I showered him with attention. Eventually he came to like addressing me as Uncle Paul.

Vincent matured to a delightful, intelligent, and multitalented man. In addition to being a superb violinist, he became a doctor and an internationally acclaimed, bestselling author. His first book, *Bloodletting and Miraculous Cures*, based on his experience in medical school, won the prestigious national literature award, the Scotiabank Giller Prize, in 2006. The book was also used to create a television series. I was most delighted, however, by his novel, *The Headmaster's Wager*. The book is based in Vietnam and tells the story of the headmaster of a famous school. Although Vincent says it's a fictionalized account, much of it rings true to me as my father's story. I always had the feeling that my father sought a woman who would love him wholeheartedly. I don't think Father ever found the woman of his dreams, but Vincent gave her to him in his book. That gave me a large degree of closure.

CHAPTER 11

HONG KONG SCHOOLS

*Learning is a treasure
that will follow its owner everywhere.*
— Chinese proverb

Considering the great admiration I had for my father, I felt badly about disobeying him the first time he made a request. Though I attended a Chinese school and spoke no English, as an English teacher Father wanted me to go to an English school, specifically his old school, the famous King's College. He approached the headmaster, who allowed me to sit for the entrance exam. I had missed two years of school, so I should have been in year eleven, but all the other candidates were much younger than me and King's College offered me a place in year seven. If I attended, I would be three to four years older than all of my classmates.

I wrote pages and pages to Father, explaining why I could not go back to year seven, even at King's College. Greatly displeased, he insisted I go to King's because it was a top Hong Kong school and English. "Never mind the age gap," he told me. I felt so bad and frightened to disobey him, but I had to do it. No more stepping backward for me—King's or Queen's college, notwithstanding. I would have been so ashamed to sit in a classroom with kids four years younger than me.

Instead of going to King's College as Father wanted, Fourth Aunt found me a school nearby. Afternoon sessions only and a lower-rated school academically, but that worked out well because I didn't know the Cantonese dialect, so I couldn't understand at all what occurred in the classroom. Except for mathematics, the curriculum differed greatly from that of China. In many subjects, I had to start at the beginning. Having to learn the complex way of writing Chinese words also proved especially challenging.

When it came to the language barrier, I most regretted missing the jokes. A jovial person with a perpetual smile, the history teacher told the class something funny every once in a while, and everyone would burst out laughing, except for me. I sat there feeling stupid and wishing I could share in the joke.

I stayed in Fourth Uncle's apartment for about six months, and had a wonderfully memorable time. Despite the lack of space, the house brimmed with books, since Fourth Uncle and Aunt enjoyed reading and cared very much about their kids' educations. I discovered a treasure trove when I dove into Western literature. Translated stories like *Treasure Island* and *Alice in Wonderland* introduced me to a world I had never imagined before. Just like Alice, I delighted in exploring this literary wonderland. For the first time in my life I could read and eat my fill. I also enjoyed being in demand with my cousins, with whom I played a variety of games, such as imaginary war; and I liked giving my younger cousin, Hao, piggyback rides. The only cloud that hung in my sky and never left me was the dark one of missing Aunt and hoping she would be well.

While in Hong Kong, I met Big Cousin, the eldest cousin of our generation. About twenty years older than me, he was married and had a child. At the time, I didn't realize his depth of intelligence. An engineer, he examined a topic by starting with the big picture and going through the entire topic logically. Sometimes I got a little impatient with the way he took so much time to look into everything. As I got to know him better, though, I began to appreciate and learn his approach. He showed me how a camera works by drawing a picture of a box and illustrating how light passes through the aperture and makes chemical changes to the films. Then he opened the camera and explained how it correlates to the theory.

I instantly fell in love with photography, which has fascinated me ever since. As soon as I could afford it, I bought a cheap camera, and I've bought many cameras over the years. I enjoy how when you look through the lens at a subject, such as a little flower, it can appear as something from an entirely different world in a photo. The camera enables you to see the various, often-mysterious dimensions of an object and you realize how much depth and meaning lies hidden in the flower.

On a visit years later to St. John's Point in Ireland, which sits at the end of a narrow peninsula that juts into Donegal Bay, I traveled a narrow road leading to a high cliff. I walked on top of the cliff covered with gigantic stones containing tiny cracks from rough weather. No soil appeared to be in the cracks, but I found little pink flowers smaller than a nail head growing out of the cracks in the stones. So tiny were the blooms that you could have stepped on them without knowing. I illustrated them larger-than-life by zooming in on the plant with the camera lens so that the tiny flowers filled the frame. To me, these remarkable flowers represent beauty and tenacity. They survived practically without soil on a cold, harsh, rocky cliff with no one appreciating their beauty, until I put the photos up on the wall of my medical office among my other prized photos. Since then, many people have commented on the stunning flowers, which to me are a symbol of the uniqueness of every seemingly ordinary person. Like myself, anyone could have stepped on the tiny flowers and crushed them, but the flowers instead went on to be immortalized in the photos on my wall so that people who came to my office could enjoy their enduring beauty.

Photographs such as these help me remember the fabric of life—from the good and challenging times, to people with beautiful hearts, to the world's magnificent scenery and events. Photography gives permanence to life and living. I enjoy taking photos to bring out the best in people by discovering certain aspects of their beauty or movement, such as tai chi poses that show energy and spirit. And then there are the practical uses of photography, for instance, taking a photo of your poses in order to identify the good points and those that need improvements. Way back then in Hong Kong as I learned the art of photography, I had no idea that it would lead me to videography and eventually producing many tai chi instructional videos and DVDs that would reach millions of people.

My enthusiasm for learning proved insatiable in the new world. I grabbed every opportunity and studied my heart out. After six months at the half-day school, my efforts paid off when I took the entrance examination for Ling Nan. Three hundred applicants vied for just four places, and to my surprise, I got a place. It was a boarding school, which meant leaving Fourth Uncle's lounge and living at the school with other students. Ling Nan sat in the middle of the mountains amidst fresh air—a welcome sight for me after months of watching the many people in Hong Kong's busier areas scurry around.

A terrace at the school surrounded by green grass overlooked the famous Happy Valley, and a goldfish pond occupied the midway. Every day after dinner, I walked down to admire the goldfish, and then I'd go up to the terrace to enjoy the heavenly sunset. At dawn on the terrace, our headmaster often joined the few of us who admired the sunrise and spoke to us and did his tai chi, which awed me with its grace. Mr. Chin was a legend. He had a PhD in law from the UK and could have been a rich and famous lawyer, but he chose to educate young people. We often marveled at his surname, which means money, and yet he gave up the chance to make lots of it to teach. This said volumes, since money represented the main religion in Hong Kong in those days, somewhat like how it is today in China.

Tai chi's power and beauty enchanted me as I watched Mr. Chin, who gave me a glimpse of tai chi's ability to offer a quiet oasis that I could take with me anywhere. This experience with tai chi proved far more positive than my first introduction that occurred when I saw a book on tai chi at a bookshop years before on a visit to the house of Big and Little Grandmother. The description of tai chi in the book as incorporating the law of nature fascinated me, but the photos of martial arts applications turned me off. Having been subjected to physical abuse, especially the Midnight Terrors inflicted on my grandmother, I abhor violence. For that reason, I put the book down quickly and chose not to read any more about tai chi. At Ling Nan, Mr. Chin's introduction to the calming and empowering potential of tai chi resonated with me.

I'd grown up in China, where privacy is nonexistent, and then arrived in Hong Kong to live wedged into my uncle's apartment with him, Fourth Aunt, their four kids, and a servant, only to leave and board at Ling Nan with thirty other boys in one room. So it's not surprising that I longed for a bit of my own space. In a daring moment, I wrote to ask Father if he would allow me to rent a small room during the next summer holiday. To my surprise, he said yes, so Fourth Uncle found me a living space. So small was the room that if I sat on the bed and stretched my arms out to the sides, I touched both walls. I soon discovered that the room was a spare toilet—and a tiny one at that. The landlord put a piece of wood over the toilet and a big piece over it for the bed. He also suspended a piece of wood to the wall for a desk. I folded it up and tied it with a string when not in use and untied it and used the bedside as a chair when I read and studied.

In that little room, I experienced pure bliss. For the first time in my life, when I closed the door, I enjoyed my own totally private world. I spent my happiest times reading. During the days of the August Moon Festival (the most significant festival in China after New Year's), I bought a box of Chinese pastries known as moon cakes. While munching on the cakes, I read Louis Cha's martial arts stories until the wee hours of the morning, only to wake up unaware of the time and resume reading.

Before he started writing genre novels known as "wuxia," Louis Cha (Cha Liang-yong) worked as a journalist. He began writing fiction when his friend, who usually wrote the serialized stories, asked him to write them as a favor when he went on holiday. Cha took over for a few weeks and his work exploded in popularity. Cha sometimes writes under the pen names Jinyong and Kam-yung, and all fifteen of his wuxia novels have been made into movies and serialized for television and radio. His books have sold over one hundred million copies. Around the same time, he also set up his own small newspaper, *Ming Pao*, which he eventually built into a major, well-respected newspaper that covers current affairs in China and Hong Kong. Reminiscent of Charles Dickens, who attracted readers from his newspaper series, Cha built his newspaper readership from a core group of readers who bought the paper daily just to be up to date with his novels. First published in 1959, *Ming Pao* has a huge following today in China and overseas.

Louis Cha's books told the stories of fictional martial arts heroes. Usually a man and/or a beautiful woman with amazing powers and extraordinary martial arts skills, these heroes performed impossible tasks. They went out into the world to right wrongs and save the oppressed and weak. Louis Cha is the king of this genre, and I often suspect his stories may have been the inspiration for Harry Potter. Most of his stories were translated into movies, with some partially adapted, such as the movie *The Swordsman.*

Louis Cha's stories caught my attention for a variety of reasons. His characters sprang to life, as did their journeys and transformations. Often Cha mixed fantasy and reality so admirably that his stories lived in the hearts of millions. One of his stories I particularly love is The Legend of the Condor Heroes (射鵰英雄傳)—not just because it is so exceptionally done. The hero and heroine undergo an unbelievable transformation of their martial arts powers, almost like well-accomplished people who experience immense transformation brought on by personal growth. They use their power to fight foreign invasion in order to save the nation and millions of lives, in the process sacrificing their own lives. The story is set in the Song dynasty and at the beginning of the Jurchen-ruled Jin dynasty's invasion of northern China. It depicts the story of the sons of two best friends: Guo Jing, who grows up in Mongolia under the care of Genghis Khan and Yang Kang, who grows up in Jin as a Jurchen prince's son. Guo Jing is honest, loyal, and righteous, but slow learning. Conversely, Yang Kang is clever, but scheming and treacherous. They eventually meet one another.

Guo Jing returns to Song with his lover to help his compatriots counter the Mongol invaders. They halted the Mongol invasion for more than twenty years, eventually losing their own lives. I love the romance, the beauty of Cha's characters, the development of personal character, and martial skill. Most impressive is that the heroes are focused on helping their country and its people. They had the high vision of helping more people—a community spirit that they saw as more important than themselves. I especially like that Guo Jing is slow at learning (I always thought I was, too), but hard work and adherence to deep principles brought him respect and a worthy life.

During the Cultural Revolution, through *Ming Pao*, Cha defied the CPC and courageously reported the truth about what occurred in China. Outside of the country, few knew of the disastrous effects and the human suffering that was occurring because of the bloody political coup by Mao as he worked to regain power after the Great Famine. As a journalist, Cha revealed the truth, which grabbed people's attention, because almost everyone in Hong Kong had relatives or friends in China. As a result, *Ming Pao* became a reliable source of information for the world about the inner workings of China. At the time, Cha took great personal risk to share the information, as CPC spies could be ruthless. His disclosure of Mao's diabolical power games (a paradox for a man famous for writing fiction) helped countless people—including me—understand the truth about Mao and Communism.

For the first time in my life during that happy summer holiday, I remained ensconced in my own little world away from discrimination, challenges, and even homework. I grabbed the opportunity to indulge in fanciful stories that resonated with me. There in my refuge, I read Cha's books and imagined myself as the hero, fighting incredible odds, taking huge risks, and growing in strength so I could right all of the wrongs in the world. I daydreamed about meeting a beautiful lady and becoming a man of respect and helping others.

In addition to the heroes in Cha's books, I respected and looked up to many of my teachers at Ling Nan. I often imitated them, maybe because subconsciously I admired my father or missed having a father figure. Whatever the reason, I always wanted to be a teacher. My class teacher Miss Lee was a smart spinster with a short chin and a bubbly personality. She taught English and liked me despite the fact that it was my worst subject. As a matter of fact, my English was nonexistent when I started at Ling Nan.

I also admired the teaching skills of Mr. Mok. Though I had never enjoyed geography, because I always thought it just involved memorizing facts and locations and I prefer analyzing concepts, he changed my mind. On the first day of a new term, he strolled in and told us we'd be studying Malaysia, and then he asked us to copy the map he drew on the blackboard. He traced a rough outline of the shape of Malaysia, and as we copied it he told us about Malaysia, acting like a tour guide. He relayed information such as that Kuala Lumpur earned its name because in the native language it meant "muddy confluence," and this location represented where the Klang and the Gombak Rivers merged.

While Mr. Mok did relay facts to us, he made it interesting. In regards to Malaysia's tropical latitude and the environment, he told us that the warm weather and rain made it a great place to grow rice and fruits like mangoes. Every two to three weeks he gave us a test, which required that we review our notes, but he never overloaded us. He shared relevant and interesting facts about Malaysia that made us think, and as a result I began to like geography.

Later on I found out from my classmates that Mr. Mok was a legend within the school. Every year his students got great marks in the school certificate examinations. The Hong Kong educational system is based on traditional methods, with the focus being on remembering facts. To teach his way, it would make it more challenging to bring great marks when the emphasis of the test is on memory. University spots proved scarce, so many parents put massive pressure on their children to do well. As a result, every year a number of young people committed suicide because they or their parents were disappointed with their testing results. One of my uncle's friends had a bright and pretty daughter, Lily. Her above-average results fell below her family's expectations. Disappointing her family made Lily so distraught that she jumped off the roof of a tall building and killed herself, which totally shocked me.

Unfortunately, Mr. Mok developed a major illness that forced him to stop teaching. The school replaced him with Teacher Chou. Miss Chou had graduated from Tsinghua University, the most famous university in China—an equivalent of Harvard or Oxford. Good-looking and in her midthirties, Miss Chou possessed a soft, beautiful voice. Of course, we boys enjoyed watching and listening to her. She also had lovely handwriting. She spent most of her lessons writing information on the board that we needed to know. It mostly consisted of huge chunks from the textbooks. At first I enjoyed watching her, but then it became quite boring.

Eventually as I learned more about teaching, I began to see that knowledge, personal charisma, and enthusiasm are helpful when it comes to being a good teacher, but these traits don't necessarily make you an effective one. Mr. Mok was an effective teacher and Miss Chou was not. I think Mr. Mok would be proud of me for writing my book, *Teaching Tai Chi Effectively*. To write it, I combined my research findings with my personal experience. I enjoy teaching immensely and take it so seriously that I studied theory and modern research on learning and teaching and analyzed many effective and less effective teachers from all disciplines prior to writing the book. I also looked closely at tai chi and medical teachers. Most importantly, I tested all the ideas to ensure they really work and are consistent with tai chi principles. I often wonder if the experience with both geography teachers sowed the initial seeds for writing that book.

After a short time at Ling Nan, I made a good friend. One of the brightest characters in the class, Win Kwan was charismatic and a smooth talker. Compared to my village background, he seemed ultrasophisticated, and I admired his easy confidence. He knew how to get along with people, although sometimes he threw his quick temper around. At first he acted as a good friend to me, but then things changed drastically.

At Ling Nan, I studied hard and within a few months I hit the top of the class, except for English. Everything came up roses, until Miss Lee nicknamed me. In ancient China, being a government official was a most prestigious position. The way to get to the high positions, apart from connections and family heritage, was the public examination system. They held the exam annually throughout the country. Bear in mind that in an entire village there might be just one person who could read and write. Only the rich could afford private tuition to enable their kids to learn to read and write, let alone pass exams. So you went to the public exam, which was administrated by the central government. When you passed the ordinary level, they called you a scholar, and to be a scholar was quite something—more difficult than getting a PhD nowadays. After that there were ascending levels, and you could eventually reach the national exam. After the final paper of the national exam, the chief examiner would select the three best candidates in the country and present them to the emperor. The emperor would choose Number 1 Zhuangyuan (狀元), Number 2 Bangyan (榜眼), and Number 3 Tanhua (探花). Those who went to the Palace Museum in the Forbidden City passed through a huge wall and past five bridges constructed of white precious stones. All the ministers and officials walked past those bridges to kowtow to the emperor and hear his decrees. Nobody ever used the middle bridge, except the emperor, and once a year the zhuangyuan was allowed to walk over the middle bridge. Zhuangyuan became the name for the highest scholar award in China.

Miss Lee nicknamed me Zhuangyuan Lam. The moniker got me into serious trouble. I didn't know it at first, but Win Kwan was quietly jealous of my academic achievements, especially when I quickly took his position at the top of the class. There were two classes for year ten: A class and B class. The top student in the other class was Ying, a pretty, tall girl with a slim and shapely figure. Ying was the unofficial Miss Ling Nan at that time. Miss Lee nicknamed her the girl zhuangyuan. The boys were all infatuated with her, and Miss Lee was heard to say in jest that that the boy and girl zhuangyuans should get together. Word got to me about what Miss Lee had said. By then I knew about the birds and the bees, and I felt quite attracted to girls. Ying was a princess, and I doubted I'd ever gather enough courage to ask her out, but Miss Lee's jest told me perhaps I would be good enough. So I thought about it for weeks, rehearsed my opening line and finally plucked up enough courage to ask Ying, "How about seeing a movie with me?" Calm and collected and obviously much more experienced than me, she replied, "Next Wednesday my girlfriend and I are going past a garden to catch a bus. Would you like to bring a friend and walk with us?" I went with a classmate, and the four of us took a ten-minute walk. One month later, I went on my first date when Ying and I saw a movie. It was a warm day, but she wore a pair of thin gloves and we said good-bye with a handshake. During that era in China and Hong Kong, absolutely no kissing good-bye occurred on the first date.

I didn't realize that Win Kwan had previously asked Ying out. The deputy principal didn't think Win Kwan good enough for Ying, however, and gave him a dressing down, telling him to stay away from her. When I went on the date with her, it was the last straw for Kwan, so he decided to make an enemy of me. A born politician, he realized that creating a common enemy would help him unite the other people, so he skillfully turned the boys in my class against me. His plan worked because of my lack of social skills and the fact that I was from China. At that time in Hong Kong, a strong current of discrimination against Chinese arrivals influenced by the CPC existed. People from China lacked the social skills and etiquette that Hong Kong people possessed. It is amazing that even many years later this discrimination lingers. There I was at Ling Nan—a socially awkward typical nerd who knew nothing about current culture in Hong Kong, and I spoke Cantonese with a telltale accent. I had also taken the top place and went out with Miss Ling Nan, so it didn't take much effort for Win Kwan to stir up jealousy and discriminative feelings from most of the other boarding students and get them to turn against me.

Hong Kong has always been associated with money and a lavish lifestyle. Many movies use Hong Kong, and particularly its spectacular and recognizable harbor, when they want to add glamour—think of 007 with his speedboat. Hong Kong hierarchy is based on money intermixed with the traditional Chinese class system. Hierarchy has been an integral part of Chinese culture since the beginning of civilization thousands of years ago. Everyone belonged to a class; you befriended people of your class and only married the same. When the CPC took over, they claimed equality for everyone based on the Communist doctrines. They destroyed the old class system, but replaced it with an even stronger class system. At the top of the heap were the CPC officials and all were strictly ranked—party members, professionals, factory workers, farmers, and so on. At the very bottom were the poison elements. Once in the bottom class, you were condemned forever.

There were so many things that Hong Kong Chinese could use to discriminate against those from China. Both cultures have strong class systems, but the two sets of classes are entirely contradictory—like yin and yang. The rich, powerful, and academically excellent are the bottom class in Communism. Those who did make the daring escape from China to Hong Kong often lost everything on the way. They arrived with no money, connections, or social status. Traditional etiquette became a lost art destroyed by the CPC and morality changed to complete loyalty to Communism. We were brainwashed. What symbolized high class in China represented low class, and vice versa.

Discrimination is insidious. It passes subconsciously from generation to generation in most cultures around the world. Very often the underlying feeling of what classes are low is planted in childhood and stays with people throughout their lives without them even realizing that it is discriminatory.

In many schools, bullying someone gives people a sense of power. Once Win Kwan made me a ready-made victim, the boys had great fun with me as their target. Hardly anybody talked to me and they played tricks on me—putting dirt on my chair, throwing my bags away, and making my assignments mysteriously disappear. Few realize the immense psychological damage to the bullying victim. It felt so lonely to be socially ostracized. Adding insult to injury, the experience brought back the horrible memories from my childhood. This time I suffered all alone in a foreign country without Aunt's comfort. The experience made me miss her so desperately. I had left my entire world behind and now my new world made me an outcast. At the end of that school year, they gave me a medallion for achieving first place for the year. I felt so depressed that I threw it out with the garbage.

Losing two years during the Empty Period and, as a result, usually being the oldest in my classes made me feel awkward. I tried everything I could to move forward. I found out that to study overseas, you had to redo the last one or two years of high school, since most universities would not accept our school certificate results for entrance (different languages among other factors). There were only two small universities in Hong Kong, and hardly anyone could get in. If I waited until I graduated from high school in Hong Kong before going overseas to go to university, I would have to do the last two years of high school again. I petitioned my father several times (long before Win Kwan made me public enemy number one) to let me go to Australia before year eleven to study, in order to save myself from having to repeat years eleven and twelve. Father felt that all of his children should complete high school before going overseas. Perhaps he also remembered that

I had disobeyed him by not changing to an English school. I appealed to Mother and she did not respond. Later I wondered if she thought me so dumb it would have been a waste of money. In my desperation, I wrote to my second-eldest brother Andrew, who already studied in Australia. He liked the idea and wrote to Father about it. To my delight, Father accepted Andrew's recommendation.

Around the time I prepared to leave Hong Kong, the Cultural Revolution spread its effect throughout Hong Kong and the student movement emerged. Riots by leftist students started, and the situation escalated so quickly that Hong Kong hit a crisis. Housing and stock prices plummeted and many people left because of fear that the Communists would take over.

As it turned out, if I had applied for my student visa a month later, it would have been impossible to get out of Hong Kong. With the mass exodus, the competition would have been so fierce that there would have been no way I could compete with my low level of English. But I did get out, and with an unexpected bonus. I escaped Win Kwan's sabotage!

I had no idea what to expect of Australia. I only wanted to avoid stepping back. Little did I know that paradise awaited me.

PART THREE

Australia

CHAPTER 12

AUSTRALIA AND SCHOOL

If you get up one more time than you fall,
you will make it through.
— Chinese proverb

My excitement about going to Australia outweighed any sadness I had about leaving Hong Kong, and the preparations kept me busy. Saying good-bye was easier, not comparable to when I left China because that experience meant leaving Aunt and the entire world I knew, and it felt so final. Leaving Hong Kong, where I'd learned to take care of myself, felt like a stepping-stone to a whole new life. I felt very sad saying good-bye to my fourth uncle, aunt, and cousins. Ying and I promised to write one another. I even parted on friendly terms with Win Kwan; we shook hands.

On the big day, I boarded the Air New Zealand plane to Sydney, Australia, for the first flight that I could remember, since I had no recollection of the trip from Vietnam to China at ten months old. Everything on the plane seemed so streamlined and sparkling clean. The stewardess served me breakfast on a tidy tray that contained just about any food I could imagine—with some items I couldn't have imagined. Like the Corn Flakes box. After careful examination, which included shaking the carton and turning it upside down, I decided that the correct way to consume the contents involved pouring the flakes into a bowl, opening a sachet of jam, spreading it on them, and eating the concoction with a fork. As I explored the food and my surroundings on the plane, I had no idea that I would one day fly on planes more frequently than many people take buses. Today I practically live in airports around the world. I even do my supermarket shopping on layovers at airport shops.

I'd met every member of my family, except for my two older brothers—Gor Gor, meaning "big brother" in Cantonese, and Second B (Andrew), the latter of whom picked me up at the airport. Jolly and all smiles, Andrew greeted me with a hug, and I felt so glad to see that we shared similar family traits. My brothers and I are like my father—with thick eyebrows and large eyes. Andrew walked with a happy-go-lucky spring in his step, and I could tell he felt glad to see me. He drove me to his home in the western suburbs, in a working people's community called Summer Hill where students find the cheapest places to rent. He and three other overseas students lived in an old, spacious four-bedroom house with a large backyard full of overgrown, healthy grass and lots of weeds. His friend swapped rooms with him so that Andrew had a bigger room to share with me.

I stayed with Andrew for a couple of weeks before school started, reveling in the beauty of the land, the clean, fresh air, and the friendly and laid-back people. The polar opposite of Hong Kong with its constant hustle and impatience, Australia exuded happiness and consideration, and it almost felt like being back in the Chinese countryside. At the shops in Hong Kong, if you didn't make an immediate purchase, the salesperson would give you a dirty look and walk away. This didn't happen in Sydney. The people were nice and what I would call country-like. I immediately fell in love with Sydney and its wonderful people, and I'm still in love forty-nine years later. Having traveled around the world and seen many beautiful cities, I still call Sydney home.

Trinity Grammar School, where I soon took up residence, was a well-established, famous private boarding school modeled after an old English-style boardinghouse system. The expansive grounds featured three football-field sized lawns, multiple school buildings, a large house for boarding, and an Olympic-sized swimming pool. Large by Hong Kong standards, the classrooms seemed expansive, and the desks proved a step above Hong Kong's and innumerable steps above China's. I'd gone from a scarred, rickety wooden desk that barely stood in China to a board on legs in Hong Kong to a spacious, clean desk with a drawer underneath in Australia.

Arriving at an Australian boarding school as a year eleven pupil, I experienced culture shock again. A standing joke among Caucasians is that all Chinese kids look the same. This is also true for Chinese when it comes to Caucasians. When I arrived at Trinity, all of the Caucasian boys looked alike to me. Most everyone had fair skin, long noses, and spoke a different language. On the very first day, a boy borrowed my dictionary, and I couldn't remember which kid I'd given it to because they all looked the same to me back then. Over time, I grew to recognize the differences. As a matter of fact, after doctoring for nearly forty years, I accumulated a patient list of thousands. I can walk into the waiting room and greet them with their Christian names even before they turn to face me.

I needed to learn many things when I arrived in Australia—the most urgent being English. Before I left Hong Kong, Fourth Uncle wrote me a note to carry with me containing some common questions, such as: "Excuse me, sir, can you tell me where the toilet is?" I found that list indispensable.

My first day at the school, I discovered they ran on a similar proficiency system to that of Hong Kong. Every subject had levels, and they put me in the bottom level for every subject. I don't know how I found this out the first day, or how I summoned the courage, but I went to talk to the deputy headmaster, Mr. Ray, and asked him to transfer me to all top classes. He failed to understand my Chinese, so Mr. Ray sent for translation assistance from a year twelve boy, Humphrey Chong, the school's first Chinese prefect. In the English school system, the prefects are selected to assist the school captain. They are essentially a minister to the prime minister in the school setting and wield a great deal of authority over the students, as well as enjoy special privileges. Only a handful of the best students in terms of sports, academics, and behavior get the honor of becoming a prefect.

A friendly and popular student, Humphrey excelled in academics and sports. In Australia we consider sports as our number-one religion, and we worship those who succeed in this area. Our gods are those like Ian Thorpe, who won several Olympic gold medals for swimming; and Pat Cash, a Wimbledon champion. Such people get more attention than our prime ministers. With this mind-set, no matter how good you are academically, you can never be a prefect without also excelling at sports.

Mr. Ray and Humphrey must have thought it presumptuous for someone unable to speak English to ask for placement in top classes. A tall man with a big heart, Mr. Ray ran the school while the headmaster prepared for retirement. He granted my request, but warned me: "If you can't keep up, you will go back to the bottom level at the end of first term." That seemed fair enough to me, so except for English, into the top stream I went. When I looked at my roster of classes, I thought how my best class, mathematics, promised to go well, providing I could understand the questions.

I didn't realize the challenges of learning English, however. It is an entirely different language from Chinese; even the names are in reverse order. My name is Lam Bon Trong in Chinese, but in English it is Christian name first, so I became Bon Trong Lam. Even before I went to Australia, a classmate told me that Bon Trong would be difficult for non-Chinese speaking people. Wishing to be user-friendly, I chose a Westernized Christian name. I would love to say that I chose Paul because it means "small" or "humble" and is the complete opposite to Bon Trong (meaning "born strong"), but the truth is that I finally found a name I could spell and pronounce with some confidence.

I know now that learning a new language is much more difficult after the age of fourteen. A neural memory located in our brains registers various sounds, and by fourteen your brain memories are set and certain new sounds will never register. Unless you are exceptionally talented in language, you will never pronounce certain words correctly and you will continue to speak with the accent of your native language. Another aspect is the overall concept of languages—especially those with entirely different grammatical structures like Chinese and English. The different concepts can be easily learned concurrently by younger children, but with adults, these concepts don't live in harmony easily within one brain. At eighteen, I struggled to grasp the various linguistic concepts, and it proved too late for my brain to convey the subtle differences in sound.

A diligent student used to hard work, I devised an effective way to tackle the language challenge. I carried a pocket notepad with me everywhere, and three dictionaries—English, Learners, and English/Chinese. I wrote down every new word I came across on my pad and checked it in the English dictionary. Often this first step proved fruitless. For example, if I looked up "dodge" and the definition read "move to and fro, change position, shuffle," I could probably recognize "to" and "and," and maybe even "change," but I would jot the rest of the words onto my pad, and again look up the new words like "move," "fro," "position," and "shuffle" in the English dictionary. It would give me several new words for each of these words, but after a few attempts I'd collect thirty or more new words and be lost. At that point, I'd use the Learner's dictionary, and this easier version often told me what dodge meant. If I still didn't understand, I'd finally use the English/Chinese dictionary. I went to this as a last resort, because I tried to avoid the easy way. I had developed the strategy of tackling things the hard way, which I found leads to the best results—in the long run, quicker, too. In this laborious way I collected many new words every single day, and I'd carry the notebook around and flip it open to memorize words whenever I had a spare moment. I even dreamed about speaking English. Before long I could read most of the math questions, which secured my spot in the top math class.

I found my biggest stumbling block to be science. Dr. Morris, who had a doctorate in science, headed up the Science Department. A legend in the school for his extraordinary academic achievements, he was one of most important persons at the school from whom to gain approval. Even to this day I have worked with many academics and prominent scientists but hardly anyone with a doctor of science. In many countries, Sc.D. is a "higher doctorate" awarded in recognition of a substantial contribution to scientific knowledge beyond that required for a PhD. Dr. Morris could have been a university professor, but he chose to teach at Trinity. Fitting the stereotype of a cranky genius, he possessed a stern voice and an eccentric disposition—demanding a great deal from his students.

In class, Dr. Morris often used his old physics textbook, of which no one possessed a copy. Most likely the book was out of print, as he neared retirement age then. Dr. Morris read questions from the book and instructed everyone to work out the answers. The top student in the school, Hanson, always came up with the answer, and I would put on my village idiot face that I'd so adeptly affected. Those times it proved genuine, because I didn't have the foggiest idea what he said.

For the first two weeks, Dr. Morris tried to be patient and helpful with me. He handed me his book, which he had never allowed anyone to touch before, and pointed out the question. "Read that, Lam," he demanded. At that point, my English still failed to be good enough to decipher what he pointed to. The fourth week he shouted at me, "Lam. You have to learn English!" I had a feeling my days in the top science class were numbered.

By the time the end of the first term neared, I'd made a few friends, including the top boy, Hanson, one of the brightest physics students I have ever met. I felt sure I'd be leaving the science class and my friends and that made me sad as I took our first class test. The next lesson when Dr. Morris handed out the marked papers, he shouted out, "Lam!" I went up and collected my paper, noticing with discomfort the looks of astonishment on the other boy's faces. Next he called out, "Hanson," and so on. All of the boys in the class knew, except for me, that Dr. Morris always arranged the marked test papers by order of results, first on top. No wonder the boys sat stunned. The Chinese hick who hardly knew English had made it to the top of the class. I felt more surprised than anyone and elated that Dr. Morris wouldn't be removing me from the class. After that, he'd occasionally shout at me to catch up with my English, but oddly, I did well in physics. Not as good as Hanson, though. I only earned better marks than him that one time.

I love the Australian culture, which went right to the heart of a village boy overwhelmed by the sophisticated Hong Kong culture. At Trinity, I really enjoyed the textbook *The Lucky Country* by Donald Horne. This introduced me to the happy-go-lucky way of Australian life. After reading the book, I found that these things stood out in the Australian culture:

- Mateship. Trusting friendships are something I've always valued dearly. Friendships, though I had very few of them, helped me survive the Communists and my time in Hong Kong. Australia places great value on friendship.

- Being down-to-earth and sticking to the truth. Australians call it "fair dinkum," meaning it is true. You hear this phrase all of the time throughout all sections of the community, especially in country towns. I have not found a phrase I love more in any language or anywhere as fair dinkum. I might not look like one to some people, but I would say I am a fair dinkum Australian.

- Tall Poppy Syndrome. Australians love to cut down tall poppies. Tall poppies are people who see themselves as superior to others. For someone who came from a rigid hierarchal system that created outcasts, I love the casualness in Australia. Here we value the average person. For example, we see our political heads and most rich people as tall poppies, unless they happen to be sport heroes. Then you can get away with just about anything. The difference is that here in Australia, we don't actually persecute tall poppies. We just cut them down to size to help them be more like everyone else.

There is so much more about Australian culture that I love; my spirit resonates with the country. I love Sydney, where I can hide and be anonymous. No more church mouse running across the street as in a Chinese village. I also love the country feeling in the suburbs where neighbors are always "mates." But mostly I love the freedom—to speak, think as you want, and plan your life. This freedom is so compelling that in later years when China opened up to the world, I met many Chinese who subsequently left China, giving up excellent jobs and good salaries to become factory workers in Australia. It helps me to understand why many of our forbearers sacrificed their lives to fight for freedom, and I thank them for doing so.

Not knowing English brings so many challenges that even seemingly minor matters can become quite embarrassing. For this reason, to this day I deeply sympathize with new immigrants without language skills and knowledge of local etiquette. For example, at Trinity the school's prefects and monitors (assistants to prefects) had power over other students, and they often made up their own rules. This meant that occasions like mealtimes became fraught with certain difficulties. If you have read some stories about bullies in the old English boarding schools, you'd understand what happened there.

At Trinity, they arranged the dining tables by seniority, with a year twelve monitor at the head of the table. Then on both sides were two year elevens, two year tens, etc., right down to the little kids in primary school. Warren, our monitor, took an instant dislike to me and my country-boy manners. He instructed us to cut our bread into four pieces before eating it, but since I didn't understand him, I continued to cut mine into two as I'd always done and gulped them down. For this piece of savagery, Warren told me to stand in the corner of the hall where the whole school would watch, which I felt a drastic and degrading punishment, so I refused. Furious, he took me to the schoolhouse captain, Reece, who happened to be a sensible person. When Reece found out that I didn't understand English, he just laughed and told Warren to cool it. Warren considered this to be a challenge to his authority, so he moved me to the end of his table below the primary school kids. I had disobeyed my father to avoid being in the same class as someone four years younger only to sit below a much younger student at Trinity. Of course, everyone wondered what I'd done to deserve such humiliation.

The incident of how I cut my bread is minor but a good example of how seemingly small cultural differences can lead to big misunderstandings between people. There are vast differences when it comes to culture and social etiquette between English and Chinese traditions. It is challenging for someone who grew up amidst Chinese culture to be aware of these differences, because when you grow up with something, you see it as normal.

The tai chi philosophy of listening to others helps bridge the gap between cultural differences and teaches various cultures to learn to understand and tolerate one another. In tai chi our first part of interaction with another person or a group of people is to feel the incoming force before we act. This minimizes quick judgment of others based on the color of skin, social class, gender, or anything else. By listening to the person with whom you interact, you can choose the appropriate response to achieve better harmony between personal relationships. Whether you cut your bread into two pieces or four really doesn't affect anybody. I love to eat spaghetti with my chopsticks. My kids make fun of me for it, and I enjoy that, too.

At Trinity, I noticed that Warren bullied other kids often by constantly pushing them around and generally abusing the power he'd been given as a monitor. My friends told me that Warren had been a nice young man before he became a monitor. This transformation supports the theory that when you give people power, the negative aspects of human nature may emerge. One study illustrates this trend. Researchers created a virtual prison environment and populated it with a group of normal, mentally healthy students. They divided the students into prisoners and jailers and gave each group a list of rules and rights. At the end of one week they studied everyone's mental attitude and found a marked psychological change in attitude, with the jailers having become more abusive and nasty.

I found boarding school challenging because of my linguistic barrier and cultural differences. I always missed my aunt, and even more so during challenging times. On November 13, 1967, at midnight in the Trinity High School dormitory, I awoke from a dream about going back to China and found myself sweating with my heart racing. Tears rolled down my cheeks as I got up to write this poem to express my emotion about my aunt, who acted as my parents and brought me up from a baby until I left China at sixteen. She was everything in my life then, and during the Great Famine I would have died if she hadn't starved herself to save me. Leaving her behind in China brought my emotional world crashing down. The experience shattered me.

The memory of my dream (originally written in Chinese—my own translation):

"Haunted by the Ghosts of the Past"
Trembling with fear
In suffocating darkness
I creep back to my village home

My heart thumps against my ribs
I am frozen between happiness
And dread of what awaits me
Recalling the sadness of parting—
My beloved aunt, the grey hairs, thin and feeble
Ravaged by time and harsh life
A hollow, empty, dark, joyless room
Faint silhouette in the darkness
Holding my breath not daring to stir her
Oh why is she so haggard and haunted?
So many long forlorn days in those cruel years since I left home!
Tap, a knock on the door
Like thunder, the fearsome heart
Jumps out of my chest
Bleeding, pumping
Cold shiver
In the deep darkness of the night
I wake up to an orchestra of snoring boys in my school dormitory
Through the mist of tears
Sad eyes in sunken sockets when I left her.

In my dream, I didn't dare wake up my aunt. When I found myself awake at Trinity with my pillow soaked in tears, I lay in the darkness of the night listening to the snoring of thirty boys, infinitely lonely.

Not long ago, I found this poem in a diary that I discovered among my belongings. I wrote in it from about the time I left China to the end of high school in Australia—a period of about four years. During that time, I had to learn the drastic cultural changes of Hong Kong and then Australia. As I looked through the diary recently, I felt amazed by the thoughts I expressed and how I put them into words. Writing Chinese is like painting a picture; every person who writes Chinese is a painter and your calligraphy reveals your personality and character. I hardly recognized my own Chinese writing at first because I remembered myself as immature, over-emotional, weak, and dumb. Looking at the poem now, I realize the words came straight from my heart. My knowledge of the character of Chinese calligraphy allowed me to analyze the strokes and see that I did actually have good strength in my character and maturity and depth. I always felt deeply for people. Back then I thought my caring feelings for people were a weakness, but now I know it is a strength.

At Trinity, one day I accidentally bumped into a boy named Murphy and knocked his hat out of his hand. Three years younger, he towered over me with his muscular frame. When he yelled at me, I didn't quite understand what he said but thought, *No need to be rude about an accident.* Generally seniority took precedence, but muscle often won out. I guess he looked at a little Chinese kid with huge glasses and saw no reason to be polite. My English prevented me from explaining, so I gestured for him to follow me to a nearby empty classroom. We sat on either side of a desk, and I put my hand out inviting him to Indian wrestle with me. Sick of being pushed around, I put every ounce of my strength into that wrestle. From somewhere deep within, I pulled up more strength than I thought I had, and I beat him. He couldn't believe it, so he put up his other hand and we wrestled again. I won that one, too.

Often people don't admit defeat gracefully, so it surprised me when the six-foot giant stood up and reached out to shake my hand, smiling. Every time I ran into Murphy after that he acted pleasantly toward me. What a much different experience than I would have had in Hong Kong. Murphy showed me a trait that is ingrained in the Australian culture—being fair and having a real sporting spirit.

By the latter part of the first year, my English improved and I managed to make my way verbally. I wanted to be with the boys and not isolated, so I tried doing things with them. The best way to prove that you are one of the boys is to break a school rule. In this case, I smoked cigarettes. Underneath the school library, the boys smoked now and then in a little dungeon-like room. I joined in, and, of course, I got caught. A kind man, the housemaster—Mr. Butler—somehow understood why I had done it. He gave me the mildest possible punishment. I had to stand at the corner of the courtyard for half an hour for three subsequent days. I deserved it, though at the time I felt self-conscious, ashamed, and miserable. One of the boys, Malcom MacKenzie, a ginger-haired six-footer with a freckled face, walked by and said softly as he passed:

"You are in deep shit, mate." The way he said it, so matter of fact and with empathy, made me feel so much better to have a "mate."

After I'd been living in Australia for a year, Father came to visit, and I felt so excited to see him again. I thought surely he'd be impressed with his newly urbane son. Father had previously been very diplomatic; I had not noticed his disappointment in me. But when he viewed me next to my older brother, I noted differences in the way he interacted with the two of us. Eager to impress him with my transformation from country bumpkin to sophisticated city dweller, I showed him around town, pointing out the post office and central station. Father had an interest in architecture and asked me the purpose of one building. I told him it was the town hall. He nodded, and to my keen eyes, the nod seemed subtly different from his other nods to my brother. Soon Andrew joined us, and I felt wounded when Father asked him the purpose of that same building.

I knew that my parents saw me as the dumbest one of their flock. It seemed that my lowly beginnings would always color their opinion of me—not to mention that we never had time to bond like most parents and children do. The excitement of meeting my godlike father turned into depression as I contemplated being a perpetual embarrassment to my family. The more time I spent with Father, the worse it became. Imagine the impact of my god seeing me as the cause of his embarrassment. I used my talent to fade into the background. No one noticed my sadness.

Just before he left, Andrew took Father and me to the musical *Fiddler on the Roof.* I went to the theater in a silent, depressed mood, but the story of the fiddler and his relationship with his daughters, their lovers, and the discrimination and persecution of the family for being Jewish fully engaged me. As the story unfolded, I identified with the characters and saw how they overcame prejudice and challenges by accentuating the joy of being alive, especially through love, resilience, and music. When the curtain fell at the end of the musical, I felt a change in my mind-set. I suddenly realized that it was up to me to enjoy my life. What a liberating feeling.

Later I discovered Stephen Covey's *The 7 Habits of Highly Effective People.* That book took me to a new world of the mind, and it changed my life. Covey really helped me to be aware of self-development and self-growth. His habits give you seven clear directions in which to grow. Especially powerful is the second habit that says you are in control of your reaction to what others do or say to you. That is the key to avoiding discrimination and being ostracized. It proved difficult not to be down when others pushed me down—or worse—ignored me and treated me like a worthless piece of rubbish. It took a beautiful story and music to bring out my inner desire to live my life with passion and vigor. I felt the power of art at that first play, and I have loved plays, musicals, and operas ever since. More importantly, I learned the power of self-awareness and self-determination, which I needed in order to live a more fulfilling life.

Always self-conscious about being older than others in my class because of losing two years to the Empty Period, I wanted to make up for lost time, so I decided to sit for the matriculation examination, which anyone could take. This exam provided a second chance for university entry after the National Tertiary Entrance Test (I was not eligible to sit for the National Tertiary Entrance Test from year eleven). To sit this exam I had to study the whole of year twelve curriculum for all of the subjects within the six weeks of summer holiday. The experience reminded me of the two weeks when I worked hard to get into the boarding high school in China. Every morning I got up and ate breakfast, as if I would be going to school. Then I'd study, have lunch, study some more, have dinner, and then study some more. While other students enjoyed their holiday time, I studied seven days a week.

At the examination I did well in all of my subjects except for failing English. Every university I applied to told me they would gladly accept me except for my English. No matter how hard I tried with English, I hit a stone wall. It takes a lot of time to learn a new language well, and Chinese and English are polar opposites. Like wine, it needs time to mature. I felt dejected and unhappy that I did not jump a year, but I cheered up a little when I went back to school and my classmates gave me almost a hero's welcome because I had already passed almost all of the year twelve subjects. No one even mentioned my failing English.

Though I felt disappointed at the time to not jump ahead and thought I'd wasted a whole summer holiday studying, the fact is that I wouldn't have gotten into medical school if I had jumped ahead one year, even if I passed English. My total marks would not have qualified me for medical school. Thanks to all of the extra studying during the summer holidays and the fear of failure again, I studied even harder. The next year, I won a scholarship to enter medical school at the University of New South Wales. What an immense blessing. I have enjoyed and been fulfilled by working as a doctor. Without becoming a physician, I wouldn't have been able to combine Western medicine and the ancient Chinese art of tai chi to create my Tai Chi for Health programs.

In the final year of high school (year twelve), Father reduced my allowance, and the boarding fees were expensive. Andrew left to further his studies in Canada, and I had to manage my own accounts. I didn't have enough allowance to cover my expenses, and like my aunt, I did not ask for more. So I moved out of the boarding school to the suburbs and Mrs. Koeppen's boarding house, where I shared a room with another boarder. A kind, Christian, German immigrant, Mrs. Koeppen was called Mum by all of the boarders. She took good care of us by cooking delicious meals on a budget and doing our laundry. Though the accommodations proved inexpensive, I had a ninety-minute commute each way, busing to the train station, changing trains once, then another bus to school. This meant working harder to compensate for the time lost to traveling.

From a young age I always worked, including chopping vegetables in China to help Aunt make ends meet. In Australia I mostly worked as a waiter. The only time I did not work full- time during the summer holidays was when I studied for matriculation. Otherwise, every year I found a full-time job during the summer holidays and a part-time job during school time. Finding a job always proved challenging, because employers don't want to employ and train someone just for a short period of time. I even went to a building site to apply for a laboring job, but they took one look at my physique and promptly showed me the door. No, I did not Indian wrestle them.

I experienced my most memorable summer job at the Market Garden. We rose at five a.m. for breakfast and then worked until nearly dark, with only a quick break for lunch. The work proved grueling. Most of the time we pulled out grass and weeds around the vegetable plants, and sometimes we thinned out seedlings. Bending down all day hurts the back, so for me kneeling down on my thongs and crawling worked the best. Later on when I had kids I told them that I crawled like a dog to pay my education.

A mean Chinese man, the boss exploited his employees. I worked twelve hours a day, six-and-a-half days a week out in the sun, and received less than half the legal minimum wage—just forty dollars a week. The job offered one perk, though—fresh-from-the-garden produce featuring the best vegetables I'd ever eaten. From working in the sun, I became so tanned that I looked like an African amongst my Caucasian and Chinese friends (that is probably why my friend, Jef Morris, who is African-American, often told everyone we were brothers).

When the day came to apply to university, my boss gave me the day off. In those days we didn't choose a university course before receiving the high school certificate. I didn't know what marks you needed for any particular course. I really didn't care what course I would take. I only knew that I had to go to university because all of my siblings had. So to not let my family down, I just did the best I could.

I sat there at the combined university admission center looking at all of the choices. I even had to ask the person next to me for a definition of veterinary science. I had a feeling I should do engineering because of my mastery of physics and math. Computer science had just emerged. Maybe I should do that, or some science-based course? Then suddenly a flash of inspiration struck me. Medicine proved the most difficult course to get into; so if I chose medicine and then didn't like it, I could always move down to a science course. But to do it the other way around would be much more difficult. So I checked medicine. And then I remembered how Mother had told me just before she left to do medicine. Perhaps that would make her happy. No one in my class went into medicine for a worse reason.

I handed in my application form and on the way out, I saw a notice about a scholarship offered for university students. The boy who told me about veterinary science suggested I have a go at the scholarship. He said they offered only fifteen places in the state of NSW (the largest state in Australia at the time with a population around seven million). I filled in the form and forgot all about it. To my amazement, I received a scholarship to the University of New South Wales Medical School.

Years later, when my brilliant daughter Andrea neared her final year of high school and contemplated what to do for her university time, she did some research and then exclaimed, "Dad, I don't believe this. It is so hard to get into medicine. Only the very top students can get in. You need 99.9 percent upwards in the tertiary entrance rank."

"Yes, it is tough," I said. "Do you want to do medicine?"

Andrea replied, "No Dad, medicine is not for me. But what I can't believe is that you got in."

Whether I deserved it or not, I made it to the place where I would have some of the most wonderful times of my life.

CHAPTER 13

UNIVERSITY OF NEW SOUTH WALES—FREEDOM!

*Deep doubts, deep wisdom;
small doubts, little wisdom.*

— Chinese proverb

As a starving child, I certainly never dreamed about being a doctor. My first encounter with a physician (apart from my infant near-death experience from diphtheria) occurred at five years old. A bicycle ran over me, leaving a small laceration on my left ankle. Cousin Zheng took me to the local hospital. I screamed with fear, so the doctor had four men hold me down so he could stitch up the wound without any local anesthetics. The experience proved especially painful and frightening. Afterward I had an image of doctors being gods, but malevolent ones to be feared.

So unhygienic were the hospital and procedure that I ended up with a chronically infected wound for six months. It looked like a permanent sore and kept getting worse. Finally, Grandmother gave me a small tube of ancient antibiotic ointment she had brought from overseas years before. The tube contained only a tiny bit, but I applied it sparingly, and in one week the wound healed completely. Nowadays because of strict dating procedures for all medications, I would never dream of using an out-of-date ointment, let alone an antique one. Even though the vast majority of expired medications are quite safe, it's best to dispose of them regularly, no matter how expensive they are. Thank goodness people weren't so strict in those days.

My time at the University of New South Wales was one of the most exciting, fun, and happy periods of my life. My brother

Andrew had left Australia, so I managed myself and had total freedom. Nobody told me what to do and nobody cared what I did. I went to lectures when I felt like it, and I lived in jeans and thongs. I thought girls would not be interested in me, being awkward, bespectacled, and skinny—so I decided to be comfortable. Unlike the more fashion-conscious students, I kept my hair long, not because it was the "in" thing to do, but because I hated getting it cut. I remembered the pain of my early haircuts from the village barber with his blunt clippers. Fortunately, many students had long hair, so I didn't stand out. After being an underdog in my Chinese village, I learned the importance of not standing out in a crowd.

The best part about that time was the complete lack of discrimination. No black label or Chinese background like in Hong Kong. At the university, everyone treated me as an adult and simply left me alone. I relished the freedom to be myself. The only negative I experienced from my poor and scruffy-looking appearance was that in restaurants they often seated me at a table next to the toilet. When this occurred, I often walked out. In those days, I hadn't yet acquired the mental balance tai chi later brought me that allows me to deal with such situations more calmly and gracefully. Interestingly, later on when I became more comfortable with myself, they didn't place me next to the toilet.

While I attended university, Father sent me around forty dollars each month. My rent at the college residence cost ten dollars a week, so to pay for the rest of my expenses, I found a job in a Chinese restaurant working three evenings and one full day every week, and I never seated people according to their attire. The money I earned also allowed me to purchase a Mini Moke—a basic car with four metal posts, canvas doors and a roof, with a virtual skeleton of a body. Eventually, the seats split and the plastic on the rear window became damaged and opaque, so I cut it out to allow for rear vision, but then the rain entered. The roof also started to rip, so I patched it up with several Band-Aids, and again the rain seeped in. I remained fairly dry when I drove fast, but every time I stopped at a traffic light, water poured down through the crack.

There I was—working, a set of wheels, a room to myself, and nobody looking at me either the right or the wrong way. It was pure ecstasy. Until one person looked at me the wrong way, and unfortunately it happened to be the deputy head of the residential college. I had grown to enjoy *Playboy* magazine. The girls pictured in the publication were beautiful and almost too perfect to be real. Photography is a divine art, and I appreciated that sort of beauty as an art form. I don't remember that the photos aroused me sexually, but I liked to look at them. I loved to see how the photographer found the best aspect of the model and brought out the beautiful aspect of a girl that sometimes even the model might not know she possessed. I also enjoyed the humor and the excellent articles.

Today *Playboy* is considered old-fashioned, and even in those days it wasn't particularly explicit or outrageous. I took out some of the centerfold pictures and stuck them on my walls to decorate my room. One day the deputy head of the residential college summoned me and said that the cleaner did not like my photos, so he removed them from the walls. The deputy head insisted that I apologize to the cleaner.

I was furious. *Playboy* was a legal magazine, and I was a fully grown adult entitled to put whatever I wanted in my room. So righteous did I feel that I demanded the deputy head apologize to me for removing my property without my permission. Of course I lost. The deputy head kicked me out of the residential college, but he kindly gave me a month to find a new place to reside. (This did not affect my schooling, as the residential college functioned independently from the educational part of the university.)

Midyear examinations loomed, and I didn't have much time to hunt for cheap accommodations for one person. To my surprise, two other college students, Tom and Hank, whom I barely knew, heard about what happened. They thought I should have the right to hang what I wanted on my walls, so they left in protest as a matter of principle. For the first time I experienced people who sacrificed themselves for principles. I found it comforting to know that such people existed.

We found an apartment for the three of us to share, which proved much easier than paying for a place on my own. That experience taught me that standing up for your rights can be challenging, but you find great friends along the way.

The next year when I walked past the college's living quarters, I saw centerfold photos on the walls and smiled. It seemed that standing up for my rights turned me into the martyr who won the rights for the other boys. Nothing compared to real martyrs who sacrifice their precious lives, but I felt good about it.

As though to reward me, my first year studies were a cinch. Essentially reviews of the high school curriculum, the subjects were designed to bring all of the medical students' scientific knowledge to a high level for medicine. I worked hard in science and math in high school, thanks to Dr. Morris, so I breezed through the year. Thinking university a piece of cake and a place to have fun, I enjoyed myself. I even started meeting girls.

My brother's best friend, Frank, one of the nicest men anyone could ever meet, wanted to introduce me to some friends, so he took me to their house. I went to please him, but when the door opened, I stood in awe of this beautiful girl. Janelle flashed me an angelic smile made even more beautiful with her welcome in a melodic voice. Her eyebrows were plucked into a high curve, like a moon in the classical Chinese fashion, and her petite figure was perfectly proportioned. She looked like a painting of a classical Chinese beauty—just like my dream of a heavenly princess.

I made many excuses to visit Janelle again. Her father was a chef, but I never met him because he worked long hours. A thin lady with angular features, her mother ran the family grocery store that sold food and household supplies for the neighborhood. People arrived at all hours, so the store had to be clean and well supplied. Janelle did all of the work in the store. When I went to see her, I helped her maintain the store while her mother sat smoking cigarettes or drinking tea. I never saw the lady lift a finger. Even in the evenings, Janelle would close the shop and tidy up, then bathe her five-year-old brother. He was old enough to clean himself, but boys are kings in some Chinese families like Janelle's. She worked like a slave while her mother, the queen bee, did nothing. When I visited, we kept busy and didn't get much time to talk. Very reserved, Janelle didn't say much anyway. I kept returning, though, because I enjoyed just watching her.

At the end of year one medicine, I asked Janelle to accompany me to my faculty's annual ball, and she accepted. We enjoyed ourselves, and I thought we'd reached a turning point. The next week I asked her to see a movie with me. She said her mother wouldn't allow it. I didn't understand what her mother had to do with it. She was an adult, and we lived in Australia. Even teenagers dated freely. Janelle told me that according to her mother's rules, she could only go out once a year, and the ball was the once a year. I happened to be the very special person for the year. Her mother would not approve of us dating unsupervised, at least not for another year or so. That astonished me.

Frank confirmed that going to the ball was truly an exceptional event from the mother's standpoint. He told me that Janelle's mother did realize her beauty and had big plans for her. Some mothers believe it is a beautiful daughter's duty to bring fortune to the family. Her mother only allowed Janelle to see boys from the medical faculty. That's why she let me see her and take her to the ball.

Since arriving in Australia, I had tuned myself to the Western world. To learn English, I forced myself to think in my initially very limited English. Soon I adopted the Western way of thinking. I love the straightforward manner and the personal independence. When I learned about Janelle's absolute obedience to her parents, it shocked my system and transported me back to the world of Confucius in China. Confucius laid down the rules for society: thou shall obey your emperor, your parents, and your husband absolutely. No room for negotiation or thinking—self-determination is considered rebellious. I told Janelle to think for herself and insist on her own rights, especially to go out with me, but she remained loyal to her mother's wishes.

I responded by saying good-bye to her.

Strangely, though her beauty overwhelmed me, I didn't feel very bothered saying good-bye to Janelle. Perhaps I never felt good enough for such an exquisitely beautiful girl, or maybe we never really connected. Beauty alone can't sustain a strong feeling. I did feel very sorry for her, though. I strongly disliked her mother's attitude and the way she treated Janelle like a slave. The fact that Janelle accepted that treatment deeply disturbed me.

At an Overseas Christian Fellowship social event I met Katharina, who was in her final year of high school. Very different from Janelle, Katharina came from Singapore and lived with her older sister, Jodie, a nurse. Where Janelle was petite, Katharina reached my forehead. She wore glasses, behind which shone beautiful, smiling eyes. Unpretentious, Katharina loved to talk and always spoke her mind. She also exhibited an innocent faith in all things good, such as insisting that her parents never argued. I couldn't accept that since I believe it's against human nature never to have disagreements, especially for couples, and I told her so. We agreed to disagree, no hard feelings. I did greatly enjoy talking to her.

I often went to Katharina's church and afterward to her house for a meal. Occasionally I helped her with her schoolwork. One day she told me she had a chemistry test the next day, but she had never studied the subject before. Chemistry is like math; you acquire the basic knowledge and build on it like a pyramid with a firm base. It's not really possible to get to the top without the base. Katharina hadn't taken the subject at her school back home, but would be taking the test with other students who had been studying chemistry for five years. It was mission impossible.

When Katharina told me of her plight, I recalled a story my brother told me about my father, the headmaster. The geography teacher at his school handed in his resignation without warning—just to show him up. There was a class scheduled for the next day, but Father had never studied geography. He crammed up on the subject the night before, and the next day he taught the lesson. The students reported the class as the best geography lesson they ever had. Katharina's chemistry test challenged me to discover if I had what it takes to follow in my father's teaching footsteps.

Right then and there, I thought hard and incorporated all of my learning and examination techniques. I structured a two-hour lesson starting with the essence of the overall concept and knowledge she needed for the first hour. Then for the second hour, I focused specifically on the most likely material that would be tested. I found it exhilarating to summarize an essential concept of a difficult subject and share it in a way that Katharina understood. More importantly, I greatly enjoyed introducing her to a new field of knowledge. It felt like introducing her to a whole new world. Best still, I experienced my first real success with teaching. A few days later she told me that she got a credit for her test. Father would be so proud of me!

Encouraged by the success with chemistry, Katharina asked me to teach her how to drive. That worked out badly for me, because a few days later Katharina told me that her elder sister, Jodie, decided she was too young to have a boyfriend and that she should concentrate on her studies and only see me in church. This surprised me, because I thought they were Westernized and freethinking. Up until then I got along well with Jodie, who had seemed to be a reasonable person. I wasn't in love with Katharina, but I really liked her. I didn't want to be confined, though, so I said good-bye to her, too. Like Janelle, I never did get to see a movie with Katharina.

When I got back to my apartment after breaking up with Katharina, I couldn't sleep, so I stayed up all night reading a novel. I finally fell asleep at five a.m. and missed all of my lectures that day. Looking back, if I had been more understanding of the concept of yielding as taught in the art of tai chi, I might have continued the friendships with Janelle and Katharina in a way that worked with their circumstances. With strong mutual feeling, we could have become close friends in time. But I was a young man, steeped in freedom and Western ideas and full of self-righteousness. I only knew to push ahead.

As things turned out, I soon met two beautiful ladies right after my second year started. Within three days of each other I came to know Lina and Eunice. They each had their charms, and my life became a dream.

I had known Lina for a while, as she was related to one of our friends. She came from a very wealthy family, and my group of friends gave me the impression that she was arrogant and spoiled. I knew nothing more about her, except that she was beautiful and seemed absolutely out of reach for me. Then on one of the rare Saturday evenings when I didn't have to work, I went to a friend's party. Though most of my friends find it hard to believe, having seen me on TV interviews, teaching, and public speaking, deep down I have always been shy and introverted. So at that party, I initially hid away, but after a couple of cheap but potent red wines, I felt less inhibited. I happened to be near Lina and started talking to her. Soon I became tired, and Lina noticed, so she suggested that I just lie on the floor next to where she sat. I lay quite close to her while she talked to me softly, without expecting me to converse too much. I felt relaxed and kept chatting with her, at one point making jokes about my grandfather's many wives. Back then I didn't realize I possessed a dry sense of humor. Lina understood my humor, however, and she had the most delightful laugh—like musical bells. She really enjoyed my dry sense of humor—despite the liquid I'd consumed.

Nearly drunk, I went home forgetting most of the night until the next day when Lina called to say she had two tickets for a movie and invited me to go with her. At that point, I recalled the fun we had had at the party and her musical-bell laugh rang in my head. I accepted her invitation and held my breath to hide my excitement.

A couple of days later before the movie date, I was at the university. The school had a large campus with ten thousand students at the time. The layout is rectangular in shape, and to walk from one end across to the next takes ten minutes. The medical faculty is at the far end of the campus. All of the medical students would cross the campus and go for lunch at a place right next to our building called the Golf House. It was like an exclusive medical students' club.

At that time, the group of friends with whom I associated were mostly engineering and science students. Our group's gang leader, Kim, said often that doctors tend to be narrow-minded people and they often associated just with other doctors and medical students. I assured him I wasn't narrow-minded, and I made a point of not associating with medical students. No Golf House for me, because I didn't know of its existence. Instead, every day I took a long walk to the mid-campus cafeteria. That turned out to be most fortunate for me.

One day lining up for lunch I stood behind a tall Chinese girl, nearly my height, and slim with soft, shiny, long hair. Her back had a beautiful line, and she had an almost rhythmic way of moving. Curious if she was as beautiful from the front, I held my breath when she turned and found myself speechless at her loveliness. Something about her hit me like lightning. I suppose it could be described as love at first sight, but I still cannot adequately describe that moment. It was the most powerful moment I've ever experienced. We bought our lunch, and I noticed she sat by herself. I have no idea how I plucked up the courage, but I sat next to her and after a while asked, "Excuse me, do you have the time?" I always wore my watch, but it so happened on that day I wasn't wearing it. Fair dinkum!

Her name was Eunice. She had a beautiful smile and talked softly with a lovely voice. Her manner was quiet, shy, and elegant—very feminine. Everything about her charmed me, and I had to pinch myself to be able to converse with her. A first year art student, she was on her way to the city to meet her mother at David Jones (a famous department store). I promptly ditched my next lecture and offered her a lift. Luckily, I had my car that day. I liked to share my possessions and on many days my friend Kim drove my car. I gave her a lift to the department store, and we made a date to meet on Sunday, just for a drive.

Inevitably, I dated both Eunice and Lina. As I got to know them better, I started to fall in love with both of them. A dream come doubly true—but I didn't enjoy it. I felt really guilty. I never felt good enough for anyone as beautiful as either Eunice or Lina, but I dated both of them. What could they possibly see in me? I didn't think I deserved either of them and found it unfair. So I told them both about the other, and it made them very unhappy, but they still wanted to see me.

One night after I took Lina home when I still lived at the residential college, I arrived at the school in the still of the night and looked at the moonlight shining on the campus lawn. As I strolled in the cool, serene air, I felt as if I walked amongst the stars. What an uplifting experience, until the thought of not seeing one of the girls hit me. This made me fall onto the ground, and I lay there in tears feeling devastated.

While I struggled to find time to work, study, and spend as much time as possible with the two girls, Katharina rang me. It was a real pain for anyone to ring a student in college in those days. Mobile phones didn't exist, and I lived on the third floor. The whole college only had two telephones for student residents, and they were located in the downstairs common room. The phones were not manned; other students had to be nearby and decide to answer the phone. Then they had to be kind enough to ring through to the sectional intercom of the floor. If I was lucky, someone from our section might come out of his room to answer the phone and knock on my door to relay the message. My room was located too far away to hear the phone ringing. Once someone told me about a call, I had to walk down three flights of stairs to get the phone. So it took a lot of time and patience to get any calls through. Eunice and Lina never told me what a pain it was, but Katharina did.

Katharina also told me that since one year had gone by, Jodie no longer opposed her going out with me. She really wanted to see me again and invited me to drop in for dinner. Perhaps this would be a more entertaining story if I had accepted, but I didn't. It was lovely to hear from Katharina, and she even told me that she discovered her parents did argue with each other and hid it well from her. I would have loved to talk to Katharina for old time's sake and to find out how she was doing as a friend, but by then I knew she wanted more than friendship. As tactfully as possible, I declined her invitation.

It took no time at all for me to discover that Lina was not arrogant or spoiled like my friends had said. Quite the contrary. She cared for everyone and never looked down on anyone. One day I went to her apartment and found she'd gone out shopping. I walked toward the shop to meet her. She had bought cod liver oil and a bottle of vitamins for me since she thought I looked pale. With my busy schedule studying, working, and going out with two girls, she knew I pushed myself past my limit. She noticed just about everything about me and looked after me like my aunt. The unspoken feeling she had for me brought back that comfort and security. Without speaking a word, she communicated that she saw me as an intelligent and caring person. I sensed an affinity with her that I had never before experienced with a girl. I felt comforted and loved being with her.

I had high regard for my friends who knew her before I did, so one day I asked, "Lina, why don't you go out with Kim? He is so smart and handsome." At first she didn't really answer, but

I persisted about her dating smarter and better looking friends from my group, until she put her hand on top of mine, smiled sweetly and said, "Look, Paul. I don't care about anyone else. I just like you." She said it so matter-of-factly, as if it was the most natural thing in the world for her to be in love with me. She would do things for me before I asked. When she came to my room, she cleaned the place up and washed my clothes. I felt funny about her handling my dirty underwear, but she didn't find anything I did dirty.

Lina sincerely praised me for my strong suits. If I did something stupid, she had a feminine way of gently showing me another way. She made me see for the first time since I left my aunt that I was a worthy person. She gave me so much. One day, however, as we walked down the street, she stopped to wipe tears from her eyes. When I asked her what troubled her, she hesitated, but then replied, "I love you more than you love me, and you love Eunice more than she loves you. I shouldn't be here." She was wrong. I had no idea who I loved more. I felt unable to compare people and feelings of love. I felt overwhelmingly in love with both girls.

Eventually, Lina left Sydney. Getting over her took a painfully long time. I often wonder how she is. I keep wishing I could send her a message or see her again. Over the years, I have sent a lot of good wishes her way. A wonderful lady like her deserves all of the happiness in the world. The way she loved me—the way she spoke with her body and her words—gave me a newfound confidence in myself that I never forgot.

Eunice had a lovely way of emanating shyness that moved me. Quietly beautiful, her eyes spoke, and when she felt happy her voice could melt me anytime. An only child of an upper middle-class family, her parents loved her very much and did everything for her. She went to one of the best English schools in Hong Kong. Possessing a talent in language and interest in voice and music, she spoke excellent English and Cantonese. She also played the piano at a high level, painted beautiful Chinese paintings, and danced and won speech competitions as a schoolgirl. Whenever I saw Eunice, an indescribable passion took possession of me. Everything about her made her irresistible to me. She was very different from

Lina in so many ways. I felt attracted to both girls for their different personalities and beauty.

In many ways, I was quite the opposite of Eunice. I had no talent that I knew of except to work hard. I didn't know much about culture, music, or higher-class etiquette, and I spoke poor English.

We also had significant personality differences. I love speaking my mind straight off-the-cuff. If there is a disagreement, I prefer to talk about it and resolve it as soon as possible. Eunice is reserved and often kept quiet about things. If unhappy about something, she often became sullen and refused to talk. I would notice the mood and ask her, "Is everything all right? Did I do something to upset you?" She wouldn't reply or would say it was nothing. Her dark mood made me feel bad and that led me to become irritated and speak loudly and shout. When I acted in this manner, she became more sullen. During this sullen phase, my world became dark and depressed—everything seemed wrong. I lost interest in everything, and I would do anything to end her silence. It took me many years to recognize that my severe reaction to this dark phase probably became ingrained in childhood. When the CPC persecuted Grandmother, she often became dark and sullen. So when Eunice did this, my mind subconsciously took me back to that bleak world where we were totally powerless.

Eventually, Eunice and I resolved the issue. She would explain what had bothered her and we would talk openly and become closer. I learned what to avoid, and I loved her more. I always felt so lucky to have her in my life and did my best to avoid things that might bother her. After I started my tai chi practice, as I progressed, I learned to control my irritation and anger. I trained myself to go into a serene state (*jing*, as tai chi practitioners call it) where the mind is quiet and calm.

From the moment I entered the University of New South Wales, life had been a whirlwind. The first half of my second year flew by as I worked twenty hours a week, partied, and spent as much time with Eunice as possible. I don't remember attending many lectures, and I certainly didn't work on anything. By the middle of the year, I realized that the second year demanded immensely more time and dedication than the first, and I had learned next to nothing.

The subjects I should have been studying were anatomy and biochemistry, and they featured many facts to memorize. I prefer to learn logic and concepts and to analyze how things work, so dry facts don't appeal to me. Anatomy is full of boring facts like positions to remember, awkward names (originating from Latin and Greek) with long spellings and very difficult pronunciations—especially for me. How do you pronounce "ventral trigeminothalamic tract" and hundreds of other tongue twisters when your tongue is fixed for monosyllabic Chinese? When you don't study and don't go to lectures, then all that stuff about hundreds of muscles on nerves, nerves on ligaments, arteries and veins, and the lymphatic system gets all jumbled up.

By the middle of that second year, I woke up feeling confused and ignorant, and I knew I had little chance of passing. I hadn't intended to study medicine anyway, so now that I had done the duty of pleasing my parents, I could change to another course, and I would still be a university graduate like my siblings. So off I went to the university counselor to discuss how to change my course.

Changing direction would have been easy the first year, but not so the second year. I'd been having fun enjoying my newfound freedom, so who cared if I became a doctor? I would be happy with any job. Australia is a country of plenty. Many cab drivers and street cleaners do well earning a living. In any case, I only chose medicine because I thought it would be easier to change to another course. Now the chance had come for me to use this choice. Perhaps deep down, I never felt good enough to be a doctor, which is why I kept telling myself I didn't intend to study medicine, anyway. Better to run back to where I belonged.

The counselor took my request seriously and called and talked to both the medical and science department heads. To my surprise, they said no, I couldn't change courses in the middle of the year. I would have to wait until the end of the year, and even if I passed my second year medicine and still wanted to change courses at the end of the year, I would have to repeat the second year. In other words, no matter what I did, I would have to repeat a year, unless I passed and stayed with medicine. She advised me to have a go. All university counselors should be like her. It proved the best advice I've ever received.

Since I had lost two years during the Empty Period, I had developed a hang-up about being the oldest in my class everywhere I went. I hated being the oldest student, and I would hate myself more if I took another backward step by failing the year.

Waking up knowing nothing in the middle of the second year proved a real shock to me. Life was good, and I felt tempted to just let go for the rest of the year and start again by taking another course the following year. Who wanted to be a doctor anyway? I wanted to have more great times, and I didn't want to spend less time with Eunice. All of the medical students were bright, and most of them, unlike me, were consistently working hard. So what chance did I have to catch up to their level? Why waste time doing the impossible?

Chapter 14

THE TURNING POINT

After three days without reading,
talk becomes flavorless.

— Chinese proverb

I decided that I didn't want to give up, so I went to lectures for a couple of weeks. What a terrible experience. I had no idea what the professors were talking about. Getting up early for a full day of lectures, then going to work drained me, so after a week I started cutting back on lectures. By the end of the second week, I felt as if I'd never catch up, and I almost decided to give up. Half a year of coursework seemed insurmountable. Besides, I had a wonderful life full of love and freedom, so why bother?

Sometimes in my life, something just happens—like a storm coming from nowhere. Such a storm suddenly hit me and an urge born during the Empty Period to do something with my life overtook me. I realized that it didn't matter whether I stayed or changed course and repeated a year. I hadn't failed the year yet, so I must give it everything I had to avoid failing that year. I'd wasted two years in China without schooling. I couldn't waste any more time. Not trying my best would be wasting time.

Once I made that decision, it became easier every day to get up early and work hard. I soon appreciated having a tight schedule and living a useful life. Gradually I began to enjoy the pressure and developed a clear purpose. I knew I had to work smart, not just hard. I have always enjoyed analyzing things thoroughly to find more efficient ways to complete tasks, so I developed a method to study more effectively.

I learned that no matter how fatigued I felt when arriving home from lectures, revising my notes proved essential. Doing so helped me remember and visualize the information and then I'd review the material again the next day. While many people might rest when they are tired and start working later, I found that my method reinforced my memory and brought up new insight. I retained more and had a deeper understanding of the contents and that resulted in much less studying time overall. More importantly, by studying when the lectures were fresh in my mind, I recalled more. Often the lecturers set the examination questions for their specialized topics, and they naturally emphasized what is more important at the lectures, which often ended up in the examinations. So I developed a skill to "predict" the examination contents.

As I started to study consistently and with the right methods, I caught up incredibly quickly. The strange names became less strange, and they began to introduce their friends and relatives. For example, one medical term gives hints to many others. The complex medical terminology revealed its logic when I spent time learning the fundamentals.

I tried to understand the reasons behind everything. Even with dry facts like anatomy, every muscle, artery, and vein has a logical reason as to where they are located and their shape, route, and position. The entire body works in perfect synergy and with immense complexity. Once you know the rules, you can apply them to everything and soon it all makes sense. The body is the most ingenuous device. Once I really understood how things work, the facts became interesting and downright fascinating. Like a gigantic jigsaw puzzle, the first pieces are difficult to find, but once you gain a good sense of how it works, the rest quickly comes together and becomes really fun.

I found it fascinating to learn that the body works in two systems, internal and external. Biochemistry is the internal on the molecular/cellular level and anatomy is the external. The two are well coordinated and work in harmony, like tai chi. The external shape is the movements and the internal is the mind and energy. When they work together in harmony, the body functions like magic.

The more I learned, the more was revealed to me. Our biochemistry tutor worked with us. A tutor is junior to a lecturer and often works with small groups. We had many tutors and a few lecturers. A lecturer often gave lectures throughout the entire year. In our year we started with two hundred and twenty students. A tutor often worked with about twenty students a couple of times per week and gave us regular tests every week, which counted toward our final mark. My friend Richard always got very high marks. He would get nine or ten out of ten, while I usually received an egg (zero) during the first half of the year. Then when I started working, I began earning five or six, despite the fact that I felt confident that I answered the questions correctly. Though medical students can be very competitive and sometimes refuse to help classmates because they don't want to be pushed lower in placement, Richard allowed me to look at his papers.

After examining Richard's work, I discovered that he wrote a lot. He gave a lot of relevant knowledge but also raved on about irrelevant things. I asked him why not make his answers pertinent to the questions. He told me that he believed the more he said the more the tutor would know how much he knew and that made his marks higher. I decided to find out and started writing more and more, and I got scores of eight. After a couple of these tests, my curiosity got the better of me and I became brave. I answered a test with long and neatly written material that had absolutely nothing to do with the questions. I received a perfect ten. This tutor did not read the test paper; he gave marks with a ruler and the length equaled the mark. I told Richard about that, but he did not believe me and continued to write his own long answers. I suspect Richard carried on the same way with the final examination, because I ended up getting a credit for the year and Richard only got a pass. Really upset, he refused to talk to me for a long time.

By the end of the second year, I passed anatomy. I had a credit for biochemistry. But more importantly, I got interested in medicine. The more I learned about the human body, the more I marveled at how the body functions and how scientists had come to understand its inner workings. I realized then that I could be a healer and help many people—especially Aunt, if I ever had the chance to see her again. At the beginning of my third year, I started out studying in earnest.

Every senior student told me that the most difficult major subject in year three was physiology. I soon found physiology, however, to be my dream science. The subject explains how the most complex creation in the universe works—the human body. Anatomy is the shape of the body, biochemistry explains the inner chemical changes within the cells, and physiology integrates the whole system the body operates. Studying physiology seemed like learning the secret of the universe. I marveled at the ingenious way the body works, interacts with the environment, self-regulates, maintains itself, and self-heals. Like the tai chi world of body, mind, and spirit, physiology is the spirit that brought the body and mind together. The beauty of physiology is that once I understood it, I could use the essential principles to work practically everything out. I found it to not be a difficult subject, but one of the most enjoyable. I used physiology during my entire medical career to give my patients better care. Later I applied physiology to all aspects of Tai Chi for Health.

Psychiatry was another third-year subject that I loved, though the school allocated much less time to this area of study. I always wanted to know how the human mind works, but surprisingly, many of my fellow students didn't seem to care. Mr. Cochrane, the psychiatry lecturer, was not popular. Most medical students are good at math and science like myself, but unlike me, they seem to find black and white facts better to work with. We have more difficulty dissecting "gray" areas like the mind, as this organ is extremely complex. You can determine with certainty from a kidney function test if a kidney is failing, but the human mind is mysterious and uncertain. As life's paradox, the mind interferes with the body, so even the most predictable outcome becomes unpredictable.

A learned man, Mr. Cochrane talked in a dry way and exuded knowledge. In order to engage with his lecture, you had to pay attention to every word he said and think about his message. Unlike most people in class, I stayed awake and became totally absorbed by the information. I wondered how the other students could fall asleep while he shared such profound words of wisdom.

Working out how people behave and the interpersonal dynamics is the most fascinating to me. I wondered as I learned about psychiatry what I would have become if I had grown up like most people with parents, siblings, and a much less challenging environment. What makes people do certain things? What makes seemingly normal people become so cruel? I had read widely on this topic and it seemed that Mr. Cochrane dangled the keys to the mind.

Sigmund Freud, the psychiatrist who founded psychoanalysis, coined the words *id*, *ego*, and *super ego*. His work changed the world. I admire him so much, and I can't believe that when he presented his paper on this concept, his fellow psychiatrists laughed so much he could hardly finish the lecture. Ego is a widely used term today, though not quite in the way he meant.

While physiology is the foundational science of how the body works, psychiatry is the science of how the mind works, and the latter is in many ways more important. Learning both of these subjects helped me to develop myself as a person, care for my patients, and interact with others more effectively. Later on these concepts provided the foundation to create and build my Tai Chi for Health programs.

Add to these subjects a healing, caring attitude, and you have the makings of a complete doctor. I've spent thirty years training doctors, and I see the importance of this trilogy. The tai chi principles relating to the body and mind are amazingly consistent with physiology and psychology. And the tai chi spirit completes the healing and caring effects of tai chi.

As I became more engaged with medicine, I'm glad I put in the extra effort, even though I initially thought I didn't care about becoming a doctor. Giving everything I had to embrace and overcome challenges changed my life. Much later I realized that I did want to be a healer the whole time. I had always wanted to heal my aunt's illnesses. But at a subconscious level I didn't feel good enough to be in a "high" position as a respected physician. I told myself I didn't want it to protect myself psychologically, so that if I failed, it wouldn't be that I wasn't good enough—rather that I didn't want it anyway.

Back in my early teens, I often suffered from pain in my neck, back, hands, and feet, especially if I carried anything heavy. I had been doing a lot of physical work since childhood, and since we had no medical care, I learned to tolerate pain well.

By my fourth year at the university, my aches and pains worsened, so I consulted an orthopedic specialist, who diagnosed me with osteoarthritis, a progressive condition that he said originated during my teenage years. Prolonged malnutrition during childhood delays the growth of cartilage, and poorly developed cartilage does not protect the joints properly. Working with heavy objects also damaged the joints without good cartilage linings to protect them. That's why at such a young age I experienced osteoarthritis, which is often called the "wear and tear" or "degenerative" arthritis.

The specialist didn't seem to be concerned as to why I had developed this condition at such a young age. He seemed in a hurry, so he just gave me a bottle of Indocin (Indomethacin) tablets to take. Indocin is a potent anti-inflammatory that would have eased the pain temporarily, but it does carry serious side effects, such as causing gastric ulcers, which can be dangerous. My sister Julia's father-in-law died from bleeding from gastric ulcers caused by aspirin, which is similar to Indocin. Worse still, on very rare occasions Indocin can cause aplastic anemia (the bone marrow stops producing blood cells), which is fatal. So I decided not to take it. Without treatment, my condition continued to deteriorate.

My future of living an active life didn't look very bright. Many people with the same arthritis have hip and knee replacements in their early forties after developing the condition much later than me. The resulting pain affected my lifestyle more and more as every year passed.

Though I studied diligently and felt happy with my studies and work, my relationship with Eunice gradually deteriorated. Our communication problem worsened. She would get upset with me or I would be critical of her. I loved Eunice passionately, which seemed to make me expect more of her, and as a result I became more irritable with our interactions. The unhappier we became, the more quiet and dark moods Eunice had, and the more irritable I became—which caused us to spiral downward. Instead of finding better ways to communicate, I started smoking.

During the second year when I dated Lina and Eunice and before I got kicked out of the residence at college, I met Danny. A tall, friendly, and charismatic overseas student from Indonesia, he never told me but I found out that he topped the engineering faculty. He went out with Josephine, so Lina, Danny, Josephine, and I often caught a meal or movie together. Danny smoked and offered me a cigarette now and then. The memory of getting caught in school for smoking and being punished for it didn't serve as a deterrent. Rather it became a symbol of defiance to authority. Danny told me that I looked really mature with a cigarette dangling from my lips. I smiled and thought he wanted to take me down the smoking track with him, but I felt too smart to be influenced in that way. I smoked occasionally just to be social with friends, but perhaps Danny's comments came back at the time I wanted to hear them. Experiencing a crisis in my life with my strained relationship with Eunice, I thought that the cool and mature me with a cigarette dangling from my lips could help solve that crisis.

Delivering self-harm gives you a sweet feeling, as though you are brave to do that. Defiance made me feel big and mature. Sometimes when I smoked, I blew the smoke out to create a virtual screen that kept out my troubles. When I got angry, I took out the packet of cigarettes and struck a match, which gave me a mature mental image. When I blew out the smoke, my problems slipped from my mind. The smokescreen worked liked magic. What's more, it made Eunice unhappy and that seemed to give me a sinister kind of satisfaction. I said to myself, "See what you did. I smoke because you make me so mad!"

Smoking made things worse, but it paled in comparison to gambling. Over the years, I often went with a group of friends to the illegal gambling joint in Chinatown. Back then only a few restaurants existed in Chinatown. The gambling joint ran one. It offered the cheapest and best food, so students flocked there. Some of my friends snuck to the back occasionally to play a few games while waiting for their meal. They played pai gow, a fast turnover game with dominoes that involved a combination of luck and skill. Every now and then I put a few dollars next to one of my friend's bets as a show of support. Sometimes I won, which I considered a bonus, but I never really became engaged.

Then one day while in Chinatown, I had nearly one hundred dollars on me—an unusually rich time for me. I felt miserable after an argument with Eunice, so I stopped for a meal and walked into the gambling joint just to forget my troubles. After two hours, I won two hundred dollars. I would have had to work for weeks to make that amount of money. I went home feeling so smart, and my friends envied me.

The cliché of the first lucky win being a bad thing proved true for me—it became a curse. I went back again when things went wrong, and in no time, I became hooked. When you are winning, you're no longer downtrodden; you are the king in full control of your kingdom. When winning, I felt on top of the world. The urge to gamble mushroomed until nothing else in life mattered. Delirious about big wins, I became desperate to gamble. At the gambling table, you feel invincible. Adrenalin rushes through your veins, giving you a euphoric feeling similar to drugs. Time ceases to exist, worries disappear, frustrations vanish, and you feel like the master of your life.

Gambling resembles a destructive worm that bores through an apple and destroys it from the inside. Before long I lost what little I possessed. The worst by-product was my loss of self-respect. I borrowed money from friends and from Eunice and went straight out and lost it all. The debts piled up, and I forgot about my studies. By the later part of fifth year, I had hardly completed any schoolwork. I stayed up all night gambling and smoking instead.

Prior to their divorce, my father blamed my mother for his smoking and gambling. I did the same with Eunice, laying the blame at her feet. I told her the frustration from our relationship led me to the behavior. A few years later when I developed some maturity, I realized it was my fault, not hers. I apologized many times over the years. Back then, however, I simply sank down further in my desperate dive to destroy myself. So lost did I become that I had no notion of how challenging it must have been for Eunice to stay with me and how much she did love me. Rather than appreciate her, I kept blaming her. Gambling proved so powerful that it threatened to destroy my life. Like an addict who would risk dying of an overdose to get a fix, I had lost interest in normal life. Even when faced with examples of others who had fallen far from gambling—like Sam, a nice, handsome man in his forties who used to own five blocks of apartments but lived in the poorhouse with his family and still gambled—nothing stopped me. Addicts are often intelligent people who cannot help themselves—like the mosquitoes flying into my kerosene lamp to their destruction.

One day, I came home at five in the morning after gambling away another night and up to my eyebrows in debt. I had borrowed money from everyone I knew—even remotely. At the time I lived in a rental apartment that was probably one of the oldest near the famous Coogee Beach. It was so cheap that three of us chipped in eight dollars per week for the rent. We heard every step the tenant above us took, and when he went to the toilet, we could hear whether he peed on the center or side of the bowl. Rather than go into my rackety apartment that morning, I walked to the beach and sat on some steps. Soon the sun rose, illuminating a beautiful scene that radiated hope and life. Amidst the beauty and warmth of the moment, I thought I saw Aunt standing on the beach. Rather than scold or accuse me, she shook her head gently and looked brokenhearted that I'd turned out like her late husband and my father. With that vision, everything about her flooded back to me—the terrible life she experienced and my dream of bringing her a better life. How did I get so off course and become a hopeless gambler?

Aunt's unconditional love and my dream for her overtook me that morning, and I buried my head in my hands and sobbed. I left the beach determined to quit gambling and did just that. I started going to lectures again and took a job driving taxicabs. For nearly six months until I paid back all of my debts, I worked nightly twelve-hour shifts from three p.m. to three a.m.

I never returned to gambling, but for a long time the bug lurked inside me. Life after gambling felt so boring, especially studying. And whenever I had difficulty at work or with Eunice, I thought about how a quick trip to Chinatown could give me excitement.

Though my father possessed a brilliant mind, he never managed to conquer his addiction to gambling. In his worst gambling experience, Father lost so much in one night that he had to work for ten years to pay it back, but he returned to gambling promptly after paying everyone off. In my father's case, he was in a low position in his family hierarchy because his father had died. I can understand how low he felt in that position and how great it would be to be the kingpin at the gambling table—much like I felt during my gambling days.

Even during the most tempting times, I kept my addiction under control. Whenever I passed Chinatown, I felt the urge to gamble, but I didn't. Years later, as my tai chi practice deepened—slowly, smoothly, and insidiously in the characteristic tai chi way—I knew the gambling bug had extinguished. I am so proud to have done what my father could not. I would have loved to turn back the clock and introduce him to tai chi so he could live a life without the devil addiction.

In 1998, I started traveling around the world teaching and spreading Tai Chi for Health. In most big cities, there are casinos. Like the pai gow joint in Chinatown, the casinos have the best restaurants. During my travels I often visited casinos to eat. As I walked past the gambling area on the way to the restaurants, I would see the same desperation that reminded me of what I'd been. I felt profoundly sad for the gamblers. Before long I stopped visiting casinos, because depressive energy can be contagious and stronger than the lure of good food.

Being addicted to gambling is like catching a serious disease. In the case of influenza, once people recover, they have years of immunity. In real life, overcoming challenges like gambling can immunize us and make us stronger.

Fortunately, I overcame gambling and salvaged my education. The clinical years are mainly the fifth and sixth (final) years. During this time, they stationed us at St. Vincent's Hospital, and we saw lots of sick patients. The more complicated and unusual the illness, the more we the students wanted to interview them to learn about their conditions. The patients would see student after student and finally become tired of us. We felt superfluous and didn't seem to have any positive things to contribute, so it wasn't a very fulfilling experience to be a medical student, but I learned a great deal. I started seeing the fascinating part of medicine when it's actually connected with a real person. For instance, two ladies of similar ages and sizes walked into the hospital one day with the same problem—a Colles' fracture, which is a broken bone in the hand. One lady appeared to be in agony while the other came in with a smile and not at all distressed. It fascinated me to see how each person made her condition unique.

This individuality became even more apparent during my psychiatric term. While the theories of psychological conditions were fascinating to read about, it was quite different seeing real people suffering from these disorders. When people are in a psychological tailspin, whether it is anxiety, psychosis, personality disorders, schizophrenia, or depression, they are like a donkey trotting in circles. Even the most intelligent and resourceful person can have difficulty getting out of it. For example, anorexia nervosa affects many young girls who starve themselves to death, like Karen Carpenter, the beautiful singer who had a brilliant career in front of her and a voice that was a gift from heaven. How could someone like her starve to death when she had so much? Similarly, why did I, after struggling with starvation and deprivation as a child, nearly throw away a promising career and a dream lover?

Interestingly, when people are deprived materially in terms of food and opportunities, they seldom experience problems like eating disorders and depression. When I went through starvation, no one suffered from anorexia. And during the Great Depression hardly anyone committed suicide. The mind is so complex. For example, how can a man become so cruel? Why did the peasants beat up my grandmother? Why did Little Uncle take such risks to bring us food and rescue us from starvation? Why did Cousin Zheng risk his life for Aunt?

Initially during my studies, I became frustrated that there weren't clear answers for these questions. It took me many years to see that as an advantage. The complexity and the uncertainty motivated me to learn more and to appreciate the challenge. Like working with a giant jigsaw puzzle, I learned to enjoy finding a new piece that fits, so that I can see the final picture better, and I finally discovered not to be concerned about completing the puzzle. Like climbing up the tai chi mountain, the key is to enjoy the journey rather than worry about arriving at the top. The more I learned, the better I would enjoy the journey and reach higher levels of knowledge and skills more quickly. This realization motivated me to help people overcome the negative power of the mind and turn things into positives. Motivating people to enrich their lives became one of the driving forces behind starting the Tai Chi for Health programs.

Part of the medical curriculum included three months' study overseas in any accredited medical school any time between our fifth and sixth year. They called it the externship. I really liked the idea of learning from a different country to gain a broader perspective of medicine, and I wanted to visit the USA.

At the time, my relationship with Eunice was rocky. We loved each other deeply, but we persisted in communicating negatively. I thought it would be a good idea for us to separate for a while so we could see our relationship more clearly at a distance.

Twenty-six years old at the time, I had yet to meet my oldest brother, Jeng, though I admired him the most. He lived with his family in New York State near New York City.

To my delight, I applied and won a scholarship to the USA for my externship at a small hospital called Highland Hospital, a part of the Strong Memorial Hospital. The Strong Memorial Hospital is based in Rochester, New York. It served as the teaching hospital for the University of Rochester, which they rated at the time as one of the five best medical schools in the US. I felt grateful for the scholarship, without which I couldn't have afforded to visit the US to learn new knowledge, meet my much-admired brother, and soul search regarding my personal life. The trip proved a life-changing time in all three areas.

I felt anxious and excited to arrive in the US, especially since I'd been brainwashed as a child to believe the country embodied the evil power of capitalism. By then I understood the various political systems and totally believed in democracy, so I looked forward to seeing what America really entailed. Save for a few expressions like fair dinkum and mateship, I experienced no language barrier. Even the Highland Hospital seemed similar to ours.

I settled in quickly and met my immediate "boss," Charlie. Highly energetic, Charlie ran his broad frame up and down the stairs many times in a day. Very bright, Charlie taught me a lot while I also got fitter running to catch up with him. Charlie took everything with absolute seriousness—a somewhat different attitude from our easygoing one in Australia. For example, after a patient received an X-ray, Charlie didn't just look at it and read the report, he took the X-ray to the X-ray department to discuss it with the radiologist. He wanted to know everything about the patient, down to the minute details.

Charlie taught me how to do an excellent systematic review. This occurs when the doctor meets the patient when admitted to the hospital and does a thorough workup to construct a medical profile. Charlie started at the top of the head and worked his way down. He inspired me to be meticulously systematic. This helped with my medical work, and years later I incorporated my tai chi principles and medical knowledge to create a series of systematic, safe, and effective head-to-toe, warm-up exercises to be used specifically with my Tai Chi for Health programs. (Thanks, Charlie.)

I enjoyed the work and the winter in Rochester. I didn't have a car, so I walked forty minutes every day through a foot of snow on the sidewalks. Nobody walked in the US, especially through snow, so it was a wonderful, quiet experience. I'd look back and see my solo footprints behind me. It also proved to be good fitness training. Try pulling your feet from a foot of snow with every step. What a great time for cool-headed meditation.

When in the US, I planned to spend six weeks with Jeng and his family before the term started. I wrote to him, telling him when I would arrive, and he said he would pick me up. He surprised me by sending a check for five hundred dollars. That was typical of generous Jeng, who always gave to others. He had left Vietnam to study in Taiwan and later earned his PhD from Ohio State University. In the US, he had a good job with IBM. The rest of my siblings regarded him as our undisputed leader and role model.

Just before the plane landed in New York, I suddenly realized I hadn't taken into account the different time zones, so I arrived one day earlier than I had told Jeng. When we landed, I called him and said, "Hey, Gor Gor (big brother), I'm sorry, I made a boo-boo. I'm here in the New York airport." He said "Oh, OK," then he hesitated for a while before adding, "I'll pick you up." Later I discovered they had a gas shortage crisis and because of the embargo, everyone had difficulty getting sufficient fuel. Jeng didn't have enough gas in his car, so he siphoned some out of his lawnmower and put it in his car so he could pick me up.

I had a wonderful time. Jeng is a very serious, hardworking person, so we hit it off from the word go. When he had time, I followed him around, and when he wasn't there I spent a lot of time with my sister-in-law Sue, who looked after their two children. Sue comes from Taiwan and also has a PhD. She has a heartwarming laugh and is very straightforward and fun to be with. In contrast to my brother, Sue likes to talk, and she is also a good listener.

Their two children were the most beautiful kids I'd ever seen. At the time, Christiana was four and Johnny was eighteen months old. We had a great time, and I'm not sure who enjoyed playing more—them or me. Johnny had difficulty pronouncing "Uncle Paul." He loved to run toward me, and I would catch him and pretend to fall down with me landing on my back holding him safely in my arms. They lived in a nice house and the family life appeared so loving and beautiful that I became inspired to build such a family of my own someday.

The separation from Eunice worked well. After the long period of being alone, I returned with an absolute burning desire and love for her. I knew there would be nothing more wonderful or important than sharing the rest of my life with her and having a family of our own.

I returned to Australia to focus on completing my studies for the final year. I applied for and got a loan from the student union. For this one and only intensive year, I didn't do any part-time jobs, but studied full time.

Throughout the latter part of medical training, half of our exam results come from the viva, a face-to-face examination with the examiner—often three of them. Even though it is fifty percent of the final marks, if you fail the viva, you fail altogether, no matter how well you did on your written examinations. The experience felt like being cross-examined in court. On the other hand, it also replicated working with real people in real time. You had to be able to interact rationally and apply your knowledge in front of patients and express it clearly to the examiners. For example, in the case of an emergency you must be able to communicate and make sound decisions. One of our brightest students did very well on his written tests, hitting the top five percent, but he failed his viva and thus the final exam. Knowing I have an accent and needed another quarter of a second to think in English, I put in a lot more effort to pronounce the queer medical words, so that the examiners would not misunderstand me. I also knew that once I became comfortable with the pronunciation of the word, I would have another quarter of a second to think of the best answer. I took my preparation seriously.

During the clinical years, the topics are more directly related to actual doctoring, like internal medicine, surgery, pharmacology, and pathology. Once I managed to learn the basics, everything made good sense. When real people were involved, it seemed much easier to me, as I love working with people. Unfortunately, preventative medicine wasn't emphasized much back then. At the time of this writing, it's still a far cry from being addressed as the center role for the future of health care. Back then almost all of the time we focused on emergency cases and fixing serious illnesses.

Ninety percent of the deaths in the Western world today are caused by chronic diseases, but we spend very little time trying to prevent them. Instead, medical training focuses on the management of the ten percent of acute cases. A vast majority of health dollars are spent on treating active disease rather than preventing it. In school, I discovered I had an interest in prevention. I wanted to help people like my aunt to build health and wellness from the onset. I also wanted to help prevent people from developing arthritis in the first place like me. I found that I like to understand the root of a problem and tackle it from the start—not just prescribe medication after the damage is done.

During the final year, I really felt that I could help people with my training, and I couldn't wait to try all of the tools I'd acquired to do so.

I applied myself diligently and passed my final year. What a tremendous feeling of relief and achievement. I nearly didn't make it, but those six long years had finally come to an end (unlike the US system, the entire Australian medical training is a minimum of six years). What a dream. Me, a doctor?

"The Dream of the Yellow Pillar" is a famous Chinese legend.

A poor man walked for miles trying to sell something to raise money for his family's dinner. He became so tired that when he came across a broken yellow pillar, he lay down and used it as a pillow, promptly falling into a vivid dream. In his dream, he joined the army and somehow through hard work and good luck he killed the enemy's general and eventually led the army to win the war. The emperor rewarded him by letting him marry his daughter. He became the prime minster, living in a huge house with hundreds of servants and wielding immense power and wealth. He had a family and grandchildren, but one day he did something that upset the emperor, who sent him to be beheaded. As he felt the pain of his neck being chopped, he woke up with a sore neck as the pillar broke. Any unreal fortune is often referred to as "The Dream of the Yellow Pillar."

Becoming a medical doctor felt like that dream of unreal fortune. Now and then I bit my finger to make sure I wasn't dreaming.

CHAPTER 15

THE RIGORS OF RESIDENCY

A bird does not sing because it has an answer.
It sings because it has a song.

— Chinese proverb

As the end of my medical student days approached, I daydreamed about practicing as a doctor and having people's lives depend on me. The hospital physicians looked so important when their beepers went off. I imagined how cool I'd feel flipping open my beeper and answering, "Dr. Lam speaking." When I actually got my own beeper, however, it didn't take long before I wanted to throw it away. I especially felt like this when I worked inhuman hours and the pager went off at three a.m.

My first hospital as a resident intern was the Royal South Sydney Hospital, a small, country-type facility with four resident doctors senior to the four interns. The hospital's specialists were our overall bosses. At South Sydney, we resident doctors got to do much more than we would have been able to in a larger hospital where there would be more supervision.

As a student you can become a nuisance to the nursing staff and especially to the patients, but being a doctor is different. In charge of people's lives, I felt useful to them. It proved a much more fulfilling role, but it did come with responsibility. For instance, on one occasion while I worked in intensive care, a senior doctor made one little careless mistake by writing .5 mg with the point hardly legible. The nurses read it as 5 mg and counted out an almost fatal dose of twenty tablets for the patient. That is the kind of heavy responsibility you bear as a doctor. The patient became ill from the mistake, but recovered. I don't know what happened to the doctor, but I would hate to be in his position.

Given the immense responsibility of practicing as a doctor, I felt excited but scared during my initial days as a resident. My first term was my favorite because I got to work in the casualty/emergency room. As a small hospital, we didn't get very many serious life-or-death cases. We treated everything from minor sunburns to heart attacks. We worked hard and shifts were tight. Every third night we had to work through, which meant going to work at nine a.m. and not knocking off until the following day at five p.m. That constituted a full thirty-two hour shift. And then every third weekend we worked a fifty-six hour shift, going to work on Saturday morning and finishing on Monday at five p.m. During a fifty-six hour marathon shift you'd be lucky to get a couple of hours of sleep per night. One night I had one hour of sleep on Saturday night and by Sunday night I felt totally exhausted. Chris, my favorite nurse, sympathized with my fatigue, and the hospital seemed quiet, so she told me to go to sleep at 1:30 a.m.

When you're utterly exhausted, you crash out, but it is not restful. Chris had to wake me after an hour because a young man in casualty demanded to see a doctor. I dragged myself down to see him, and he complained of inability to sleep due to discomfort from a very mild sunburn. I gave him a prescription for an anti-inflammatory cream, but with his unending frivolous questions, he prevented me from leaving. Thinking back, I now realize he probably felt lonely and wanted to talk to someone. Exhausted and not in a sympathetic mood at the time, I finally told him to go. When he commented how doctors should care for patients, I replied, "I don't. Bye." I admit to feeling good as I stormed back to catch another nap. Don't tell the medical board!

So taxing was the residency that at the end of the year I had one week off, and I only have a vague recollection of what I did during those days. It's amazing how lack of sleep can accumulate over a year and then catch up with you. All I remember is getting up to eat when hungry and then going back to sleep. Even when awake, I just slouched around the house. The whole week I remained in a stupor, but at the end I snapped back to normal. Nowadays I am glad to report that such inhuman hours are no longer legal. The young doctors I've trained over the last thirty years have never had it so good. They complain about their work—if only they knew.

I learned so much during my year as a resident intern. I loved seeing patients with different types of ailments, and I liked how I could help patients straightaway. They might need stitches or to have a sprain checked out, and I could do that right then and there. We could fix most conditions, which gave me the immediate satisfaction of being able to help people. I found it immensely fulfilling to alleviate pain and improve people's health. My aunt suffered from many different conditions—most likely due to poor nutrition and injury from hard work and stress. I always wanted to help her feel better. Once I committed to medicine, I hoped that one day I could care for her.

The memory of being held down by four men to get stitches at six years old always haunted me. When I became a doctor, I promised myself that I'd never scare children in that way. If I stitched up a child's wound, I used all of the techniques I learned from Aunt to relax the child and gain his or her confidence and used the least painful and traumatic procedure. Everyone is different, especially kids. They are certainly not like adults in smaller size. They think differently and their bodies function differently. Kids have a seventh sense. Even when scared, they can feel who cares for them. When treating children, I moved gently and slowly but always so they could see me. Rather than overwhelming them, I sent them in my mind quiet and sincere thoughts of goodwill and gave them an occasional smile. If they could talk, I'd try to gently engage them by asking simple questions. I keyed into how they reacted to me, which showed me what approach to use. Many parents expressed amazement at how their children happily chatted away with me as I sutured them. Dispelling fears for the kids can be challenging but very fulfilling work for me.

In order to learn various skills, we completed different terms during residency. I also greatly enjoyed obstetrics. I found bringing new life into the world an incredibly uplifting feeling. I felt differently about anesthesia. Not being able to talk to patients dampened the experience for me, but I learned to take care of them in every possible way. Fully anesthetized people are unaware and don't feel anything. Their hands can be hanging out and get hit by something or their skin can get caught in between changing beds to the surgery table. An anesthetist must look out for everything. Most importantly, I learned how to resuscitate someone, including intubation (inserting a tube into the trachea to flow in oxygen) to save a life. Knowing this made me feel more competent as a doctor, although during the following thirty-nine years of medical practice, I never had to use this skill except during the anesthetic term.

Despite the exhausting internship, during my residency Eunice and I decided to get married. When I returned from the US, we had no doubt that we loved each other deeply and wanted to share our lives together. So we took a weekend off to tie the knot. Being a rebel against ceremony and believing that love is more important than formalities, I initially planned to just take some friends out for dinner and register at the registry. We couldn't afford a ceremonial wedding anyway. But Eunice told me that since her parents only had one child, they wished to have a proper wedding with their friends in attendance, so they gave us six hundred dollars and we had the wedding at the Mandarin Restaurant. Though arranged hastily, the ceremony turned out lovely. Stunningly beautiful in her wedding gown, Eunice made me feel like the luckiest man in the world.

We invited sixty guests that included a mixture of our friends and parents' friends. My classmates Edward Young acted as my best man and Rodney Young emceed. We had no paid photographer, but my good friend and another classmate, S. N. Un, did a great job of photographing the wedding. I even bought a suit for the occasion. We enjoyed a short honeymoon. I took Monday off while my friend Dr. John Grey did my work for me. Then I returned to the exhausting residency.

When I did my surgical term at Prince Henry Hospital, I initially worried about cutting people open and working inside a live body, but once we started surgery, the horrified feeling left and I found myself concentrating on doing a good job. The experience also caused me to admire the beauty and ingenuity of the internal body in action, and I found that I enjoyed working with my hands and had good dexterity.

I completed my surgical term at Prince Henry under the legendary surgeon Dr. Geoff Pritchard. A tall, happy, and charismatic man, Geoff's philosophy, which he shared with many surgeons, is that surgeons fix patient problems and see them to recovery—that's all. A magical surgeon who effortlessly completed complex surgeries, Geoff didn't always use conventional instruments. Legend has it that he could use hooked forceps to do any procedure. At that time my registrar was David Sonnabend, a brilliant doctor a few years senior to me. David served as my immediate boss/teacher and Geoff served as the boss and teacher for both of us.

Initially, things started off on the wrong foot with Geoff. The first day when we were all scrubbed up (in surgical gowns), and it was around lunchtime, I asked him when we would have lunch. He replied, "Paul, we don't have lunch here." I later learned when Geoff recalled the incident at the year-end doctors' dinner that at the time, he thought of me as wimpy and trouble. Back then doctors were supposed to be tough. They worked fifty-six-hour shifts and didn't worry about something as insignificant as lunch. He had no way of knowing, however, about the potentially debilitating hunger pangs that overcame me.

Geoff, if you are reading this book, let me tell you why I was paranoid about lunch. Due to the years of starvation, my stomach had shrunk. I could not eat a lot at once and found it impossible to go a long time between meals without developing awful and desperate pangs of hunger. For me, like millions of Chinese who survived the Great Famine, the traumatic experience of nearly dying from lack of food left long-lasting, nasty consequences. I used to get hungry frequently, which greatly distressed me. The hunger sent me back to the hellish time of waiting to die. For that reason, I snacked between meals to avoid the pangs. Fortunately, the surgery nurse kindly told me about sandwiches available in the surgeons' common room, so I slipped out and ate between cases.

Over the years, I became more tolerant of feeling hungry. It gradually developed into three waves. The first wave is easy to handle. I acknowledge it and let it go. This enhances my appetite and improves the taste of food. It takes from sixty to ninety minutes to reach the second wave. At this point, the hunger becomes quite uncomfortable, and I am anxious about food. If I stay calm, however, the anxiety for food gradually subsides. If I still have no food after another hour, I experience a third wave that brings rushing back the old desperate and helpless feelings of starvation. This stage creates irritability and causes me to seek food like a vulture. For that reason, I try to avoid the third wave.

Starvation did give me advantages. Because I don't eat big meals, I can keep a steady body weight. I used to feel embarrassed about being skinny and small, but now I've become comfortable with it both physically and mentally. When I started my frequent global travels to teach tai chi years later, I initially ate out a lot and gained thirteen pounds in a couple of years. Though people didn't notice my weight gain, as I still appeared skinny, I felt uncomfortable and sluggish. So I took care to lose the extra pounds, which made a great advertisement for tai chi's weight loss effect.

When David went on two-week's leave after I started the surgical term, no one of the same seniority replaced him, so I took over his duties. The paper and administrative work involved in coordinating Geoff's operation list proved onerous. The job required a lot of time and meticulous planning and checking. I spent many extra hours doing that. We didn't get overtime pay in those days, but working long hours came second nature to me. I felt happy to be useful. I found it especially challenging to care for patients and do as good a job as a senior doctor like David. An efficient physician makes sound decisions without taking risks with patient health. It's hard to get the balance without the experience.

Working hard enables you to overcome many challenges. I spent much time and effort with each patient. I did thorough history taking so that I could anticipate any potential problems. With each case, I researched the procedures and possible complications after surgery. Then I read up about all of the signs and symptoms of these complications. Combined with thorough knowledge of each patient's condition, I managed the cases without unduly worrying Geoff by asking his advice too often. As a bonus, I learned a great deal about surgery and patients.

How I managed David's workload during his absence pleased Geoff, who commented about the excellent job I did in his speech at the year-end dinner. "When David went on leave, Paul had to take over David's job as well as do his own," he said. "I anticipated a nightmare, with Paul calling me every night, but by the end of the two weeks, I hardly noticed any difference," said Geoff. "Good job, Paul. Feel free to ask me for a reference anytime."

Geoff liked me so much that at the end of my term he invited Eunice and me to dinner at his house. He took me around his landscape and showed off his garden full of Australian natives all chosen for their hardiness. Geoff shared with me his secret for healthy plants. He planted them and watered for the first three days, and then left them alone. If the plants toughed it out and survived, they earned a place in his garden. If not, he'd done his duty. I suspect all surgeons' gardens have only Australian native plants.

One of the most modern and up-to-date facilities in the area, the Prince of Wales/Prince Henry Hospital, where I also worked during my residency, possessed a state-of-the-art intensive care unit. A kind man who found turning people away difficult, the director of the ICU took on any patient, such as an eighty-four-year-old man with cancer that had spread throughout his body. The man should have been sent to rest peacefully in the ward or in a hospice, but the director admitted him to the ICU.

In my eyes, when I worked as a resident intern, the ICU resembled a dehumanizing torture chamber. Patients had monitors and tubes inserted into every conceivable part of their bodies. One to the vein for an intravenous drip, one to the artery for arterial pressure, one to the deep vein inside the lung for special pressure measurement, a tube to the penis to collect the urine, one to the lung if the patient could not breathe, and one through the nose to the stomach.

The machinery of advanced technology is essential for life-saving procedures, but that experience showed me that I love working with people and prefer not to dehumanize them. I decided to work with real people in a gentle manner to help them overcome their conditions and avoid getting sick. Unfortunately, a high percentage of the patients in the ICU passed away, which made it a depressing, gloomy place. After that experience, I'd had enough of hospitals, so I decided to pursue what I love most about medicine—being a family physician. A family doctor is almost like a member of the family. We can conduct ourselves in a quiet, gentle manner and help many people. Back in school, many of my colleagues thought being a family physician (general practitioner in Australia) boring and reserved for the "leftover doctors." I knew I would love the work and find it exciting, though.

I couldn't wait to get started as a general practitioner—but I was not quite ready.

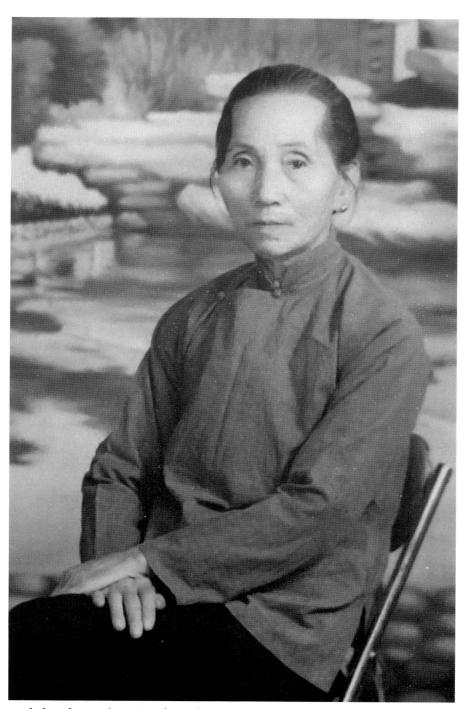

My beloved Aunt (Ma Xiang) sits for a rare photo.

A ceremonious affair, my parent's wedding united two families. Paternal grandmother sits to the left of father and Big and Little Grandmothers appear to the right of my mother.

The Lam family living in Vietnam. Pictured [from left, front row] are my sister Celia and, in the middle, Foreign Grandmother. Aunt Lotus is located seventh and Mother is the eighth. Back row [from left] pictured are Fourth Uncle in the sixth position, with Father in the seventh position, and my sister Julia in the tenth position.

Grandmother's stately eleven-room house in the 1930s during its prime.

Big and Little Grandmother pictured with Little Grandmother's son before my grandfather's mysterious death.

I'm pictured here a year before I left China in 1963 with Big Grandmother and my cousins, Li [left] and Zhi.

A fear of haircuts made me appear fashionable during my undergraduate days.

Father's official portrait during his prime in 1963.

My mother.

Meeting my father for the first time in Hong Kong in 1964. We're standing on the Star Ferry crossing Victoria Harbor.

My first meeting with my mother in 1964 in Hong Kong included a professional portrait of us together.

Pictured is my sister Celia when she visited me in Hong Kong for the first time on her way to study in the USA in 1964.

I felt such pride to show my sister Julia around Hong Kong when she visited me in 1965 on her way to study in the USA.

The worn patches on the knees of my pants show the long, grueling hours I spent crawling around the Market Garden weeding and harvesting in order to pay my educational expenses.

Eunice and her parents saw me graduate from medical school in 1974.

My happy wedding day.

Holding my toddler son, Matthew, filled my heart with joy.

Matthew announces the arrival of his baby sister, Andrea.

Loving siblings, Matthew and Andrea enjoyed playing together.

Andrea tries out tai chi for the first time.

It filled me with such pride to see Andrea participate in her first documentary produced by the Australian Broadcasting Commission.

Cousin Zheng proudly posed for a photo with his grandson Yong-lin when I visited China in 1990.

My first tai chi teacher and father-in-law, Mr. Lum, practices with me in 1990.

Doctors diagnosed Cousin Zheng with lung cancer soon after we posed for this photo in 2007.

Showing my tai chi friends the extensive damage to Grandmother's once stately home proved a moving experience for us all.

Sixty years later, my first school stands derelict, though the beautiful carvings depicting the building's history survived.

The perpetually cramped storage room in 2011.

Here I'm pictured with some of the winners of the Third International Tai Chi Competition in 1993 in Bejing.

Pictured with me at a Tai Chi for Arthritis workshop in May 2000 on the beach in California are Professor Vincent McCullough [middle] and Ian Etcell.

Climbing up the stairs of the Great Wall of China in 2006 with video equipment in tow was a piece of cake, thanks to tai chi.

The 10th Annual USA Tai Chi Workshop held in Terre Haute, Indiana, 2011.

The 15th Annual Australian Tai Chi Workshop held in Sydney, 2012.

After my tai chi workshop in China in 2014, we toured the famous Wu Yi Tea Mountain and practiced tai chi there.

Sharing tai chi with my mother prior to her death in 2014 truly connected us, despite the separation in my childhood.

Here I am in Sydney in 2015, enjoying becoming stronger and more flexible with each passing year.

CHAPTER 16

BREAKING THROUGH THE BAMBOO CURTAIN

One happiness scatters a thousand sorrows.
— Chinese proverb

During my internship, the exhaustion resulted in some strange and revealing dreams. One night I woke up from a vivid one about Aunt. In the dream, I saw a deep sadness in her eyes. Sitting up in bed, my heart aching and mind racing, I thought about how I longed to see her. Twelve years before when I left under threat of death, there'd been no hope of ever returning. But the world had changed.

It was 1975 and Mao was very ill. The new leadership was more moderate and encouraged some interaction with the rest of the world. I realized that going back, while still scary, would no longer be a life-and-death matter. The hope of seeing Aunt again kept me awake that night with excitement.

The next morning, I brought the idea of visiting Aunt up with Eunice.

"Oh, no, it would be dangerous. I know how much you feel about Aunt, but don't take the risk." She looked so worried that I came to my senses and agreed.

But the thought never went away.

The next year Mao died and things looked even more stable in China. I talked with Eunice again. She could see how desperately I wanted to go, so she agreed and insisted on coming with me. While I was scared for her, I knew that the fact that she was born overseas would make her less at risk for detainment than me. I decided to become an Australian citizen before I went, and I got my passport and visa. I also took out a bank loan for the big event.

Back then a medical resident's wage added up to less than a factory worker's, but doctors had good credit ratings, so I qualified for enough money to finance the trip.

Despite my longing to see Aunt and the thrill of excitement I felt at the prospect, the fear of the Chinese government remained deep and palpable. I knew being an Australian citizen was no guarantee. As a matter of fact, Chinese officials detained a journalist friend of one of our prime ministers for years because he reported about the true China. If they possessed any records of my escape from the country thirteen years before, they could throw me into a cold, dark prison cell and everything I'd achieved through hard work, the freedom I enjoyed so much, my friends and love for my wife, and my medical career could all be torn away.

Those who haven't experienced a life under Communist rule may find it hard to understand how fearful and even paranoid people become. The Communists encouraged and even forced friends and family to spy on one another. Parents had to watch what they said, in case their kids inadvertently said something unintended, as kids do. For example, if a child told another child that his father became angry because his boss had shouted at him, the father could be thrown in jail or killed. Children being children, you never knew what they might say or do. In Australia—where I fortunately didn't have to worry about the consequences—my eight-year-old son, Matthew, told his classmates: "My father is really rich." That filtered back to me, and I asked him, "Hey, Matt, why did you tell people I'm rich?"

"You opened your wallet and I saw a fifty dollar bill inside," he answered innocently.

In China, if you said something that seemed even vaguely against the party, it could land you in jail. A remark, however inoffensive, against Mao Zedong could condemn your whole family to death. My older distant cousin had a schoolteacher friend who, when marking a student's paper, put a red mark through an incorrect answer. The red ink also happened to touch the word "Mao." This slip landed him in serious trouble. He narrowly escaped imprisonment but lost his job and any chance of getting a new one.

Given the potential danger of returning to China, however,

I thought through every possible scenario in order to help ensure my return to Australia. I could pretend to have amnesia about leaving the country or say that my parents thought of the idea, and as a child I simply did what they instructed. I finally compiled a list of all of my friends, especially anyone who might have the remotest access to politicians or people in power. I gave the list to my father-in-law, who might be able to use it to petition to get me back if the Chinese detained me. I knew very well that the list most likely would be useless, but having done something slightly alleviated my fear.

Entering China from Australia back in 1976 proved a much different experience than today. Back then, most Chinese had never seen a foreigner. Eunice and I had no idea how the experience would be since no one we knew had ever attempted to go to China.

I took two week's leave from work, which was all I could afford. When we crossed the Chinese border, it was very quiet, since few traveled to China. Two stern-faced officials took us into a tiny run-down room for what seemed like ages. Eunice sat next to me feeling very anxious and lost, as she didn't understand the official language. I felt like a spy interrogated by the Secret Police. They wanted to know all about my relatives, including their names, addresses, and what they did—basically their entire life histories. Then they wanted to know everything about me, including my family and friends, where I had been every year, and what I did at various specific times. They asked everything about my life except what I had for dinner the day before. If I'd recorded that interview, this memoir would be so much easier to write.

During the interrogation, they viewed me with such suspicion that I began to sweat and tremble as I did years before as a child at the mercy of the Communists. I felt just as powerless then. What if they found out about my escape? All of the horror stories I'd heard about the Cultural Revolution ran through my mind, including that of a friend sentenced to hard labor over a triviality and a cousin who made an innocent joke and underwent brainwashing—an experience so terrible he said he would have committed suicide if not for his two beautiful children. Just when I opened my mouth to confess what I ate for dinner the day before, they cleared us. So at that point, from Sydney to Hong Kong took one day, and from Hong Kong to Guangzhou, which should have taken two hours, took another full day.

Then more fun.

They required us to report to the Guangzhou police where we underwent another two hours of similar interrogation. Still no questions about dinner, but everything else. Later the Guangzhou police gave us permission to go to Shantou—a city close to my aunt's village (where the grandmothers lived) in the same province of Guangdong. They allowed us to purchase a one-way air ticket from Guangzhou to Shantou but didn't give permission for us to buy return tickets from Shantou back to Guangzhou.

This time around, I no longer sweated with fear. Instead, my frustration mounted. I had already obtained a visa and had full governmental permission to go to my home village, Anbu, so why did they need to interrogate me and get new permissions at every step? Finally I joined the long queue for an air ticket to Shantou. The long queue was not because many people could afford to fly. We waited because though the airline office opened at nine a.m., they sold no tickets until ten-thirty a.m. We were standing patiently in line while the ticket salesgirls drank tea and chatted amongst themselves. When they finally felt ready to sell tickets, they moved at a snail's pace and and treated us in a condescending manner, as if we were begging for money rather than buying tickets.

"No you cannot get a ticket to go to Shantou today or tomorrow or the next day. You must wait three days," the ticket salesgirl told me. Public servants in China are considered the public's bosses. When I asked why I had to wait three days, she gave me a dirty look that warned me I'd better behave or I wouldn't be getting a ticket at all. When we finally boarded the plane three days later, most of the seats were empty.

My burning desire to see my aunt met with many such frustrating stops and interrogations. As a citizen of the free world for thirteen years, I'd forgotten the exasperation of living as a prisoner of unpredictable bureaucrats. Fear kept me in check, though. I obeyed orders and answered questions, no matter how ridiculous.

When we arrived in Shantou, I had to first report to the city police to answer all of the questions again—except these were even more ridiculous and irrelevant. A ferocious policewoman put me through hours of nasty questioning. When she decided to give me an even harder time and demanded that I translate into Chinese all of the street names in Australia where we lived, and in the US where my brothers and sisters had lived, I lost my patience. I'd been in China for four days at that point and though my aunt lived within walking distance, they still hadn't allowed me to see her. My two weeks were quickly running out. At this realization, for a split second all of my fears evaporated as anger possessed me. I stood up and almost shouted at the ignorant woman, "I can't translate these English names into Chinese. It is not possible. It is a different language. What do you need them for anyway?" At that point, my cousin Zhi and her husband grabbed me by the sleeves and yanked me down into a chair as they apologized profusely for me. Fortunately, the policewoman seemed to wake up from her stupidity and decided to let it go. Or perhaps sending me to jail threatened to give her an inordinate amount of paperwork.

She stamped my paper and waved me away to go to Anbu, but that wasn't the end of the line yet. Normally, a neighbor overseer would come next to interrogate everyone, but my relatives skipped that step by giving the overseer a gift. Almost done, I still had to get tickets to go back to Guangzhou so that I could return home to Australia. I spent the entire next day in line waiting to buy one-way tickets back to Guangzhou. After all of the rigmarole—an extremely frustrating entire week wasted on interrogations and senseless delays—I ended up with only two nights to spend with my aunt.

Mao's Cultural Revolution had just about ended, but reminders remained. Every adult female still wore the same nondescript style of dark, shapeless, loose-fitting clothing and had the same bland hairstyle of Mao's wife, Jiang Qing. The only difference was some clothing was more threadbare than others. Every man also had the same severe haircut and wore dark, depressive clothes. What a dreary scene. No smiling faces. Just grim, miserable expressions like a black-and-white walking dead movie.

When we finally got onto the bus to Anbu, we walked to the back and sat in the only two empty seats. Every single passenger turned to stare at us. It reminded me of the scene in *The Graduate* when Dustin Hoffman stops the wedding and persuades the bride to leave with him. He and the bride in her full regalia sit at the back of the bus and every head turns to look at them.

The anticipation of finally seeing my beloved aunt overwhelmed me when I walked into the village. Before long, just about every kid and some adults in the neighborhood followed us—about fifty curious people. So thin were the children, they appeared to be walking skeletons. They looked at Eunice and me with our Western haircuts and clothing as if we were extraterrestrials. I can still see in my mind's eye the man who rode past on his bicycle and craned his neck so far around to look back at us that he fell off.

Unaware of Western social etiquette, many of the villagers walked right up to us, stared into our faces, and pulled at our clothes. Good thing I didn't go with my Caucasian friends. We would have caused a riot. At first Eunice and I felt awkward, but after a while it became annoying and then scary. Privacy was an unknown concept.

By the time I reached the front yard of our little storage room where I had grown up with Aunt, children jammed the entryway. When I finally squeezed into the room filled with wall-to-wall kids, I saw my aunt and experienced the most incredible moment—like in the movie *Ghost* when Sam Wheat is able to return briefly to earth to see his wife. Tears flooded my eyes and my vision blurred. I couldn't see Aunt properly, but I could feel and hear all of the kids pushing and shoving and yelling at each other. Without thinking, I assumed my doctor's voice and shouted, "Kids, get out!" A moment of stunned silence followed and a few adults (who were not part of our family) looked puzzled. Then I shouted again. With shock on their faces, they ushered the kids out. Finally we had a little privacy.

When the room cleared and I focused on Aunt, it shocked me to see how tiny she appeared, especially since I'd grown considerably over the thirteen years since leaving. So overwhelmed did I feel about seeing her that I momentarily forgot Chinese etiquette and tried to hug her. Aunt ducked away, which brought me up short, until I remembered that in China touching and hugging broke the rules of etiquette.

It took both of us a few minutes to adjust and reconnect. Aunt appeared mystified at my transformation. The small, scrawny boy who had left her more than a decade before had returned as a much taller, mature man with a beautiful wife. No doubt she wondered if I was the same child she had raised. Aunt appeared older and even thinner, with more deep worry lines etched into her face. She wore a shapeless dress that hung on her small frame and initially stood in awkward silence trying to connect with me. Then I motioned for us to sit down. When we did so, all of my pent-up feelings of love overcame me and I addressed her as I'd always done. "Ah Aunt . . . ," I said, choking back tears. She smiled and replied, "Ah B, you are so tall." We smiled at each other and instantly slid comfortably back to those days when we depended on each other to live.

Those two precious days flew by as I also met my cousins and saw some of my old classmates. My cousin Zheng still had Paul Newman's facial features, but was much skinnier and shorter than I remembered him. We bought warm clothing for him and his four daughters and wife. I always thought of Zheng as a tall man and bought him extra large size clothing. The Chinese silk coat I got him hung over his knees. I apologized for getting the wrong size. Pleased to get the coat, he was at pains to assure me that it suited him perfectly and insisted now he would never have cold knees in winter! Zheng had the same beaming smile I remembered, but the deep lines on his forehead revealed a man with heavy responsibilities.

Knowing full well what it was like to starve, I found it especially sad to see the intense hunger of Zheng's malnourished daughters. I was glad to be able to offer them enough food during our visit. We brought with us as much food as we could, such as preserved dried meats and portable cakes. We also gave them vitamin tablets and money, the latter of which we turned in for food rations. The kids and Zheng and his wife went everywhere with us during those two days. When we brought them to restaurants, his daughters gobbled down their food as though it might disappear the next second.

Eunice found the experience awkward, as she didn't speak the local dialect, so she couldn't talk to anyone or understand what we said. I tried to translate, but I became so emotional while engaging with my relatives that I couldn't explain everything to her. People behaved much differently than Eunice was accustomed to, as well. In those days in Chinese villages and even now, they spit loudly in public and even in each other's homes. And they smoked in your face.

The unhygienic and poor surroundings greatly shocked Eunice, who had never seen anything like it. After thirteen years away from the extreme poverty, during that first visit I also saw the filth and unhygienic surroundings through different eyes. As I walked the neighborhood reminiscing, I noticed that the village seemed impossibly dirty and bare. The pond we used for swimming and bathing looked like a cesspit. Desperation hung in the air, like the time of the Great Famine. So depressing and desolate were the surroundings, I found it hard to imagine I had survived all those years in those conditions.

The hotel where Eunice and I stayed really showed the differences between China and the Western world. We checked into the one and only hotel in the nearest town center, and it was the worst hotel I have ever seen. The "shower" dribbled cold water and the once-white sheets had browned. The worst was the filthy drinking glass on the table. I asked the service person to change it, but she looked at me as though I was a man in prison asking for a banquet and feather bed. "What do you expect?" I heard her say under her breath. "Clean it yourself."

Though we found the room inhospitable, when Aunt stepped in, her eyes brightened and she exclaimed, "What a beautiful room. Like a palace." That remark hit me hard. How spoiled had I become? Had I forgotten where I came from?

Except for the clothes we wore, Eunice and I gave away just about all of our belongings before we left China. Though I'd finally experienced my dream come true to go home and bring Aunt a better life, I left with a heavy heart as I thought of her and the kids, weak and skinny.

I tried very hard to visit Aunt every few years. With a big mortgage and a young family, returning was a significant expense. I reminded myself that I lived in Australia and my prime responsibility was to my family. I could lower my standard of living to help Aunt and Zheng, but my family was entitled to the same standard of living as our contemporaries. Eunice chose not to return to China for many years, but she was always understanding of my desire to help my family.

After that first trip, I returned many times to China and conditions gradually improved with less officialdom to tussle with and better communication and understanding of Western culture. On the second visit two years later, my relatives told me I had insulted the whole neighborhood by shouting at the kids to get out, because in the village, everyone has rights to everyone's business. For that reason, they avoided me. To ease tensions, my niece Shu Wan, the eldest daughter of Cousin Zheng, who was closest to my aunt, asked me to buy lots of candy. Then she walked around to all of the neighbors, giving out candy and apologizing for my behavior. She assured them I wasn't the ogre I appeared to be. It took another few trips for them to forgive me.

Today China is changing at lightning speed. It's hard for me to imagine that Shu Wan is now the mother of two university graduates. Although China appears Westernized and much freer than before, it's sobering to note that the country is still under total control of the Communist Party and the same dictatorial system that caused the deaths of millions. China has been on a rapid path to prosperity and modernization, but the country's people still have little or no say regarding the political structure.

CHAPTER 17

FAMILY PRACTICE AND LEARNING TAI CHI

The gem cannot be polished without friction,
nor man perfected without trials.

— Chinese proverb

I knew that more experience in the family medicine field would make me a better general practitioner (GP), so I started working as a locum (substitute doctor) at various practices. Doing so gave me more experience and a job to earn money. With Eunice's blessing, with my first paycheck, I increased the amount of money I'd been sending to Aunt, Zheng, and his family.

In small country towns where there are fewer specialists and advanced facilities, the GPs, or family physicians, have to do more than in big cities, such as deliver babies, perform surgery, and take more comprehensive care of each patient and family. Because small-town patients have fewer choices of doctors than city people, they tend to follow their GPs directions more closely.

I took up a locum job in Condobolin, where Evonne Cawley, the Wimbledon tennis champion, grew up. (During my time there, I treated her grandmother.) Michael Clark, a wonderful GP who loved practicing in a country town, headed up the group of dedicated family physicians there.

The practice supplied me with a car and a small apartment. On the second day, my car broke down while on my way to the medical offices. I got out and tried to figure out the trouble when two cars pulled up behind me. The drivers offered to help me. The first one said he'd give me a lift to the medical office and the second said, "I will get the mechanic to take care of the car."

Their friendliness and helpfulness warmed and impressed me, but curiosity prompted me to ask, "How do you know who I am and who owns this car?"

"Everyone in town knows a new doctor is here," one of the men said.

While I liked being recognized and appreciated the help, I also felt uncomfortable at his remark. Then I realized that my mind had transported me back to my village—the country town where everyone denigrated us as a landlord family and forced us to hide in the little storeroom. I realized then why I enjoyed the anonymity of cities. Even though on a conscious level I knew my experience as a country GP couldn't compare to China, that incident made being a GP in a small town less attractive.

I greatly enjoyed working in the country, finding it fulfilling and educational. Michael became so impressed with my performance that he asked me to join the practice on my second day at work. The offer tempted me, but I also knew that Michael's wife found the small town with its lack of social life challenging. I thought of Eunice, who loves art and culture, and how she might have the same challenges as Mrs. Clark, so I turned down his offer.

After graduation from medical school, my arthritis worsened. My first trip to the Thredbo ski resort revealed what the future had in store for me. On a weekend ski trip organized by the Overseas Christian Fellowship group, I fell in love with skiing. With the help of gravity and a pair of skis, power and freedom coursed through my body and mind and my spirit soared as I took flight and glided rapidly through the snow. The experience reminded me of being able to control my direction and speed in life. After only a couple of hours of skiing, though, my pain ran deep. By the time I got home, I could hardly walk or move. On Monday morning when I shuffled into work, my receptionist, Linley, took one look at me and told me to go home; she'd cancel my appointments. I'd never taken off time from work, but felt greatly relieved to do so that day. Later Linley told me I looked so bad she thought I might die, so she took it as her duty to "save the doctor's life."

It took many weeks to downsize from the severe aches and pains to the usual daily discomfort. The experience showed me how bad my arthritis had become and that I had to do something about it. I had found a new way to fly—I wanted to ski again. I recalled hearing years before in my village in China that tai chi helped arthritis. I also recalled the headmaster at Ling Nan, Mr. Chin, doing tai chi at sunrise every morning. I decided to give it a try and started looking for a teacher.

Back in 1976, finding a tai chi teacher proved difficult. I went to one teacher's class, who taught me the classical Yang style and Push Hands. I didn't feel right about him, though. He had a nervous, jittery way of talking and moving that didn't seem consistent with my image of a tai chi practitioner. His dirty fingernails also bothered me, but I didn't decide to stop practicing with him until my father-in-law, Mr. Lum Wan Kwai, told my wife that the teacher was not a good tai chi practitioner. I respected my father-in-law's judgment and went looking for another teacher.

I met another teacher, an engineer and very nice man with clean fingernails. He told me about his tai chi journey. He had learned a variation of the Yang style from a famous tai chi master, who placed much emphasis on relaxation. He invited me to his class where I saw that many of his students closed their eyes and assumed hunched postures, moving about almost formlessly. That didn't look right to me either, and the complete lack of structure made me feel uncomfortable. I debated about whether to join his class when my wife told me that her father said he was no good either. Then I got curious and asked what Eunice's father knew about tai chi. She told me that he had practiced tai chi since her childhood and had studied under a famous teacher, so I asked if Eunice's father would teach me.

My late father-in-law was one of the nicest and most unassuming men I have ever met. Born in Australia and educated in Hong Kong, he later married and lived in Hong Kong for many years. He and I share similar backgrounds. Like me, he had ties to China and grew up without his parents. His father died when he was just a baby, and his mother put him in boarding school and didn't seem very interested in him.

So unassuming was Mr. Lum that he had never told me—but I later found out—that his teacher, Yang Shou-zhong, was hailed as one of the most famous, if not the most famous tai chi master in the world. Yang Shou-zhong was the eldest son of Yang Cheng-fu, the grandson of the creator of the Yang style tai chi. Among the many styles of tai chi, Yang is by far the most popular. The tai chi world regarded Yang Cheng-fu as the father of modern tai chi, as he brought the practice to many people in China in the nineteenth century. My father-in-law and his friends were Yang Shou-zhong's first group of students. Together a few of them paid for the down payment on Yang Shou-zhong's apartment. As a result, this group benefited from special teaching from the great master.

Yang Shou-zhong taught my father-in-law personally for years until Mr. Lum moved from Hong Kong to his birthplace in Australia. During our tai chi lessons, my father-in-law told me a great deal about Yang, including his personality, power, and mannerisms. For example, the tai chi master took small, almost measured steps when he walked, and he possessed a seemingly unlimited capacity for food and alcohol, yet kept a slim figure. Yang felt strongly about mastering the movement "Waving Hands in the Clouds." He believed this movement to be one of the most powerful in the Yang style, and he felt that people who failed to do this movement well were just monkeying about. That inspired me to use the "Waving Hands in the Clouds" frequently in my Tai Chi for Health programs, especially in the Tai Chi for Diabetes program, where it is the featured movement.

At the time of my lessons, Mr. Lum was in his late sixties and retired, but he looked much younger than his years. Slim, agile, and shorter than me, he possessed the skin of a twenty-year-old. Like a Chinese scholar, he exuded a gentle and learned manner. He shared his knowledge without reservation. I visited my father-in-law's small lounge three times a week, where he gave me lessons.

We always started our lessons with a little talk about family matters. Since I did not grow up with a father, and Mr. Lum did not have a son, we developed a close father/son relationship. I respected him as a father, but he respected me as a doctor. In those days, the Chinese community regarded doctors with great respect, as well as a little fear. So we were always friendly and cordial. My mother-in-law would bring me a cup of tea, and when I finished it, we started my lesson.

Like most traditional teachers, he did not do any warm-up exercise. He would start by leading me with the movements we had learned and teaching me new ones. He would show me the entire movement once, then I would copy him several times and then we moved on to the next movement.

Mr. Lum was soft-spoken and moved slowly and gently, yet exuded an inner power that I didn't understand then, but could feel. I would try to imitate him, but I only managed to do the movements without the power. Every once in a while, he offered corrections, but he seldom checked my progress or offered praise. He often talked about his teacher and what he taught him. Mr. Lum was fond of telling me about the inner powers of the great master Yang. For example, Mr. Lum told me that at the practice drill of Pushing Hands when two people push each other to experience the opposite force, Mr. Yang would suddenly push a student's feet away with a subtle, almost invisible movement that sent the student back as though pushed by an immense force. But he always ensured that the student fell back toward a safe space and grasped him before he fell. Yang focused on internal energy (*qi*) and force (*jing*), yet only on rare occasions and only to his close students explained how to generate inner energy and internal force.

I learned the entire classical Yang 108 Forms. At that time, I had no idea that I possessed a better-than-average memory. I kept coming back for more tea, corrections, practices together, and questions and answers. I felt very fortunate to have the opportunity to have learned from my father-in-law, and the teaching of Master Yang through him. I found it really enjoyable to hear about the legendary Yang firsthand, as by then I had read all of Mr. Lum's tai chi books (some of them rare and almost antique). What a gift to be able to learn from such a close link to the creator of the most popular tai chi style.

I especially enjoyed discovering how the ancient practice benefits your mind. The uniqueness of tai chi comes from its ability to integrate the mind, body, and spirit (not in a religious sense, rather the positive inner sense of well-being and harmony). In many sports and types of exercise, people often say you deteriorate after a certain age. For example, in tennis a competitive player is considered old at thirty and performance tends to wane with time. In an art like tai chi that draws from inner wisdom and strength, your life experience augments the depth of the art and your progress is never hindered by age or physical conditions. The more you learn, the more you improve, no matter at what age.

Being a traditional teacher, Mr. Lum never told me that I was a fast learner. However, as I progressed in tai chi, he came out openly to encourage me to expand my horizons and learn other forms and styles. In this regard, he was highly unconventional. Traditional tai chi teachers often insist on absolute loyalty. Later when I began teaching tai chi, one of my workshop participants told me her teacher expelled her from his school because she studied my instructional DVD.

The benefits of tai chi did not come easily to me. Years of malnutrition and emotional abuse had significantly weakened my physical condition. Prior to studying tai chi, I thought myself uncoordinated and poor at any sports. In the early years when we underwent persecution and discrimination in China, I avoided interacting with others, including group sports. Once in Hong Kong and Australia, I focused on learning a new language and studying, so I remained inactive. Because of this, at the beginning of my tai chi journey, I needed to work three times harder than other practitioners in order to gain the same level of fitness. I practiced regularly and made progress, however my poor immunity caused me to develop a viral infection every time I reached a slightly higher level of fitness and that resulted in lowering my fitness level again. It seemed to me that my much weakened immunity and health had become deeply entrenched, and any effort to make changes met with much resistance from my body.

Later on when I began teaching my Tai Chi for Health program, I observed that many students gained benefits very quickly—sometimes within weeks. These observations were substantiated by the largest study to date of Tai Chi for Arthritis. Led by Professor Leigh Callahan from the University of North Carolina, the study showed significant health benefits for people with all types of arthritis. The researchers presented the landmark study at the American College of Rheumatology Annual

Meeting in November 2010. In the study, 354 participants were randomly assigned to two groups. The tai chi group received eight weeks of lessons, while the control group waited for tai chi classes. The group performing tai chi experienced significant pain relief, less stiffness, and better ability to manage daily living. More importantly, subjects felt better about their overall wellness, as well as experienced improved balance. I constructed my programs specifically to improve health and wellness. Many other medical and tai chi experts further enhanced them. The tai chi I originally practiced with Mr. Lum represented the traditional tai chi taught by people who didn't understand medical conditions. That is another important reason it took me so long to gain the same health benefits.

Despite the challenges back then, I persevered at learning tai chi. By the second year, I noticed my pain had subsided, and I developed increased muscle strength. I could hold my doctor's bag and do house calls without problems. I also came down with fewer upper respiratory tract infections. Before tai chi, I got sick every two weeks, catching every cold and flu bug from my patients. It took me a week or two to recover, and then I picked up a new bug. After several years studying tai chi, I noticed that I became sick much less often, and by the ten-year mark I hardly ever got any cold or flu. In the case of something really virulent, I would feel it starting to affect me, but I would only feel unwell for half a day, and by the next day I woke up feeling back to normal and energized.

The most powerful effects of tai chi for me were the mental strength, inner confidence, serenity, and intrinsic joy practicing gave me. As I grew with my tai chi practice and reached more advanced levels, I incorporated the tai chi principles into my daily life and got to know and like myself better. This occurred when I became more aware of my attacks of insecurity and learned to better control my emotions. I became more mindful of my emotional state and better able to manage it. For instance, when I first started my practice, I became annoyed when patients left my practice to go to other doctors. My insecurity would torment me about what I did wrong. In later years, I could assess the situation rationally. My analysis would usually show a good reason, like distance or family influence.

As I learned to accept, cherish, and improve myself, I used that skill to interact with others and to accept, cherish, and care for them as well. I became able to absorb and redirect incoming forces—especially angry ones, which enabled me to help my patients, friends, family, and tai chi colleagues to develop their inner strength.

I worked as a locum in many areas, including Cremorne, Sydney, a plush northern suburb filled with many doctors where I didn't feel needed. So instead, I decided to set up my practice in the south where I found just the right kind of people—mostly hardworking middle class. With the help of my late mentor, Dr. Robert Clark, we drove through many suburbs until we found the smallest one in Sydney called Narwee. It possessed a country-town feel but still lay within the Sydney metropolitan area. It seems that the universe chose that area just for me. Many years later I discovered that Narwee is an aboriginal (Australian native) word for "sun." Twenty-one years after establishing my practice there, I created the Tai Chi for Arthritis program based on the unique and powerful Sun style tai chi. That led to the Tai Chi for Health programs that have helped millions of people around the world. The creator, Mr. Sun Lu-tang, a visionary of his time, was the first tai chi master to promote the health benefits of tai chi in his book *A Study of Taijiquan*. Although not as well-known as the Yang style I learned at the beginning of my tai chi journey, Sun style is ideal for healing and relaxation, as it is easy to learn and suitable for almost anyone. How serendipitous that I introduced Mr. Sun's tai chi style to help so many people from a place named sun.

Once we chose a suburb in which to set up my practice, I started looking for properties to rent. As I drove through South Bexley, which is about a ten-minute drive from Narwee, I found a cluster of five shops. The shops included a little post office where Lyn and Phil Curtis had a franchise—a grocery store and a pharmacy, the latter of which is crucial for a family doctor to have close by. The grocery store owner owned a small two-room house behind the store and wanted a doctor there, so he made the rent very attractive. At the same time, we also found a nice and bigger shop in Narwee on the main street that also featured a reasonable rental rate.

I had a dilemma about which practice location to choose. I've never been good at choosing, so I took both. I'd start in Narwee and see patients from nine to eleven-thirty a.m., and then I'd drive to Bexley for an hour. I'd have a super quick lunch and make some home visits, then do another hour in Bexley and return to Narwee. On top of that full day, I did my own after-hours home visits.

Kind and always helpful, Robert taught me a great deal about running a practice. A brilliant man, he told me that he breezed through medical school but found when he started working that he had an aversion to touching patients. He enjoyed talking to people and loved getting to know them, but his dislike of touching patients caused problems, as it didn't match well with most branches of medicine. In his practice, Robert worked three full days with a partner, Martin Simpson, working the other two. (Martin had an interest in filmmaking and later became a well-known documentarian.) Australia is a worker's country. We greatly respect worker's rights and the Labor Party often leads the government. Workers are well paid with lots of fringe benefits, including a compulsory one-month holiday plus sick leave, double pay for public holidays, and overtime. Often employees refuse promotions as managers, because they only get slightly more pay, but no payment for overtime, so they end up being paid much less than hourly workers working the same number of hours.

A receptionist is the most expensive running cost for a medical practice, so unlike most physician's offices, Robert and Martin didn't employ one. They paid a reasonable rent and shared costs proportionately, splitting the profits. I found it to be smart business, and I learned a lot from them about all aspects of running a practice. I couldn't do what they did, however. Within a couple of months of starting my own practice, I hired a full-time receptionist. I like to focus on patients, not on paperwork.

The year after I started the family practice, I received a late night call about a sick young man. A smoker with a fever and cough, he looked quite unwell. I did a thorough examination and took a full history. I suspected he had pneumonia but couldn't be sure without the use of hospital equipment, such as an X-ray machine. I told the relatives to call an ambulance and take him to the hospital right away. I wrote a referral letter, then left.

Unfortunately, the family failed to follow my advice and decided instead to let him sleep until the morning. The next day they called me to say that he never woke up. The subsequent autopsy showed that he had died from pericarditis, an infection of the membrane surrounding the heart, which is rare and difficult to diagnose. The fact that he died devastated me. As soon as I heard, I stopped everything and rang Robert. Like a good doctor, he listened intently while I poured my heart out. Then he told me that all doctors make mistakes, as we are human. He said he would have done the same thing. "You can't do more than telling people to go to the hospital, Paul," he assured me. "If they don't, then it's not your fault." The way Robert listened and empathized with me made me feel so much better. Still, the responsibility for life and death decisions remained a burden.

I started my medical practice squatting, which means starting from ground zero. In Australia, you aren't allowed to advertise medical practices, so it can take a long time for patients to find you. The first day that I opened, two people wandered in, but the second day nobody came. The word did get out, however, so I gradually got patients.

I practiced in a conservative area, and the people didn't like change. Initially, only those unable to get an appointment with their regular doctor came to me. They would ask apologetically, "Do you mind seeing my son, Johnnie? He is very sick, and we cannot get an appointment with our usual doctor."

Like my aunt, who could stop a baby from crying in an instant and to whom all of the neighborhood children flocked, I know how to get along with kids. Many parents marveled at how the kids stopped crying when they walked into my consultation room, which made my chest swell with pride. Parents who brought their children to see me when their doctor couldn't see them would often return and tell me, "Sorry, Doctor. Johnnie only wants to see you. He refused to see our other doctor." Eventually, the adults switched to my practice, too.

I especially loved it when the children I treated grew up and brought their own kids to see me. In one case I am really proud of, I cared for five generations of a family. I will never forget the young woman who brought her baby in for an immunization and told me, "Dr. Lam, you are looking after my baby, me, my mother, my grandmother and my great-grandmother." What a special moment.

The best aspect of being a GP that beats working in any hospital is how I had the privilege of becoming the consultant and friend of entire families and positively impacting their lives. This experience fulfilled my passion for teaching, since it gave me the opportunity to educate patients about their health and lifestyles and help them to understand how to take control of their own medical conditions. Later I took the teaching further by becoming a clinical supervisor and lecturer for postgraduate doctors at the University of NSW.

Over the years as I learned more about family medicine, I saw what an impact a family physician can have. At one conference I attended in the nineties when the medical community considered transplants the pinnacle of modern medicine, the transplant team talked about their multimillion-dollar budget and the number of heart transplants they handled—around sixty patients per year. On average, each patient got four or five extra years of life at the cost of many hundreds of thousands of dollars for each person. In most cases, it came with a significantly reduced quality of life. Patients often had to take steroids and underwent maintenance medical supervision.

Studies show that a family physician can give an average patient four or five extra years of quality life just by helping patients manage their weight, blood pressure, cholesterol, lifestyle, and diabetes, at around a few hundred dollars a year—a fraction of the cost of a heart transplant patient. One family physician takes care of thousands of patients a year. The number of extra healthy years GPs give their patients adds up to many more than what a heart transplant team can give. I often share this information with the doctors I train, because I want future GPs to be proud of what we do.

As soon my practice became established, we decided it was time to have a family. I was overjoyed when Eunice became pregnant with our first child. It turned out to be a son, whom we named Matthew Wei-Sun Lam. In Chinese, "Wei-Sun" means "great life." I thought of that name while showering, which is when I often make the most important decisions. I wanted him to have a great life.

Our beautiful boy, who possessed a happy and contented nature, enchanted us. I worked long hours, leaving home at eight-thirty in the morning and sometimes not returning until nine at night. My wife felt a little nervous about handling a small baby, so I gladly offered to bathe Matthew when I got home. I also did anything else necessary, such as changing his nappy (diaper), even though it didn't smell so great. I enjoyed seeing him clean and comfortable. He stayed awake until I got home to bathe him and put him to bed. No matter how busy or stressful my day, I always looked forward to coming home and seeing my son's smiling face. Holding him in my arms made me indescribably happy. I wanted to be the best father possible. When I had my child in my arms, I felt so much love for him; I could not imagine anything separating us.

In 1979, when Matthew was ten months old, my practice was going well, but finances were tight. Eunice didn't work, we paid bank loans for the medical practice and our house, and we had the expenses of a baby. One day a very flashy-looking BMW drove up outside of the office and parked. In came a casually yet expensively dressed young man who turned out to be a great salesman. He quickly discovered my love of photography and asked if I'd heard of video cameras. At the time, VHS was very new and having your own camera was unheard of. No wonder he could afford to drive a BMW; he talked me into buying a video camera!

The camera itself weighed twelve pounds and had to be used together with a portable VHS recorder that weighed twenty pounds. Every time you wanted to make a video you had to carry thirty-two pounds of bulky equipment, as well as a tripod and chargers. At four thousand dollars I couldn't afford it, but he had a ready-made finance contract that would be paid off in two years. In one of those crazy moments, I signed the contract, much to Eunice's dismay.

My peers all had better cars than us, but I had a video camera, and as I videotaped my children, I never missed having posh cars. You can't buy such precious footage with any amount of money. I had no idea how in later years video would significantly change my life.

By the time Matthew turned fourteen months old, it became clear that he failed to meet developmental milestones. I took him to a pediatric neurologist who diagnosed him with a language receptive disorder. He could hear perfectly, but the language center of his brain found it impossible to process the meaning of words. He failed to understand what we said and couldn't say anything meaningful. An average child says *dada* and *mama* at around twelve months old and knows what the words mean. (Yes, most babies say *dada* before *mama*.) By two or three years old, they are completing sentences. Despite intensive speech therapy and our tireless efforts, Matthew did not say a meaningful word for a painfully long time. We talked to him until our mouths went dry. I bought every tool possible that could help. My brother Jeng even bought him a car that would respond to a simple word command like "go." In those days that car was top technology. Nothing worked. He went along happily uttering meaningless sounds. We smiled at him, but our worry deepened. I had patients not speaking at two years old who ended up in institutional care when they grew older.

As the months went by, our concern for Matthew's future deepened. One day I went to a lecture by a speech therapist, who experienced a disability herself and overcame it. She used her experience to set up a therapeutic center. I became so impressed with her work that we sent Matthew to her center. He received care from Jill Haddock, one of the best therapists at the center. Eunice drove him across the city to sessions for many years—a challenging and time-consuming task in busy Sydney, especially in peak traffic.

At three-and-half years old, Matthew finally uttered his first word—*horse*. I still don't know why his first word was horse. We don't have one nor do we talk about horses.

About the time Matthew uttered his first word, Eunice gave birth to our daughter, Andrea. Our children looked almost identical as babies, but they grew into two very different people—in looks, behavior, interests, and so many other things. Most importantly, they are great "mates," which means so much to both of us, who grew up without siblings. I often carried both Matthew and Andrea, one on each arm, and felt an overwhelming sensation of our love and energy as one.

CHAPTER 18

PARENTING AND TEACHING

If you always give, you will always have.
— Chinese proverb

W ithin one year my practice grew, and I couldn't keep up with two locations, so I sold the Bexley practice and extended my time in Narwee. It made me happy that many of my Bexley patients stayed with me and made the drive to Narwee.

As my practice got busier, the patient waiting time lengthened. Medicare started two years after I began practicing. New to Australia, socialized medicine caused some controversy. Like most doctors, I believed in free enterprise and private medicine, and I didn't like the idea of social medicine. The government required doctors to conform to Medicare and offered incentives for using the bulk billing procedure. That meant patients signed a form and the doctor submitted the form to the Medicare office in order to get paid by the government. While this did give the government direct control of doctors, it brought some benefits, including eliminating accounting tasks and bad debts. Much as I like private medicine, the idea of not taking money from my patients appealed to me. It felt like I delivered service on almost an honorary basis. For that reason, I joined bulk billing, which made my practice grow even more quickly.

I knew if I wanted to deliver good medical care while cutting down waiting time and costs, I would have to work out more efficient ways to practice. Like in my student days when I devised a smart way to study so that I could also work and enjoy life,

I needed to find ways to be a good doctor, husband, and parent. So I spent time discovering methods for efficiency and effectiveness.

I don't like wasting anything, especially time and food. Time is life's most precious commodity; we can't get it back once it's gone. Since hunting about for a pen or stethoscope is a waste of time, I became extremely well organized in my work environment and with my schedule. Every piece of equipment had a place and could be accessed quickly. I also learned to interview, examine, and treat patients efficiently. I made time for them when required, but my procedures were clear and straightforward and respected everyone's time.

I learned to reward "good" patients. Most people are considerate, and many of them would offer a quick exit after waiting a long time to help me get caught up on my schedule. I would make a point of taking more time with the most considerate people. Patients often think of mind-related problems like stress or depression as not "real" sicknesses and don't feel right bringing such issues up with a busy doctor, so they often skip mentioning those problems. By giving patients time to sit down and chat leisurely with me, however, I helped with many serious mental health conditions. For example, I assisted a middle-aged man whose wife left him and the kids. Devoted to his children, he worked extra hard to take care of them. They were happy with the situation until several months later when his wife returned and wanted to take the kids away from him. The man felt devastated. I spent a great deal of time with him and subsequently with the children and his wife. I eventually helped them sort out their situation for the best outcome. Instead of a fight and divorce, which is where they'd been heading, the couple reconciled and the family reunited.

I quickly came to distinguish serious from frivolous conditions. As a result, I learned to say no in a nice way so that I could free up time for the considerate and seriously ill patients. Through painstakingly encouraging good behavior, I cultivated a wonderful group of loyal and considerate patients.

Being a GP proved rewarding in many ways. I have met so many incredible people. One day I shared with a longtime patient, who I had always believed to be a teacher, about how my father had lived as a refugee in Hong Kong since Vietnam's fall. I mentioned my desire to help him immigrate to Australia where the living conditions would be much better. To my surprise, the patient told me he not only worked for the Immigration Department, but he oversaw Hong Kong migrants to Australia. John gave me useful information and dropped off an application form. I didn't ask for or expect any special treatment, but later my father told me that his application went amazingly smoothly. The Hong Kong office even gave him a chair while he waited. He had talked with many refugees trying to migrate to Australia but never heard of anyone being dealt with so easily and pleasantly.

I love teaching, so by 1982 I gained a position at the Sydney Institute of General Practice Education and Training as a clinical lecturer, training family physicians (registrars) at the postgraduate level. Later I became a lecturer with my university (University of New South Wales). Not only did I learn how to teach family physicians effectively, I also got to work with them on practical and real-life matters. I found as I taught that the secret is the tai chi principle of listening to the incoming force. In teaching it translates to understanding the learners' objective.

One of the most charismatic and intelligent young doctors I ever taught was Kevin Wong. A very talented pianist, he studied under Neta Maughan, my daughter's teacher. At the crossroads of choosing to be a professional pianist or doctor, he took up medicine—a gain to patients and a loss to music lovers.

On one occasion, Kevin made a house call to Elma, an older lady. Afterward, she told me that she liked Kevin because of his knowledge and kindness, but his offhand attitude bothered her. In tai chi, we learn to listen to the incoming force and understand the perspective of others, which in this case is how the patient feels. To the doctor treating a patient with something minor, like a cold, it is natural to feel lighthearted about the matter, but to patients the issue is of the utmost importance. That is why I curb my sense of humor when speaking with patients. I told Kevin that a doctor needs to look at the patient's point of view and recognize that everything, no matter how minor, is important. It pleased and impressed me a week later when Elma rang to apologize about what she said about Kevin and wanted me to know that she found him to be a wonderful doctor.

In 1995, I began seeking a partner to share the overwhelming patient load and to enable me to spend more time with my family and on tai chi. I asked one of my best trainee registrars to join my practice. A foreign graduate from the Philippines who worked in that country prior, Dr. Richard Cue was older than most locally graduated registrars. All foreign graduates needed to take more training to gain an Australian license, so he came under my tutelage, though he is only ten years younger than me. Our patients liked Richard, and I liked his gentle manner, life experience, and caring attitude, so I considered inviting him to join my practice.

During his training, an older man with a hearing problem came for an appointment. I received a phone call from a journalist who wanted to arrange an interview with me about tai chi, so I took the call and talked for a length of time while Richard spoke with the older man, who eventually asked him, "Who is Dr. Lam talking to and what about?" I heard Richard reply, "Oh, he just sold you for twenty cents." That impromptu remark clinched my decision. I invited Richard to be my partner, and it turned out to be a great decision. We worked very well together. He is hardworking and never once complained when I walked into his office and announced that I would be taking two months off to teach tai chi. From 2000, I began teaching tai chi for six months out of each year, and I could never have done that without his help.

The longer I experienced tai chi, the more in tune I became with my inner self and the more effectively I could use my instincts as a doctor. One day, Chris, a healthy man in his late thirties, sat in the waiting room. As soon as I saw him, something about his appearance bothered me. In the consultation, he told me about a gastric ulcer he'd had for twenty years that would bleed a small amount intermittently but always got better. His medical history clicked with my instinctive discomfort—his color was much paler than normal when I first saw him, though it had returned to normal when we went into the exam room. I checked him out as thoroughly as I could and everything seemed fine, but I advised him to go to the hospital. He remained unworried since he'd had many similar episodes, some even more severe. I called his wife into the office and pressed her to take him to the hospital. She did straightaway, and thankfully he went. Tests showed an extremely low blood count. If he had failed to go that night, he would have been in serious danger. Later he and his wife came to thank me for saving his life.

My keen desire to learn more about the human mind drove me to study psychiatry and psychology with great gusto. Sigmund Freud's psychoanalysis introduced me to new territory of the human mind. I also enjoyed learning about Dr. Aaron Beck's Cognitive Therapy and Dr. William Glasser's Choice Theory. The deprivation during the Empty Period left me with a nearly insatiable thirst for knowledge, especially of the human mind. I am drawn by what makes people like Mao and Hitler cause the death of millions of people and what causes seemingly normal people to act cruelly.

The Empty Period also left me with the desire to develop myself, often referred to as self-growth. This is the process of learning life skills that help you understand yourself and your purpose in life in order to work out the best ways to be a more effective and fulfilled person. I learned much from great thinkers and researchers like Stephen Covey, Martin Seligman (leader in positive psychology well shown in his latest book *Flourish*), and Mihaly Csikszentmihalyi (leader of studies on flow). They are brilliant explorers of the mind who often couple their theories with ingenious research work that shows how individuals develop themselves personally and achieve greater life fulfillment. The more I learned these theories, the more surprised I became at the similarities between self-growth concepts and tai chi principles.

In his book, *The 7 Habits of Highly Effective People*, Stephen Covey influenced me with his philosophy to be proactive and responsible for yourself. His philosophy can be compared to tai chi development, which involves proactive thinking and being responsible to practice regularly. Covey also stresses goal setting and prioritizing. This resembles the tai chi practice of setting goals to incorporate tai chi principles in the tai chi forms and prioritizing time for regular practice. When it comes to dealing with others and the community, Covey advocates understanding others first and working at win-win situations. This method resonates with the tai chi practice of listening to the incoming force and absorbing and redirecting the force to create a harmonized or win-win situation. His last habit relates to self-rejuvenation. Tai chi teaches you to revitalize your *qi* (the internal energy that improves all aspects of health, according to traditional Chinese medicine). Studying Covey's paradigm-changing concepts helped me to develop my tai chi and personal growth.

Tai chi is created based on the law of nature. The formal name of tai chi in China is tai chi chuan, or according to the Pinyin system, *tai ji quan.* The meaning of tai chi is infinity. The ancient Chinese believed that the universe started as a vast void, which is *wu ji*, then suddenly the infinite universe formed, which is tai chi. This resembles the big bang theory that many scientists currently believe. Everything in the universe is made of yin and yang. They are polar opposites, yet complementary to each other and tend to harmonize with each other. For example: the moon and the sun, softness and hardness, and night and day are yin and yang. They are opposite but complementary, and when yin and yang are in harmony, nature is serene and calm.

The human mind works much like nature. For instance, anger and calm and sadness and happiness are yin and yang. When yin and yang are in harmony, human beings are balanced and healthier in mind and body. Things that are perfectly balanced and in harmony are at peace; being at peace leads naturally to longevity. A well-harmonized person exhibits this balance by his or her tranquility and serenity of mind. However, no one is in perfect balance, just like no one is perfect.

Our modern world has created unbalanced minds and bodies. We experience excess stimulation and stress and are moving too fast. Many people possess sedentary jobs and don't take part in sufficient physical exercise to balance the body. Tai chi builds serenity by offering a slower pace that provides regeneration of energy and relaxation. At the same time, tai chi exercises the entire body, from all muscles and joints to all internal organs and even the mind.

The philosophy of tai chi's martial arts application proved revolutionary in its time. It didn't encourage fighting blow to blow and blocking and hitting back harder to win over your opponent.

The ultimate purpose was to harmonize with your opponent. Tai chi movement does not start with aggressive attack, rather with listening to the incoming force, yielding, absorbing and redirecting that force, and utilizing the incoming with your own force to reach harmony. Yin and yang interact and harmonize. Harmony is the healthiest outcome for human interaction, as it improves people's health, fosters healthier communities, and creates a more sustainable and healthier world.

Even more important than developing my practice, tai chi, and myself, I did everything possible to help my children develop as they grew. Matthew and Andrea are the most wonderful gifts of my life. Love can be unlimited and take many different forms—for example man and woman, father and child, and friends. In many ways, the core of love is the same despite the various forms. I loved watching and helping my children grow and mature and sharing in their happiness and when necessary, their pain. I knew that they were dependent on Eunice and me, and I wanted to give them the best care possible. My focus was on their long-term well-being and empowering them to live happy and fulfilling lives. So I studied the most effective ways to bring up mentally and physically healthy children. Concepts like Covey's habits, Seligman's positive psychology, and Csikszentmihalyi's being in flow are useful principles to embrace for their potential to enhance development and fulfillment in life.

Often the more difficult ways of reaching goals are more effective in the long run, and I have a knack for finding them. As a baby, Andrea woke up crying from her afternoon nap. I preferred her to wake up happy, so to encourage that I waited quietly outside her room around the time that she usually woke up. If she awoke crying, I waited a few minutes before I went in to pick her up. When she woke up without crying, I went in immediately to play with her and gave her extra attention. One of the most effective rewards for children is attention. The opposite—deprivation of attention—is the worst of punishments. Even scolding kids is a form of reward because that gives them attention for undesirable behavior. That is why punishment can have the opposite effect. After a couple more times of rewarding Andrea for waking up happy, she always did so. It took considerably more time to encourage this desirable behavior, but the many hours I waited patiently for the happy moment to come were worth the effort. In the long run, I had a happier and better-behaved child. I didn't physically punish my kids but used rewards for desirable behavior. And I seldom scolded. Instead, I pretended to ignore them.

Matthew's speech problem made me worry that he might turn out like Younger Uncle. Drawing on the knowledge I acquired studying human development, I researched ways to help him. I believe that everyone has unlimited potential, and I became desperate to unearth his so he could live a normal and fulfilling life. Gradually, I concluded from various studies on learning that creating an environment of respect and support would be most beneficial. By giving him respect, he'd be more likely to develop self-respect and confidence. Not telling him what to do but supporting his ideas would encourage him to develop his own thinking ability and problem-solving skills. This tactic develops empowerment, and it is much more difficult than just teaching him what to do. It meant treating him like a peer.

When Matthew turned twelve, I began disciplining myself to treat him like a peer. I found it especially challenging to watch him make all sorts of mistakes and wrong decisions. Instead of correcting him, I watched his progress and would only offer suggestions if he asked, as I would for a friend. I knew all of the right answers, but I had to hold myself back and never discouraged him from trying out new ways. How I disciplined myself to step back impressed Eunice, who often said, "You are taking so much from Matthew." Which meant being tolerant of his difficult behavior and unexplained outbursts. This tolerance resulted in him becoming more confident and developing his own way of learning. The tactic paid off many years later, and I'm glad I persevered.

High school loomed for Matthew and fortunately my old school, Trinity, offered an excellent education. Gaining entrance into Trinity proved as difficult as getting into an Ivy League school in the US. Parents usually enrolled their kids at birth, and then the school selected the best for entrance when the time came. Fortunately the school had a policy of admitting children of former students. We felt so happy Matthew got into Trinity, because that meant he'd get the best education possible. It especially pleased me that he attended the same school as I had.

Matthew worked very hard at school. He is talented and developed an interest in graphic design, which compensated for his speech challenge. Despite his hard work, we knew that he would be challenged to get minimum marks for Tertiary Entrance Examination points to study graphic design at good universities. Matthew exceeded our and the teachers' expectations at the end of high school, but his marks were still short of the minimum set for a place in all universities. This news made Matthew angry and depressed. After several weeks, however, he accepted his fate and enrolled in a private graphic design college more open to paying students. Unexpectedly, the University of Western Sydney also sent him an offer to enroll. When they had interviewed him regarding entrance into the school, one of the interviewers was the head of the graphics department. Matthew's high school project of designing a sports shoe impressed the interviewer so much that they offered him a place despite his being short of minimum marks. Matthew loves sports shoes like Nike. He devoted an enormous amount of time and energy to the project. He even wrote to the owner of Nike for his comments and interviewed doctors and physiotherapists about his own design for a sports shoe. The project didn't impress his high school teacher enough for high marks. Matthew thought the project a waste of time until it earned him an exceptional offer from the university. Like I've always believed, hard work is never wasted.

Matthew experienced a dilemma. The university offer was exceptional, but we had already paid a large, nonrefundable sum to the private college. At that point we were comfortable dealing with him as a peer, so we left the final decision up to him with the caveat that he not consider the money—only the education aspect. He chose the university.

The university years challenged Matthew. In his second year, for instance, the lecturer in charge of the main subject, design theory, told students that they must include citations for their end-of-the-year essay. Because of his speech problem, Matthew developed a habit of ignoring things he didn't fully understand, so he failed to include citations in his essay. Despite the fact that Matthew had gained good marks throughout the year and had written a quality essay, the lecturer failed him on the subject solely for not including citations. On that rare occasion, I decided to step in, so I talked to both his dean and the lecturer, explaining the reason for Matthew's mistake and supporting it with medical evidence. They said if Matthew had told them at enrollment, it wouldn't have been a problem. I explained that Matthew didn't wish to broadcast his disability and that he had worked hard and proved he could do well his first year. It was quite unfair, in any case, to fail a student for an entire year for missing one single instruction regarding citations. If they reassessed him, even giving a heavy penalty he would have passed the year. The subject teacher did not bother to reassess the paper, however, because he got a new job, so Matthew failed the major subject of the year. The department did let him carry the subject, which means he progressed to the next year, but he had to redo the subject and complete the full third-year curriculum. They also warned him that no one ever passed the third year carrying this subject—what a way to set students up for failure. Matthew worked hard and became the first student to break that record by passing all subjects.

The next year he went on to gain a high distinction for book design. His graduation was one of our proudest moments. Matthew's achievement confirmed my belief that no matter how hopeless things may seem, there is always hope, and that working hard can overcome most, if not all, challenges. Everyone has unlimited potential.

Though she looked almost the same as Matthew as a baby, Andrea Suk-Jin (meaning "an English rose") grew up to be very different. She started talking at the normal age and from then on she talked nonstop. When she was four, I took her ice-skating. She could hardly stand up and instead of trying to balance as I held both of her hands, her eyes darted everywhere as she gave me a running commentary on the other skaters. I tried not to be embarrassed as she called out, "Hey, Daddy, look at the fat lady coming toward us."

What happened with Matthew proved much more embarrassing. He didn't like ice cream, which is unusual for a child, but we were used to his contrariness. When he was six years old, we were in the Westfield Mall, which is a big shopping center. I saw a shop selling New Zealand natural fruit ice cream. It looked so tempting that I tried to convince Matthew to have one, but as usual he refused. As I walked around holding Matthew's hand and eating my own serving of delicious ice cream, I noticed people giving me funny looks. Then I realized that everyone must have thought me a mean father eating ice cream while depriving my son. That realization made the ice cream not taste as good anymore.

Andrea loves ice cream and never did embarrass me in that way. In fact, she brought a great deal of honor and pride to the family. She wanted to be involved in everything. One day when she was nearly five, as Eunice played the piano Andrea climbed up beside her and happily played random notes. For fun, Eunice began to teach her. To her surprise, Andrea finished the entire elementary grade book within a week. She obviously possessed talent. We looked for a teacher and found a very nice lady, Jean McVeigh, who ignited Andrea's deep love of piano and music. Miss McVeigh quickly saw Andrea as a prodigy, however, and urged Eunice to find a better teacher. (Despite no longer being her day-to-day teacher, Miss McVeigh kept in touch with Andrea until she passed away in her nineties. She always attended her concerts and provided encouragement. Andrea treated her like a dear, respected, and loved grandmother and teacher.)

Eunice has always loved music, so to discover her daughter to be ultratalented felt like a true gift from heaven. She put all of her energy into seeking out the best possible teacher for Andrea and found Neta Maughan, one of the most famous teachers in Sydney. After auditions, they accepted Andrea as a shared student with Neta and Kathryn Lambert. For eight years, Andrea studied with both teachers. Neta is a genius of a teacher who knows how to bring out the best talent in kids, while Kathryn, a previous student of Neta's, is meticulous and technically faultless. After some study, Andrea began entering competitions and won a good number of prizes in the Sydney Eisteddfod. Her performances amazed Eunice and me, and we felt so blessed with this wonderful gift from the universe.

I knew nothing about music, so I felt lucky to hear Andrea play as she became educated in music. For me, I discovered a new and beautiful world. I went to concerts, met many musicians, and learned about music and the musicians' lifestyle. When Andrea was thirteen, ABC (Australian Broadcasting Commission), the national government TV network, started a national competition called ABC Quest. Each state had a judges' winner and a viewers' winner. Then all of these winners competed in a national contest to find the overall winner.

Andrea entered and played Shostakovich's Piano Concerto no. 2, a bright and exciting piece that is technically challenging but easy for the audience to understand and enjoy. She won the state final and subsequently won the national final. I still remember when they announced the winner on TV and showed Andrea in a red dress playing her piece. It was the most beautiful music I had ever heard!

After winning that competition, Andrea became well-known nationally and had many opportunities to perform with major orchestras and solo recitals. Three years later at sixteen, she won the ABC Young Performers Award on piano, the most prestigious national competition for people under thirty-five years old.

I deeply believe Andrea loves performing. She enjoys sharing her inner beauty through music, and doing so brings out her best. She has a deep, delicate artistic beauty in her soul, and I have been moved so many times with the flow of that beauty through her music. This is not just father bias. Many of her fans are also moved to tears. Just about every one of her concerts in Australia sells out way ahead of time.

I feel the same enjoyment I believe Andrea experiences when I do tai chi performances on TV and in workshops. My tai chi growth helped me overcome feelings of inadequacy and allowed me to engage my mind and body on the inner beauty of tai chi—putting me in the state of flow. The more I merged with the spirit of tai chi, the better my performance and enjoyment of it.

Though it might seem surprising, living with an exceptionally talented child can be more challenging than helping a child with disabilities. Parents of prodigies feel lucky and proud, but there are immense challenges involved with helping your child excel and reach optimum performance, yet still develop his or her personality and life as a "normal" person. What can make the job of raising a prodigy especially difficult is when each parent tries to assist using a different method, which creates destructive division. If the child fails in any way, the parents blame one another, and that creates even more division.

I believe that parents, like teachers, should learn how to empower and not discipline. Empowerment is much more difficult to accomplish but works better in the long run. The process of empowerment facilitates learners to develop their own intrinsic rewards. The most challenging part to empower others is to change yourself. If you can change yourself and your attitudes, then you're better able to empower others. Parents would be more effective in helping children understand where they want to go in life and to set goals, motivate, and discipline themselves to work toward their goals if parents do the same first.

Both overwhelmed by the sheer depth of Andrea's talent, Eunice and I had a strong desire to support our daughter, but we gradually developed different ideas about how to guide her. My belief led me to use positive methods, including encouraging self-motivation and praising efforts rather than focusing on external outcomes, such as winning or losing.

The Chinese culture of upbringing focuses on criticism and sometimes even punishment as the most accepted tool to help children develop. Eunice was brought up with this culture, so she didn't agree with my positive approach. "That will ruin Andrea," said Eunice. "She will become big-headed."

Typical Chinese parents apply strict discipline and push the kids to work hard. Eunice didn't push forcefully, but she did apply gentle pressure. For example, she showed her displeasure when Andrea didn't practice, and then refused to do things for her, like drive her to a competition, so I took time off to take her. Then Eunice would blame me for spoiling her efforts.

Eunice is an accomplished musician with a deep understanding of the artistry. When she criticized Andrea's mistakes, I had no clue of their merit. I could personally feel the beauty and spirit of Andrea's playing, but technically I knew nothing. When I gave praise on Andrea's performance and it conflicted with Eunice's criticism, she thought my praise confused her.

Keen to help Andrea, Eunice and I worked even harder to assist her in our own ways, which brought more conflict. I tried to facilitate Andrea's understanding of where she wanted to go as well as encouraged self-motivation and discipline, which would help her develop inner strength and a sense of fulfillment. Anytime I attempted to share my approach with her, however, she turned her back and refused to listen to me.

Andrea is brilliant and quicker and smarter than me. She is also very sensitive and could always "smell" that I planned to talk about what she called a "D and M" (deep and meaningful) topic. I would strategize about how to gain her open-minded attention and think about how to stay nonjudgmental with no pressure. For example, I would ask:

"How did the competition go for you?"

Her answer would close the door. "Good."

"Were you happy with your preparation?" I persisted.

"Yes."

"Were you happy with the outcome?"

Silence.

I knew I put my foot in the wrong place, so I would often stop, smile, and leave things there. Other times I would push further, though, and say, "You know, winning or losing doesn't matter; it's the progression and self-satisfaction of the effort you put in that matters. Eventually if you continue to progress you will get to where you want to be."

"I know that, Dad," Andrea would say, irritated with me. She is very knowledgeable and knew just about every theory, but knowing something and incorporating it into your life can be two entirely different matters. I've learned many painful lessons, and my life experience has helped me develop my inner strength and self-discipline. I wanted so badly to share my precious life experience with my children, and that is when I made even more mistakes. Like most people, when in an upset state, Andrea felt everything seemed like more criticism, and she was confused by my and Eunice's different approaches, so she shut her mind and got upset. Both Eunice and I persisted with our ways. We could not help ourselves.

It pained me to see my talented daughter become frustrated because she limited herself. In turn, I felt frustrated that she wouldn't open her mind to my suggestions, which I thought could help her. No matter how much effort I made working out a way to communicate with her, it almost always turned out badly. Eventually, I understood and kept quiet. Other than that, we are a wonderfully loving father and daughter.

At eighteen, Andrea left home to study at Yale because she had the chance to study under a great teacher—the head of the piano department at Yale—Boris Berman. Mr. Berman is a brilliant teacher, pianist, and a wonderful person. He and Andrea developed an excellent mutual affectionate teacher/student relationship. She's been living in the US since, attending Yale and later marrying a wonderful, loving man named Evan Wels. They met at Yale where Evan also studied music. Later he became a choral conductor and music teacher in a NYC school. When they were planning their wedding, Andrea objected to formal dress for the fathers: "My dad would not be comfortable wearing a tuxedo. He has never worn or owned one," she said. She wanted me to be comfortable and to totally enjoy the happy occasion. She is very considerate about my likes and dislikes.

Several years after moving to the US, Andrea came home to Australia for a concert tour. As I chauffeured her around, she asked me, "You know those D and M talks, Dad?"

My heart sped up, and I replied, "Yes?"

"I feel like I can talk to you about that now."

I became so excited I thought I might have an accident, so I pulled over to the curb and asked her, "When?" I felt overjoyed when she said, "Anytime."

We were close to Sydney's Central Park, so I parked my car and we walked along, talking about her goals in life and her satisfaction in performing and sharing music. We also discussed challenges in her future, including making a living as a musician. I felt so happy, as though all of the birds from heaven sang for me. Finally at that moment my daughter and I connected mentally and spiritually.

Andrea and I would often joke about her taking tai chi lessons, because when she had the flu at twelve, I told her that tai chi improves immunity. She hated being sick so much that she agreed to learn tai chi from me. Unfortunately, after a few lessons she decided to call it a day. I tried every gentle persuasive technique I knew and even resorted to bribing her with ten dollars, but to no avail, so I yielded.

At twenty-five, thirteen years after the first few lessons, when she came home to Sydney for a concert tour for two months, she asked me to teach her tai chi. I thought she wanted to humor me, but she did actually want to learn tai chi, so I started giving her regular lessons. In no time, Andrea learned the Yang style 24 Forms and moved on to the Chen style 36 Forms and my Tai Chi for Arthritis program. I was in heaven. She is so talented—a teacher's dream. Anything I said she did quickly and well. She possesses such great body awareness that she performed beautifully, as though she'd learned tai chi since childhood. Even more exciting, she understands the inner energy and picks it up naturally. Evan came to see her in Australia, and I taught him Tai Chi for Arthritis, too. Teaching them was certainly one of my most cherished achievements.

A couple of years after renewing her interest in tai chi, Andrea joined me at the filming of my instructional DVD for the program *Tai Chi for Energy*, a combined set of Sun and Chen style movements. Words cannot describe my happiness. Andrea came for the first day of the three-day scheduled shooting; she portrayed one of my students in the DVD. She could only join the filming for one day, because the next few days she had to practice and rehearse for her performance with the Sydney Symphony Orchestra at the Sydney Opera House.

During the third and last day of filming, she and Eunice came to pick me up for dinner. We had run into some problems at a difficult sequence and were running out of time, as we had to finish the filming that day. I mustered all of my physical and mental strength and started all over from a long way back. We did the job splendidly but did not finish until eighty-thirty p.m. I walked out of the studio tired but excited, apologizing to my girls for being late. Andrea looked happy and said, "D, I felt so exhausted after just one day of filming, but you did three. You direct, teach everything, and work nonstop for three full days. Before you came out while we were waiting, everyone (other assistants) dragged themselves out of the studio looking so tired, and here you are bouncing out of the studio full of smiles and energy."

I felt so great at her comment. I wanted to throw Andrea in the air like a baby and catch her. Instead I smiled and said, "Sweetie, I am always happy and excited to see my beautiful daughter."

And that is the truth. I always am.

Totally unexpectedly, Matthew applied his wonderful design skills to all of my tai chi instructional materials—books, videos, CDs, and DVDs. His designs brought a touch of class to the products of my passion. Matthew possesses incredible visual ability. He has amazing eyes that see things graphically, which make his designs outstanding. His work has significantly contributed to my success.

One day during his lunch hour at his place of employment, while Matt fit in some work on my Tai Chi for Osteoporosis cover design, Matthew's boss walked past and saw what he was doing. "Matt, I should have known," she said. Matthew was perplexed, because he knew he'd done nothing wrong, since he was working on his lunchtime. Then she (Tracy) told him she had arthritis and had been using my program, which gave her great relief from pain. She hadn't connected Matthew as my son until she saw him doing the design.

Andrea and Evan also added to my success by working with their musician friends to create the *Tai Chi Music* CD for me. Music is composed mostly to capture your attention or to take you to a relaxed state. Tai chi creates inner energy and a special rhythm, so most music does not work for tai chi. I wanted tai chi music to carry a special tai chi energy with the unique tai chi rhythm. The best way was to have it composed and performed by musicians who have an understanding of tai chi and a high level of musical talent. Andrea and her colleagues were the perfect people to do just that. Both Andrea and Evan knew my Tai Chi for Health programs. The musicians composed and performed their pieces to my tempo and energy as I performed tai chi.

How wonderful to have both of my beautiful children honoring me with their artistry.

CHAPTER 19

THE FINAL GOOD-BYE

When you drink the water, remember the spring.
— Chinese proverb

In 1986, I received a letter from my niece in China, Zheng's eldest daughter. Back then it was difficult to call the village and impossible for my relatives to call me. The news Shu Wan's letter relayed sliced through my heart. Aunt suffered from cancer of the esophagus. My receptionist, Joanne, came in and found me weeping uncontrollably. When I finally regained some composure, I canceled appointments and got the first air ticket to China.

During the long flight, I felt waves of deep sadness followed by an urgent desire to see if I could do something—anything. When I arrived, Shu Wan told me they'd known about her condition for a while, but Aunt hadn't wanted to worry me.

Aunt still lived in the storage room. When I walked into the dark space, my eyes struggled to adjust as I approached her lying in the shadows. The feeling in the tiny room almost choked me with its desperation, and tears welled up in my eyes as I lifted her bony, cool hand. She looked almost like a shadow. Through my blurred vision, it seemed like we'd returned to the time of the Great Famine with Aunt skin and bones and struggling to survive starvation.

The next day I took her to the hospital in Shantou, the biggest nearby city with a better medical facility. What a terrible experience. As a physician, I'd heard horror stories of patients in hospitals being treated badly and how unequipped and understaffed hospitals can sometimes be, but those stories paled in comparison to what I experienced in China. The hospital was noisy, unhygienic, unimaginably crowded, and hostile. When we arrived, I introduced myself to the nurse and told her why I came. They considered it a big deal to have a doctor visit from overseas back then, so they treated us like VIPs. The nurse found two chairs for us, and I helped Aunt sit down.

My aunt hadn't been allocated a specialist, so a junior hospital doctor entered the room where we waited. The nurse started to introduce me, but before she had a chance, the doctor pointed to me and demanded, "Is he the patient?" When the nurse shook her head, he grabbed my arm and proceeded to drag me out of the chair so he could push me out the door. Before I recovered from the shock and delivered a tai chi punch, the nurse explained that I was a doctor visiting from Australia. Instantly his manner changed. He asked me to sit down and became helpful.

The doctor showed me Aunt's X-rays and reviewed her case history. She'd been having difficulty swallowing and couldn't afford the hospital fees, so she went to Chinese herbalists and other alternative practitioners for a number of weeks. By the time she received an X-ray, it showed advanced cancer of the esophagus that had become inoperable and untreatable. This cancer grows in the esophagus (the eating tube), eventually blocking it completely so no food can get through. As a result, the person dies from starvation.

I cursed the gods at the cruelly ironic fate they had dished out to my beloved Aunt! My whole life I desperately wanted to find a better life for her, and I would have done anything for her. I could finally buy her anything she wished to eat, but she could not eat. I am a healer, but I couldn't heal her. Despite my medical degree, I was as powerless as I'd been twenty-two years before.

I stayed in China as many days as I could at Aunt's side. Frail and weakened from hunger, she sat and gathered all her energy to talk to me. Before I left, I took her thin hand in mine and struggled to hold back my tears. I knew our parting would be absolutely forever this time. Aunt sensed my despair and reassured me, "Ah B, don't worry, there is an experienced, old Chinese doctor in a faraway village. I will go and see him. He will save me. I will be all right."

I broke down silently within myself. I can't remember for how long I said nothing, but eventually I regained my composure and replied, "That's a wonderful idea. I'm sure he will be able to help you. Before I go, is there anything I can do for you?"

"Ah," said Aunt, "I'm just a useless old woman. I never did take good care of you. Thank heaven you got out of China in time. Don't worry about me. You are a good man with a kind heart. You have taken care of me and my family. I know you will continue to take care of the children. I am very grateful to you, but I have nothing to repay you. I will return [via reincarnation] to pay you back in my next life."

I wanted to tell her how wrong she was. She had starved herself and saved my life. She made me who I am, and I will forever be in her debt. I longed to insist that she could never be a useless person and that her love was the greatest gift that any human could give. But I couldn't say anything. I just nodded slowly, in my heart feeling torn.

Why did my beloved aunt have to survive the Great Famine and then years later starve to death in a time of plenty? I thought about how her fate was not only terrible from the physical deprivation and poverty standpoint, but she never received the respect she deserved. My aunt always called herself useless, and she would die thinking of herself that way. I knew she would be happy knowing that she made me who I am. She gave me a caring heart that drives me to help others. She could never be a worthless person. How I wish she would know that!

Aunt sensed my deep pain and sadness about her impending death. She smiled at me, and at that moment I knew she understood what I felt. I could see in her eyes that she would do anything to make me feel better. As always, she didn't care about her life as much as my happiness. Her death approached, but the strength in her eyes somehow comforted me, just like how she consoled me as a child.

Aunt died peacefully ten days after I left. I received another letter a month later with photos of the funeral ceremony. For many years after receiving that letter, I avoided grieving the loss of Aunt, as it felt too painful to even think about. In some ways, I'd already mourned her loss when I left China. It took a miracle for the world to change and for us to meet again, so perhaps in my unconscious,

I waited for another such miracle. When I met Dr. Pam Kircher while building my Tai Chi for Health program and learned about her book on the subject of near-death experiences and how the purpose of our lives is to learn to love, she and her book helped me to grieve for Aunt. I became able to go through the various stages of grief, including denial and anger and letting go without holding back the tears and pain. My family's support greatly helped me in the process of acceptance. Dr. Kircher's experience gave me hope that there might be life after this life. I will see Aunt again.

Twenty-one years later, a letter arrived bearing the news that Cousin Zheng had lung cancer spreading throughout his body. I dropped everything and went home to see him. On my previous visits to Cousin Zheng, I usually stayed at a hotel in Shantou and only met with him briefly. Often he came to meet me in Shantou. This time I stayed by his side in the little storage room for an entire week. We didn't talk much; we often just sat there. During his naps, I talked to his daughters, sons-in-law, and grandchildren.

When he had the energy, we spoke about pleasant memories from times past. My visit passed slowly and sadly. The day before I left, we both sat there feeling melancholy. Then I remembered how he loved fishing in the old days, so I started talking to him about it. The mention of fishing made his eyes sparkle and his posture straighten. His energy level changed. He no longer looked like a man in the terminal stages of lung cancer, but came back to life and transformed into the young man who loved fishing. This prompted him to want to climb onto a stool, which he did with the assistance of his tribe of four sons-in-laws holding him. As they supported Zheng, he reached up into the little loft and took out a bag filled with about ten fishing rods. I've never seen anything like them before or since.

The old Chinese fishing rods were made from pieces of bamboo, string, small pieces of reef for buoyancy, and each possessed a hook. Fishing rods in the Western world have a reel, rod, and a line threaded through little hooks so that you can cast it out and roll the line back. Zheng made his own fusion rod. The handmade rods were unlike the smooth and polished rods you would buy at a shop. He used different sizes of bamboo, joining them with hand-welded metal rings. He also welded some metallic pieces that functioned as a reel. Highly innovative, the rustic and crude rods reminded me of impressionistic paintings—very hard to recognize what they were meant to be but artistic in their own right. Zheng showed great pride in his adaptation of a Western technique to his rods and became excited and pleased when I admired his handiwork.

Having the rods out prompted Zheng to share his favorite fishing stories. As he spoke, I felt the spiritual connection that had faded between us when I left China rekindle. Even though I'd returned many times, those rushed visits never brought back the closeness we once shared growing up. For once, I saw life through Zheng's eyes and realized how challenging reconnecting must have been for him since I left as a small kid fifteen years his junior. Once weaker, smaller, and clumsier, I returned as the benefactor supporting him and his family. Not to mention the immense changes in my life and the world. These changes meant we had very little in common, and it must have been emasculating for him to receive my financial assistance. At that moment with the fishing rods, recent years faded. Only love remained between us. I sat there holding back my tears but feeling good that we reignited the love that would last forever.

Zheng passed away peacefully two weeks after I left. He experienced no pain until the very last day. His loved ones surrounded him and made his final time comfortable. They took turns bathing and massaging him. Zheng withstood all of the humiliation of the black label and gave up countless opportunities in order to stand by his adopted mother, my aunt. What a brave and loyal man.

CHAPTER 20

BETTER HEALTH TAI CHI CHUAN

*Teachers open the door,
but you must enter by yourself.*
— Chinese proverb

Since early childhood, I have admired teachers, and I always wanted to teach. It's in my blood. My father was a famous teacher. Twenty-five years after the Viet Cong took over the Vietnamese government, forcing his school to close, Father's alumni numbering in the thousands are still active around the world. In fact, his magical teaching skills inspired a student to help him set up his school in the first place.

In a way, I considered myself a failure for becoming a doctor rather than a teacher. After going through the Australian high school system, I chose not to teach because I observed little respect for teachers. I suspected that with my small size and Chinese accent the kids would have given me a really hard time. I'd stand a better chance teaching in an Asian country where teachers are respected and students are more eager to learn. At that time, though, I didn't know much about teaching methods. I also had no idea that effective teachers can overcome many challenges.

Nonetheless, my desire to teach persisted. When I discovered an opportunity to teach postgraduate doctors through the University of New South Wales, I grabbed the chance with both hands. Over the last thirty years, I've gained much fulfillment and learned a great deal about teaching from instructing postgraduate doctors.

During my years in practice, as I personally discovered the many benefits of tai chi, I started recommending that my patients give it a go. One of my patients and a good friend, Scottie Porter, had arthritis, so I sent him off to learn tai chi. A year later he came in for a check-up. I asked him about his tai chi progress, and he complained about the difficulty he had with the teacher, especially with the fact that what the teacher instructed him to do worsened his condition. Out of the blue, I heard myself saying, "Come to my house. I will give you some lessons."

After a few months of private lessons, Scottie encouraged me to start a school. Knowing my busy schedule, he offered to do all of the organizing work, leaving the teaching to me. That proved an offer I couldn't refuse. By coincidence, his brother-in-law, Tim, also my longtime patient and friend, had helped build a scout hall near my medical office. Tim arranged for me to rent the scout hall for a nominal fee, and Scottie and I started our school.

First we needed to decide on a name. Scottie insisted that we call it Lam's Tai Chi School. I felt equally adamant about not using my name. After growing up under the Communist system and Mao, who the people revered like a god, I saw how such glorification led to an abuse of power, disregard of human life, and the death of millions. I am opposed to any personal glorification, especially to me.

Then one day I came up with the perfect name while bathing. Until I left China, I'd never experienced a shower. A long, hot shower is one of my greatest pleasures in life. Like Archimedes in his bath, I relax under the warm water and let it cleanse my mind and me. When I'm in the shower, brilliant ideas often pop into my head. During one of these showers, the name for my school came to me: Better Health Tai Chi Chuan. The name summed up my tai chi vision. While the practice is well known throughout much of the world as tai chi, in China where tai chi originated, the right name for it is tai chi chuan. Tai chi provides the perfect way to develop *qi* and as a result achieve better health and a more fulfilling life.

My first class contained eight students, all of whom came from word of mouth. The class included Scottie and Ian Etcell, the husband of one of my receptionists. Ian came along out of curiosity. He possessed excellent body awareness and a keen sense of biomechanics, plus an amazing talent. Before long Ian got hooked on tai chi. He became a close colleague and developed his own tai chi to an extremely high level. Over the years, I've learned a great deal from my students and my colleagues—especially from Ian.

Better Health Tai Chi Chuan opened as a local school, and many of my patients joined. We enjoyed learning and progressing together. Right from the beginning, we made the school nonprofit, because as one of the instructors said, "There is no profit to be made from teaching tai chi, so we might as well forget the profit and we will enjoy teaching more." A few years later, to further our tai chi study, I organized an annual trip to China for training, which I continued to do for a number of years. Our school features an academic approach. We practice diligently and quietly, working on improving ourselves but never worrying about expanding the school. Over time, we've attracted many like-minded people who enjoy the open-minded approach and seek the true depth of tai chi.

Our students develop in their chosen directions. Some like competitions and have represented Australia, winning many medals in major international competitions. Others choose to share their knowledge of tai chi, like retired teacher Pat Webber, who came to class for the first time to give her sister-in-law moral support. Her sister-in-law left within a couple of weeks, but Pat stayed on. Twenty years later Pat is one of our most experienced and respected master trainers. She has trained hundreds of instructors, who have in turn trained thousands of participants. Doctors had previously diagnosed Pat with osteopenia, a condition where the bones thin and the condition usually progresses to osteoporosis. After practicing tai chi, Pat's doctor told her that her bone mineral density test has shown an improvement over the years instead of deteriorating like others with the same diagnosis. Tai chi has given so many of us significant health benefits.

Motivation can be a challenge, even for a well-disciplined person like me who likes to work hard. So many things were happening in my life, including attending to my busy medical practice and spending time with my family. When could I find time for practice? How to motivate myself? I answered this question by setting up a regular routine in the early morning. I arose before the rest of the family and did my tai chi. Having a routine makes it much easier to adhere to practice. On the occasions when I really didn't feel like practicing, I forced myself to go to the practice room, practically pulling my arms and legs to start moving. Once I started, after the first five or ten minutes the tai chi became so enjoyable that it took on a life of its own. The rest of the day would be more pleasant and productive. Those times set me up for future recurrences. I knew if I practiced, I'd feel better afterward. At a practice session I often feel wonderfully "in flow," forgetting time and space and totally engaging my mind and body. In this state, my aches and pains disappear and my mind is serene. The feeling is so wonderful that it always pulls me back to regular practice.

In a very real way, my arthritis pain is a blessing. When my busy life prevented me from practicing regularly, my pain worsened, which served as a reminder and powerful motivator to do more tai chi.

At the end of the day, practicing tai chi has much to do with self-control and the personal desire to complete a task and carry out one's own plan. The Empty Period when I had nothing to do and no stimulation made me appreciate any opportunity to learn and to persevere with the tasks ahead of me. If I didn't continue and accomplish my goals, I felt my life wasting away like the "Song of Tomorrow" poem that I'd written down for De all those years ago. Tai chi is something I can do anytime, anywhere, and at any age.

I often tell myself: "JUST DO IT." And I do.

I used to be more impatient and preferred fast movements, which is why I loved skiing. Because I'd been deprived of opportunities, I wanted to make the most of every moment. As I matured, my tai chi helped me understand the concept of inner harmony. Being patient is the yin and excitement represents the yang part of nature. Yin and yang complement one another. Rushing through something when the time is not right is against nature. When I started tai chi, I felt impatient with the slow movements. The long period of time learning and practicing tai chi before gaining any benefit challenged me. My patience improved as my tai chi progressed, however. I enjoyed it so much that I wanted to learn more and more. Like climbing up a beautiful mountain, I wished to see the view at the top.

I had the good fortune of working with my friend Ling Wong

in San Francisco. Ling has practiced tai chi and martial arts since childhood. He told me about his brilliant teacher, Professor Men. With encouragement from Mr. Lum, I wrote to Professor Men Hui Feng and his wife, Professor Kan Gui Xiang, both teachers at the Beijing Institute of Physical Education and the most famous tai chi teachers in the world. Fond of Ling, they responded quickly and encouraged me to visit them. I got a bank loan to make a trip to Beijing to train with them.

When I first met Professor Men, he asked what tai chi form I wanted to learn, and I told him I preferred the traditional Yang taught by my father-in-law. I commented that if he could improve upon that style, I'd appreciate it. He said, "Show me." So right there on the street in an empty corner, he squatted down and watched me do my Yang style form. After I finished, he said, "Oh . . ."

The blank look on his face reminded me of Chinese tradition and custom. Traditional tai chi teachers don't focus on what the student wants. The teacher teaches whatever he or she wishes to teach, and the student must accept it wholeheartedly. I realized by Professor Men's reaction that he expected me to follow his lead. At the time, China had just opened up to the outside world. Professor Men had probably heard that overseas teachers were more student-orientated, so he asked me what I wanted to learn out of politeness, but when I actually told him what I wanted, he didn't know how to respond to my request. In this respect, I have an advantage over Westerners. In addition to knowing the Chinese language, I understand the culture.

I knew what I had to do, so I said, "Professor Men, I am here to learn. Whatever you wish to teach me, I will be honored."

After that, whenever in Beijing, I switched from a Western mode to a subservient Chinese manner. That meant absolute, unquestioning obedience to my teachers. Often close students take care of their teachers' personal needs, like my father-in-law who paid a significant sum for his teacher's apartment. I did my part by giving my Chinese professors as much of my personal income as I could.

One year Professor Men asked me to bring him a video camera, which cost a great deal in those days. At the time, I struggled to build up my practice and support my family, and I carried a heavy mortgage. I paid two thousand dollars for the camera, which constituted more or less the equivalent of a good secondhand car. On top of that, a video camera entering China attracted a two hundred percent tax. Luckily, I found a way out of the tax. I knew the Chinese customs officials were immensely more lenient toward Caucasian foreigners. I traveled with a group of students, so I asked one of my Caucasian students to carry the camera in his luggage. The customs officer smiled at him as he walked past and didn't look in his bag, but he did search mine. I had a small radio in my case—just a cheap thing, but they wanted to tax me on it. I attempted to reason with the customs official, but he remained determined to make me pay high tax for it. Fortunately, my foreign students who had all passed through customs waited for me. Curious about the holdup, they waved to me from the other side. When the customs officer realized I had so many Caucasian friends, he changed his attitude and let me pass through. This is when being a Westerner is an advantage.

In Beijing I learned various styles of tai chi and a different approach and focus. They placed great emphasis on competition aspects. With competitions, aesthetic value is crucial. At first I didn't care too much about the external aspects, as tai chi is an internal art, which is what attracted me to the practice in the first place. However, I'd already made the decision to follow the teachers' instructions totally, so I did.

Once I made a committed effort to follow the teachers, good things happened. There is a power in the universe that seems to pull us toward positive outcomes. I noticed that when I worked hard, a positive outcome occurred sooner or later. Sometimes it took many years to appear, but hard work always paid me handsomely in the end. When I got the external appearance of the form just right, it began to resonate with the internal components and increased my internal energy. This allowed me to gain a deeper understanding of integrating the internal and external.

With diligent work, I learned many different sets of tai chi, including the most popular 24 Forms, the Combined 42 Form, the Combined 48 Form, the Sun style 73 Form, the Chen 36 and 56, and the several sets of Sword Forms. I liked the diversity, which enabled me to discover the depth and height of tai chi from different perspectives, like looking at the elephant from different angles. Fortunately, I possess an exceptional memory, though I didn't realize that until years later. I memorized the set of 73 forms in one day. The depth of tai chi, however, came after a long time of diligent and continual practice. The key to tai chi is the true understanding of the principles common to all styles and forms. And that understanding only comes with sound knowledge and consistent, mindful practice. It is a lifelong, revealing journey climbing the magnificent tai chi mountain. As you climb, the views keep getting more spectacular and the air fresher, although neglecting practice can make you slip back down.

One day Professor Men said to me, "Paul, you should enter the 1993 International Tai Chi Competition in Beijing."

I replied, "Huh?" I am not a competitive person, but the teacher wanted me to enter the competition, so I did.

At that time, my brother Andrew and his family from Canada were visiting me in Sydney—a rare occurrence in those days. I'd already committed to the competition, so I had to say my good-byes and leave for Beijing in the midst of the visit.

We went a week in advance to train. Competitors were allowed to enter a maximum of three events, and I chose the Combined 42 Forms, the 42 Sword Form, and the Chen style 36 Form—three of the most fiercely competed sets. I had no idea in what standard of the competition I stood. I only chose these forms because I liked them. Winning hadn't entered my mind. The 42 International Competition Forms is a combination of four major styles, namely Yang, Chen, Sun, and Wu. Professor Men and Professor Li created this form for the International Tai Chi Competitions. I took a team from our school that chose different sets, like me, totally on personal preference.

In an international tai chi competition, there are five judges for each event. The chief judge is positioned in the center and the other four are placed in each corner. The scoring system is complicated, with many strict guidelines. The highest and lowest scores are eliminated to remove any extreme opinions and then the middle three scores are totaled and divided by three. Even a decimal place or a second decimal place can make the difference between first and second place, so competition is fierce.

At forty-five, I was one of the oldest competitors. A mature category for those over forty existed, but my teacher wanted me to be at the main events. I had no idea of my chances and didn't care about winning, so it didn't faze me to compete against younger professional tai chi practitioners and athletes.

During the pre-competition week, I began training really hard. The second day, my muscles ached so badly that even walking proved painful. Turning over in my sleep felt like agony, so I learned to lie still and move as little as possible. They held the competition in the summertime, whereas previously I'd only visited Beijing in the winter, because it is the quiet period in my medical work. Australia is opposite when it comes to seasons compared to many other countries. Our winter is summer in most other countries, and winter is the busiest season in a family practice. I had no idea that the summer in Beijing would be so dry and uncomfortable. At every training session we sweated profusely, each drinking two large bottles of boiled, cooled water. The days were more exhausting than our usual training.

By continuing to train so hard in such hot weather I risked injury, and it concerned me that the painful muscles would hinder my performance. However, we had one week in Beijing, and we had the best teachers available. I urged my team to take advantage of the opportunity to train with the excellent teachers, never mind winning or losing. Having decided that, and as I continued to train hard, something uncomfortable started sneaking into my head. I started thinking more seriously about injuries and about my fellow team members. The training we did, especially for the competition, put a great emphasis on lowering the stance. This meant stretching to your limit, and sometimes past, which could lead to injury. That practice is inconsistent with my method of learning tai chi for health.

At that point, I reviewed my real purpose of my tai chi journey. I started tai chi as a way to help manage my arthritis. As that became well managed, I enjoyed it so much that I allowed my approach and goal to change. The competition's increased potential of injury stood directly opposed to my original goal of health and harmony;

health remained at the heart of my tai chi venture. Putting all that aside, however, I pressed on with my training. When the competition arrived, my muscles felt so painful from training that I had to take analgesics for pain relief.

Like the Olympics, the ceremony and atmosphere inspired awe. The mayor of Beijing opened the ceremony, and a full military band played with more than thirty countries represented, all marching under huge banners announcing their homelands. As we marched into the arena, with the band playing and the spectators cheering, it felt electrifying. We brimmed with pride at representing Australia.

So excited were we to be at the competition that our team won several silver and bronze medals. I won the gold for the Combined 42 Forms and silver for the Chen 36 Forms and the Combined 42 Sword Forms, respectively, and had the highest total score.

The medal presentation and the closing ceremony were incredibly exciting, especially considering my surprise at winning. Like the Olympics, but on a smaller scale, they called the winners onto a stage to receive their awards. When my turn came, I was surprised that I barely remember walking up to receive the award from the mayor. At the conclusion of the ceremony, all of the gold medal winners, including me, demonstrated our winning forms. I was glad to be able to stay in the serene *jing* state and performed better than I had during the actual competition. The euphoria from the entire experience infected me with the competition bug.

When I returned to Sydney, my brother Andrew was still at my home. He immediately asked about the competition.

"Did you enjoy yourself?"

"Yes, I had a wonderful time."

"How did you do? Close to the average?"

"Better than the average."

"Really? That's good. How much better?"

"A gold and two silver medals."

Andrew appeared suitably surprised and impressed. It felt so good to boast to my big brother!

PART FOUR

The World

CHAPTER 21

TAI CHI PRODUCTIONS

Do not fear going forward slowly;
fear only to stand still.
— Chinese proverb

We came home to Australia from the tai chi competitions to a heroes' welcome. I proceeded to push aside the uneasy feeling about injuries and focused on promoting tai chi through competitions. At that stage I didn't yet have a clear distinction between the traditional tai chi and what would later become my Tai Chi for Health program. My intention at that time was to spread the word about tai chi, since it had benefited me so much. Later I saw the need for creating special programs based on traditional, authentic tai chi that incorporated modern medical knowledge and current teaching methods. At that stage, however, I just recognized the effect of competition on bringing attention to tai chi and helping to spread the word about the art.

With my encouragement and training, many of my students competed, and a number of them represented Australia in national and international competitions and won many medals.

Because of our students' involvement in competing, I joined the AKWF (Australian Kung Fu Wushu Federation). I chaired the New South Wales Wushu Committee and became one of four members of the medical committee for the World Wushu Championships.

Later, AKWF and other organizations asked me to chair their judging panels to promote competitions within Australia and internationally. I accepted the positions with the aim of steering the competitions toward the internal aspects of tai chi. Tai chi is one of the most effective and certainly the most famous of internal martial arts. The ultimate purpose of internal arts is to improve internal energy. With tai chi the type of internal energy is integral to health and harmony.

A few years went by, and I started to see things more clearly. The emphasis for the competitions was on aesthetics and athletic and gymnastic abilities—because those skills understandably draw the attention of spectators and are easier to judge than internal aspects. While internal health and harmony provide the receiver with spectacular benefits, they aren't spectacular for spectators. I did my best to fight this trend, but after several years of swimming against the tide, I realized that the fundamental differences would always exist. I decided to resign from all of the positions and focus entirely on building Tai Chi for Health.

Ironically, while I didn't care much about winning the gold medal, it helped me start Tai Chi Productions, which ended up making a significant contribution to the health and harmony of many. It all started one day in 1992 when a student asked if he could videotape me while I taught so that he could follow me when he practiced at home. Video photography was in its infancy, but I did have one of the earliest video cameras, and I knew something about videoing. When he asked, I quickly responded, "No, you cannot, because videoing is not just about pointing a camera and shooting. What comes out would be very different."

Later I reflected on this and felt bad for refusing. This started me thinking about my first video project. Once I did some research, I discovered the immensity of the task. There are so many aspects to consider, including lighting, background, voice, script writing, acting, editing, and filming. Not to mention funding. Most of us know that making a movie costs millions of dollars, with teams of experts. Creating a video is similar to making a movie and most like making a documentary.

Even for smaller projects, all professional productions have teams of experts working on each of the individual aspects. For example, when we filmed the revised instructional DVD *Tai Chi for Arthritis* twelve years after the first, I collaborated with the Arthritis

Foundation in America. We rented the ABC studio, and a team of lighting architects designed a specific lighting system so that the lighting appeared clear and soft to show the full dimensions of all participants without any shadows. During the filming, two full-time lighting technicians stood by to adjust for each scene. The same went for the sound recording, cameraperson, background design, and many other aspects. Just as you see hundreds of names on the credit list at the end of a movie, a good video production requires similar expertise and expense.

Despite the complexity and enormity of creating a video, even from that first video in the '90s, I never felt daunted. I desired to share my tai chi with more people, and I knew that I had a limited amount of time to teach face-to-face. Video offered an ideal way to reach more people. When I decide to pursue a project, I put everything into it.

I couldn't afford any professional setup. I thought that we could overcome the cost factor with enthusiasm and hard work, thinking that a good homemade video could achieve the same goal. I wanted to do this project as well as possible, as there's no point in doing something poorly, so I learned as much as I could about video production.

In those days, you couldn't type the title or any wording into the screen unless you had expensive studio equipment. One of my friends used an affordable yet time-consuming method for creating titles and instructions. We bought sheets of preprinted letters and he drew lines with a pencil to ensure that all of the letters were straight. Then he painstakingly stuck the letters on pieces of white paper, rubbed off the pencil marks, and we shot them. Just for the name of each form and the most pertinent instructions we required twenty pages of text, which took days to assemble.

We started by choosing the set of tai chi to instruct and found the filming location and worked out the method of presentation for instruction. The position of the camera had to be consistent to make it easier for viewers to orientate themselves. Since it took days to film the 42 Forms set, we ensured the camera angle, the lighting, and everything we did would be consistent throughout. The challenge is to always put yourself in the position of the viewers. There are many viewers with different learning patterns, skills, and resources, and ideally I wanted the videos to be useful to people of all skill levels. It's a real challenge to give useful material to advanced tai chi practitioners while relaying information that's easy enough for novices to learn from—all without face-to-face communication.

Talking to a camera is much more difficult than addressing a group of real students. With video, you must talk naturally, clearly and concisely, while also appearing at ease. To make matters more challenging, English is not my native tongue. To practice prior to videotaping, I drew a circle on a piece of paper, put it on the wall at camera level and spent months talking to the circle on the wall as if it were a camera. I used a stopwatch to time each segment, as videos have a limited length. By doing this, I planned every second so the video would be clear, unhurried, meaningful, and useful to viewers. If you know a second language, you most likely realize how much more challenging it is to focus on thinking clearly and at the same time trying to pronounce the words accurately.

Preparation prior to creating the video took nearly a year, even with the help of my team of volunteer assistants. By the time we filmed, we'd clocked a total of six hundred hours, or about four months of full-time work for one person. When you watch a one-hour documentary, it flows quickly. It's hard to imagine that it takes a team of hundreds of people working full-time for a year to produce this one-hour show. That first video experience taught me a great deal about producing a video and prepared me for the next phase when I graduated to professional production. Even today, I still practice talking to a circle on the wall months before every new DVD. Preparation and hard work always help for each project, and it improves my tai chi. At every phase, I check everyone's tai chi forms, especially my own. A key to tai chi is body and mind integration. Often you think your body is upright, but that isn't the case on the video screen. Looking at yourself at every angle helps to integrate the body and mind. The immense effort of making the video user-friendly and useful within a limited time frame also greatly improves my teaching technique.

I felt so happy with the first video production that I sold it to our students cheaply at thirty dollars a copy. It disappointed me that the person who asked about videoing me didn't buy one. That taught me that you can't count on people to purchase your product, no matter how much love you put into a video and how well the job is done. This didn't dampen my enthusiasm, however. I learned a great deal from the project and gained enormous satisfaction completing something that continues to help people with tai chi.

In the '80s, *T'AI CHI Magazine* from the US was about the only tai chi publication available. Hardly anyone had heard of tai chi in those days. The owner/editor of *T'AI CHI Magazine*, Marvin Smallheiser, a visionary man, worked hard to deliver quality articles, and the magazine carried advertisements for videos and other products.

My urge to share the power of tai chi with others inspired me to write articles for *T'AI CHI Magazine* before I started making videos. My forte has always been math and science, so writing is something I find challenging. I wrote a number of articles for *T'AI CHI Magazine* and for media outlets, including newspapers. By writing the articles, I got to know Nancy Kaye. She came to my workshop because she liked my articles. Prior to retiring, she worked as a magazine editor. We became great friends and she cowrote my book, *Tai Chi for Beginners and the 24 Forms*, with me. She often challenged me to think more clearly about the concepts and ideas before I put them down on paper. Nancy loved to ask me challenging questions like what something means and how it links to the next point. She would say: "This bit is boring. Let's write it again," which greatly improved my writing.

Tai chi is an art of doing, so video is much more effective than words to show how the art should be performed. After the homemade video project, I became hooked, but I didn't feel satisfied with its quality. To reach more people, I knew that I needed to invest in professional production. Driven by passion and a burning desire to share tai chi with as many people as possible, I jumped into video production, throwing financial considerations to the wind. Without any knowledge of marketing and no idea if a market existed for tai chi videos, I set up the company, Tai Chi Productions, for the sole purpose of producing tai chi instructional materials.

In the '90s, video production was prohibitively expensive. A ten-minute introduction would take four days of studio time, and a studio charged around five hundred dollars an hour. The industrial experts gave a general estimate of the cost of producing a video at one thousand dollars a minute, which meant a standard ninety-minute video cost around ninety thousand dollars. That didn't include the price of cover design, duplication, and packaging. Even today with technological advances and cheaper equipment, a professionally produced DVD still costs around one thousand dollars a minute, although twenty years ago one thousand dollars bought you a lot more. If you're lucky enough to get a distributor to take your product on, at completion most retail distributors only pay a ten percent royalty to the producer. In 1994, when I completed the first professionally produced video at a retail price of twenty dollars per video, to recover costs I would have to sell forty-five thousand videos! In those days, ninety thousand dollars would buy a high-end, two-bedroom apartment in Sydney. I clearly couldn't afford that kind of cost.

Determined to produce professional quality video, I knew there must be a way to cut costs. In my search for an affordable professional video company, I must have called just about all of the video producers in Sydney, with no luck. Finally, I found at the end of the phone a deep, no-nonsense voice with what turned out to be an Austrian accent. Anton invited me to visit his studio converted from his garage. A tall man with a meticulously organized workspace, I clicked with him straightaway. I love organized people, but most importantly, Anton agreed to work with me to save on costs. He offered to show me everything my team and I could do to cut costs. With that understanding, I gathered enough money through yet another bank loan to start our first two professionally produced videos.

With half a year of meticulous preparation by my enthusiastic tai chi team completed, we chose to film the Combined 42 Forms. I decided on that set because I had won the gold medal with those forms. Though I didn't think that winning a medal necessarily meant I was an effective teacher, everyone I spoke to was impressed with the achievement and advised me to use "international gold medal winner" as the marketing pitch.

I booked Anton for two days of filming, but he said we needed three days, so he scheduled another day a week later, saying we could cancel at no cost. We were so well prepared, however, that we completed the filming in two days. Since I had another day scheduled, I decided to do the 24 Forms, because it's the most popular tai chi set in the world. My enthusiastic team supported me in this decision, and we worked like crazy to prepare for the second title. The six hundred hours of hard work we already spent on producing the home video version of the 24 Forms came in useful. The entire filming proved a most satisfying experience.

My dream came true. I felt like a movie director, project manager, and tai chi instructor combined.

By the end of the filming, I flopped down on the steps of the stage feeling exhausted yet satisfied. Anton saw me sitting there and said, "That's just the beginning, Paul. The hard work is just starting."

"What?" I asked, thinking I didn't hear him right.

"The production is just the beginning; the selling is the really hard work," he replied.

"I don't care," I blurted out. "I feel so good about having done it. I don't care if no one buys it."

In reality, I should have cared about people buying the videos. My friends and students would buy about fifty, which meant I had to find a way to sell thousands of copies to pay for the costs. Considering that I hate selling anything, doing that promised to be challenging.

I wanted to make the videos available for everyone, so the best way seemed to be selling them through retail channels. To do that I needed to find a video distributor. I didn't know anyone in that industry, so I worked my way through the telephone book, searching high and low and spending numerous hours in vain. Chinese culture says that if you are good enough, people will come find you, and if your product is good enough, people will seek it out. Certainly this Chinese saying is not right. After months of trying, I got nowhere regarding distributing the videos. My time would have been better spent teaching tai chi to real people.

Most distributors worked with large companies like 20th Century Fox or Disney. They weren't interested in me. David Carradine knew a lot less about tai chi than me, but he had no problem finding distributors for his tai chi video. I hardly ever managed to get past the receptionist to talk to a manager. The rare times I did, I got nowhere.

The video market is a small, closed world reserved for the big producers and blockbusters, or famous people like David Carradine.

Not good at giving up, I decided that there would be a better chance to enter the retail market if I produced a video for total beginners. Like a gambler throwing good money after bad, I worked with my team and Anton to produce the next instructional video, *Tai Chi for Beginners*, featuring a simplified program based on the 24 Forms. Then undaunted by my previous futile efforts at selling my videos, I knocked on distributors' door again. Still no luck.

One day after six months of numerous, futile calls, someone did call me back. Ron Glover was a part-time, semiretired distributor who worked with Jamie MacKinnon of Video Unlimited from New Zealand. They ran a relatively small company and were willing to give me a try. They did warn me, however, that tai chi videos were new, and they had no great expectations.

A few months later, Jamie informed me that he'd made a breakthrough to get my video included in the *Reader's Digest* catalogue for Australia and New Zealand. A few more months later, *Tai Chi for Beginners* made the best-seller list. That earned me sufficient royalties for paying my bank loans' down payment, and more importantly the opportunity to meet the Australian catalogue manager, Keith Anderson.

Keith liked my intention to help others through tai chi, so he introduced me to other *Reader's Digest* managers around the world. As a result, *Reader's Digest* Canada took up my title the next year, and they became my lifeline. Both *Reader's* royalty checks paid much of the costs of producing the videos, but inclusion in the catalogue proved sporadic. The main catalogues only go out once or twice per year, and you never knew if *Reader's Digest* would pick your title. They deleted any titles that didn't sell well.

A couple of years later, Video Unlimited failed to break in anywhere else, so I decided to take up the challenge again. Jamie warned me: "Paul, the video market is very close—almost like a family—an outsider has no chance of breaking in. Good luck if you want to try." I believed him. I'd discovered the impossibility of selling videos prior to him giving me a chance. But I had to have a go and start the sales journey again. Giving up has never been my strong suit. I didn't understand why I did it. I love my job, family, and my tai chi school. I had a wonderful and busy life, so why—as Eunice would put it—punish myself?

Back in those days, international phone calls were very expensive. Despite the expense, I took the risk and started calling overseas. Not unexpectedly, it ended up that I wasted a lot of time and money on those overseas calls. Jamie was absolutely right—there was an impenetrable barrier in the video sales market.

One day in 1996, I received a letter from Peter Young, a well-known tai chi teacher from Manchester, UK. Peter organized annual international tai chi and wushu championships in Manchester. Peter invited me to be a judge for the coming competition. To take a week off work and pay for the airfare and expenses would be a pricey venture, so I hesitated. Understandably, Eunice didn't support the idea. She knew the numerous barriers I'd hit without much return. To her a doctor is someone important, but a tai chi teacher is a "nobody." She found it hard to understand why a "somebody" would try so hard to be a "nobody." Certainly the financial aspect of tai chi teaching looked bleak, and I was a successful family physician making a good income. I felt guilty for having spent so much money on my passion, but the thought of using the invitation to break into the UK tai chi community and video market tempted me. Should I venture out and see what I could gain or cut my losses? I got my answer when Keith Anderson called me one day out of the blue and offered to arrange an appointment with his counterpart at *Reader's Digest* UK. I had called the UK manager several times prior without success. Grasping at any excuse I could find to go, I reasoned that seeing someone face-to-face gave me a much better chance of success. If I could get my video in *Reader's Digest* UK, that would cover the cost of visiting.

I told myself I'd work longer hours to make up for the loss of income for my family. Working twelve hours per day didn't worry me, as my arthritis remained well controlled and I felt healthier than ever. I worked hard to maximize my schedule so that I still spent time with my beautiful family, worked as a doctor, practiced tai chi, taught, and even sold videos. In order to find time for these pursuits, I went without watching TV and movies. When it came to reading, which I love, I only read personal and children's development books.

How exciting to visit Europe for the first time. The flight transited at Singapore and then London, finally flying on to Manchester. All total, the journey took more than thirty hours. Peter, a strong and energetic man, waited for me at the airport. He greeted me and firmly shook my hand as he said, "We have a judges' meeting in ninety minutes. Are you ready?" After arriving at my hotel, I showered, changed, and went to the meeting. The next day they invited me to chair the tai chi competitions. What a great experience to meet many tai chi practitioners from outside of Australia. No matter where tai chi people are from, there is much similarity. Most tai chi practitioners are kind and caring and share the same enthusiasm. How satisfying to meet the people who read my articles and used my videos. When they came up to tell me how my work had helped them, I forgot the financial challenges and the numerous rejections.

After the competition, I left for London with just two days left to sell. I don't recall anything I saw in London, as my mind became full of video sales. Everything in London cost a great deal of money, especially accommodations and hotel telephone calls. I sat in my tiny, expensive (but cheapest I could get) bed-and-breakfast room thumbing through phone books. I found fifty-five companies that sounded vaguely related to the video business and made fifty-five calls.

Imagine being a successful and respected doctor with an always-packed waiting room sitting in London making cold calls to companies where the people on the other end of the line said disdainfully in a typical English high-nose fashion: "Tai chay? What's that?" "Who are you?" "No, we don't know you. Did you have an appointment?" "We don't talk to salesmen." "We are too busy."

No one knew me and nobody wanted to talk to me. How low could I go? Eunice was right, I thought. A doctor is somebody, a tai chi teacher is nobody, and a tai chi video salesman is worse than nobody.

One person did end up meeting me—a lady in charge of a small book club that sold via catalogues. She kindly offered to take two hundred copies at a seventy percent discount. That thrilled me. The profit of selling two hundred videos just about covered the cost of my two-day hotel room stay. Success at last. Just as I prepared to leave, she hesitated for a few seconds and then told me, "By the way, I know a couple of people in the video business who just started their own company. Here's their phone number. Why don't you give them a ring?"

I thanked her, not feeling hopeful, as I'd experienced rejection so many times. But then I thought, *I've made fifty-five calls. Why not fifty-six?*

I walked miles around London to save the expensive taxi fare in order to meet Kim and Garry, the two good friends who owned Quantum Leap. To present myself well, even though it's not my favorite thing, I wore my leather shoes and a suit and tie. When I returned to my hotel after the meeting, I gasped to find my right sock full of blood. A careful examination revealed the cause. I had fractured my right third toe at a young age, and it never set properly since we couldn't afford a doctor. As a result, I have a crooked toe. The nail of that toe rubbed against the adjoining toe during the hours of walking and cut into the skin, causing it to bleed. Incredibly, I felt no pain while walking. So I can truly say that I've shed blood in the process of promoting Tai Chi for Health.

Fortunately, all the bloodshed proved worth it. Kim and Garry took my titles and gave me a fair contract. Quite different from the other larger distributors, their contract shared profit with me after the cost. With this contract, if my titles didn't sell, I would get nothing back, but if they sold well I would get a much better royalty than from the big distributors.

At that time in London, I had no idea how important Quantum Leap would be. My main hope rested on my last trump card, a meeting with the manager of *Reader's Digest* UK. When I met with Eric Davidson, it took less than ten minutes. He asked me a few questions about my videos and then said, "I will take them up." After we finished, I felt so excited that I practically ran all of the way to Harrods, the famous department store, and celebrated the success with an expensive lunch. I paid eight pounds sterling for four Irish oysters.

Riding on the euphoria of my success in the UK, the next year I set off to conquer the US. My mother, brother, and sisters lived there, so I considered it half a home to me. The English people tend to be reserved, but Americans are friendlier. I felt more confident about breaking in there.

In the US, I made more than a hundred telephone calls, only to be greeted by a recording on almost all of them. I left multiple messages, but hardly anyone called me back. In the US, people have a nicer way of communicating. Instead of saying, "No, go away," they say, "Thanks so much for considering us. We will call you back. Don't call us."

Once again I remembered Eunice's words. I could stay in Australia doing my job as a doctor, which I truly enjoyed, and I would be well paid. So why did I put myself out there? I couldn't answer that question. Instead I kept cold-calling, even though I hate it. I like talking to people, but calling and trying to make sales makes me feel insecure and fearful of rejection. Despite my discomfort, I urged myself to keep going, because no matter how hopeless things appear, there is always hope if you try. Only if you give up will nothing happen. So I kept calling.

The day before my scheduled return home, while talking to my sister Celia at whose house I stayed, she said, "Hey, Paul, I forgot to tell you that somebody returned your call yesterday. Here is his phone number."

Named Wellspring, the relatively new company had a special interest in health-related videos, so I met with them. The success with *Reader's Digest* and Quantum Leap impressed Wellspring and the company took up my titles. That last-minute meeting turned out to be a winner from which I received substantial royalties for the next few years.

During my venture to the US, I considered *Reader's Digest* USA my trump card. I made several efforts to meet their manager. With a sound referral from Keith and my successes with his UK, Canadian, and Australian compatriots, I expected it to be easy, but sadly they never took up my titles.

After the immense amount of time and effort spent producing and selling videos, I felt lucky to recover most of the costs. My videos did get distributed and my dream of them being used by many people to help them gain better health did come true, but in too small a number for me to recover the full cost of production—never mind the time cost. Professionals often measure remunerative worth in terms of an hourly rate, but that's a concept that tai chi teachers forgo.

I did eventually reach a much larger number of viewers with my videos and make a good profit that allowed me to continue producing more instructional materials and participate in unpaid projects, but that didn't come until much later. First I had more work to do.

CHAPTER 22

TAI CHI FOR ARTHRITIS

> *Give a man a fish and you feed him for a day;*
> *teach a man to fish and you feed him for a lifetime.*
> — Chinese proverb

I am so sensitive to motion that even watching waves on television makes me nauseous. On a trip to Florida, I became so sick on the plane that by the time we touched down in Los Angeles (the layover before Florida), I could hardly stand up. As I tried to crawl out of my seat, an elderly couple who were longtime patients and happened to be traveling to Florida, saw my plight. Together they pulled me up and helped me walk down the stairs and off the plane. Later they told me I looked so pale they thought I might pass out at any second. It made them feel good to help their doctor for a change.

I found surviving flying meant keeping my eyes closed most of the time and practicing seated tai chi frequently. Like having arthritis in my early teens, the motion sickness curse turned into a blessing. When my life becomes busy and I neglect my tai chi practice, the arthritis pain worsens in response and that reminds me to practice regularly. The realization that the motion sickness requires closing my eyes forced me to think about my life, and this soul-searching time often leads to amazing discoveries.

One day in 1996 as I flew home from the US, I experienced a long period of soul-searching during the fourteen-hour flight. While contemplating, a thought flashed through my mind. I experienced arthritis since my early teens. As a family physician and acupuncturist, I possessed the qualifications to practice

Western and traditional Chinese medicine. And I had extensive knowledge of the various styles of tai chi. Given all of this, it made sense for me to create a special tai chi program for individuals suffering with arthritis. Until that time, I hadn't thought about the importance of people with arthritis having access to a specially designed program. This epiphany resulted in the beginning of the journey to what would eventually be called Tai Chi for Health that transformed my life and that of many others.

By the time the plane touched down in Sydney, I had chosen the style and forms for the Tai Chi for Arthritis program and worked out the steps.

As happens, once home I got swept up in work and life. A few weeks later, however, one of my longtime patients, Judith White, came in for an appointment. For several years I tried to talk Judith into learning tai chi to help her arthritis and hypertension (high blood pressure). Judith told me that a few days prior to her appointment, she finally attended a tai chi class with her daughter. She didn't continue, however, because she felt the class too difficult for her, and she explained why.

During the first lesson, the teacher spent half an hour talking about tai chi theory while all of the students stood still. Fascinated at first, Judith became overwhelmed with the yin and yang and five element theories. Worse, standing for so long made her arthritic knees ache. Finally the teacher started teaching, but only one warm-up exercise for the rest of the lesson. They swung their arms back and forth while the teacher corrected them. At the end of the lesson, both Judith and her daughter felt exhausted, and Judith's knees hurt badly from standing still and performing the same movement too many times. The last straw came when the teacher told them that tai chi is very complex so they must practice daily and not expect to gain any worthwhile benefits for the first year. Judith and her daughter left the class feeling demoralized.

When Judith recounted her tai chi lesson, I felt annoyed with the teacher. What a wasted golden opportunity. Two keen students felt discouraged right from the first lesson. Judith wasn't the only one to complain to me about the ineffectiveness of tai chi classes. Many of my patients tried tai chi on my advice and gave up for similar reasons. Worse still, some with arthritis found that the lessons aggravated their condition. Some traditional teachers don't know how to teach tai chi effectively and fail to safely instruct people with chronic conditions like arthritis. How discouraging and incorrect to tell learners they won't benefit from tai chi for the first year. Studies later done on what would become my Tai Chi for Arthritis program found that participants can see significant health benefits as soon as eight weeks.

Judy's experience fueled my enthusiasm for developing a tai chi program for arthritis and an accompanying video. I realized that not only did we need a safe, effective, and easy-to-learn tai chi program; the teaching methodology badly needed modernization. Much of new research on learning had by that time unearthed more effective teaching methods.

Over the years, I've learned different aspects of tai chi and analyzed them all medically—from traditional forms and their martial arts aspects to competition forms. I've enjoyed everything I've learned during my tai chi journey, as well as the wonderful health benefits I've gained. I forever remain fascinated with reaching the highest level of tai chi. I see the journey like climbing a mountain. I want to discover what it feels like to reach the top and how to get there, and I strive to help my students reach the tai chi mountaintop with me.

After years of exploration, I discovered that the secret to tai chi is the principles. No matter what form and style of tai chi you do, the principles—control of movement, good body structure, your internal state of mind, breathing, weight transference, and situation awareness—are the same. Principles stay true regardless of time. Tai chi principles are the core values derived from the collective wisdom of many tai chi experts. Every single tai chi movement incorporates most if not all of the principles, which means a tai chi set, which is a flowing sequence of forms, no matter how short, can bring about the full power of tai chi. This constituted our basis for constructing the Tai Chi for Health programs. We used only twelve Sun style movements for Tai Chi for Arthritis, yet it incorporates all of the tai chi principles and delivers many benefits to the mind and the body in a relatively short period of time.

Tai chi helps me to interact and work more positively with others and enables me to harvest synergetic energy from a team. In order to develop the Tai Chi for Arthritis program, I knew I needed a team of experts, especially an authority on arthritis. Professor John Edmonds, one of the most respected rheumatologists in Australia and the head of the Department of Rheumatology at St George's Hospital of the University of New South Wales, seemed like the ideal person. Often my insecurity makes me feel threatened about approaching well-recognized experts. For that reason, it took me some time to call John. When I finally met with him and explained my intentions, he said in his authoritative way, "Paul, there is no evidence to show tai chi works for arthritis. However, I do encourage my patients to exercise, and your tai chi looks gentle and safe. I know some of my patients like tai chi. On that basis I will support you for now. Eventually you will need research studies to prove it really works."

Once Professor Edmonds agreed to join, I invited a group of tai chi colleagues to participate, including Julie King, a software engineer with excellent analytical skills and Michael Ngai, a brilliant IT professional with a knack for seeing the big picture of a project. He came to tai chi in his early forties when he experienced severe neck pain radiating to his arm and diagnosed as a cervical nerve impingement. His neurosurgeon recommended surgery. Michael told me that the surgeon said casually, "It's no problem, we just go into the neck, cut off the bits of disc, and you will be as good as new again." Michael researched the subject and found that surgery of the neck is far from a simple matter. It involved many intricate nerves, muscles, and ligaments in the affected area. He decided to find an alternative to surgery. Within months after he started learning tai chi, Michael's neck pain and all of his nerve compression symptoms disappeared. As happened with my arthritis, Michael reported that his condition motivated him to keep practicing, because the pain returned when he stopped. As a result, he became very efficient at tai chi.

I also recruited Ian Etcell, who possesses an innate talent with biomechanics and a keen curiosity to match. He can dissect any movement, make sense of each part of it, and combine all of the facets to show the complete picture.

To add clinical experience, I also invited to the team Dr. Ian Portek, a brilliant rheumatologist, and Guni Hinchey, a senior physiotherapist specializing in rheumatology.

We started by defining our objectives, which were to create an easy, safe, and effective set of tai chi for people with arthritis. The program should also improve balance and thus prevent falls, as many elderly with arthritis fall and seriously injure themselves. We also wanted to improve relaxation for participants. People who are more relaxed can deal with their arthritis better, which holds true for most conditions. A more relaxed person also feels less pain. (In the case of diabetes, for which I later created a program, studies have shown that blood glucose control improves when people are more relaxed.) The arthritis program must also be accessible and enjoyable and keep the learner's interest. And above all, the set must contain all of the essential tai chi principles in order to deliver maximum health benefits within a short period of time.

We carefully chose each movement for its healing properties, safety, and pleasure of practice. Each movement had to flow smoothly in accordance with tai chi principles. The set starts with a gentle stretch of the joints and muscles, followed by more expansive movements to develop the energy and flow, gradually building up to a climax, and then slowly winding back down to the starting point. The tai chi set flows in the rhythm of nature in full circle.

We conducted tests with diversified groups of learners. Guni, our physiotherapy expert, suffered from an old ankle injury that caused arthritis to set in her ankle. She volunteered to be one of the guinea pigs. We became really excited when she reported that her pain reduced and mobility improved after practice.

After a year, we were ready to produce instructional materials for the program, including the video. I asked Professor Edmonds to explain to the viewers what arthritis entails. He agreed, but wanted the right of final approval at completion of the video. This condition worried me, because in the days of linear editing, to change something, no matter how small, meant taking all of the footage apart and reconstructing the video. That could mean many thousands of dollars for which I couldn't budget.

I questioned him about his stipulation. "John, I'm only asking you to talk about arthritis. Why do you need to worry about the rest of the video? I am the tai chi expert and a physician. I know what works for arthritis. Do you know that if you don't like something, I must start editing from the beginning, and it will cost me a fortune?"

John did not blink an eye when he replied, "Paul, if I appear in the video that means I endorse the project, so I must be sure that everything on the video is absolutely correct." A tough but reasonable request when he put it that way. I worked extra hard to ensure everything in the program and on the video was absolutely correct and safe. Fortunately, John approved the entire video at completion.

As always, while working on the project, I looked for ways to improve the quality of my productions. One of my tai chi colleagues knew a documentary director with ABC TV—Warwick Freeman. He agreed to help us for a significantly reduced fee. Warwick brought more professionalism to our production, contacts, and a new studio. He introduced Ken Sparkes, a top voice synonymous with Australian radio. Most Australians recognize his golden voice.

The way Ken studied the Tai Chi for Arthritis script and put his emotions into the words fascinated me. His voice alone seems to tell the story. A tall man, Ken looked like any other man of stature, until he talked into the microphone. He sounded more like a tai chi authority than me. Warwick's enthusiasm and professionalism gave a magical touch to the video, and it flowed beautifully. However, he brought unforeseen new challenges. During the process of filming, Warwick met people whose lives had been transformed and decided to include some of their real stories in the introduction. While these real-life stories touched the viewers, I didn't realize that official organizations such as the Arthritis Foundation and medical associations have a deeply ingrained suspicion of personal stories. Personal testimonials are widely used by commercials, and they are not scientific evidence. The addition of testimonials resulted in our meeting tough challenges when we tried to gain support from various arthritis foundations.

Out of respect to Warwick's experience and my obsession with perfection, I did not watch the clock during production of the video. Warwick also decided to use the famous studio that works with major TV networks. As a result, halfway through I found myself in deep water financially. I responded by negotiating and doing everything possible to cut costs without cutting quality. The studio gave me a plan to pay by installments while I obtained a second, larger loan from the bank. This proved an especially challenging time for a family man with a mortgage and obligations. Despite working even longer hours in my medical practice to make up for the expense, it became necessary to sell our investment property in order to get our heads above water. Under the Australian system, self-employed professionals like me must invest for retirement, because we won't be entitled to any pension. I felt very guilty that my passion negatively affected my family.

Despite the financial trouble, we did complete the video to the highest quality. I am a stubborn man when a project is involved. I won't abandon a project without a huge fight.

Fortunately, the video sold well through *Reader's Digest*, the Arthritis Foundation (later), and retail markets around the world. Over the subsequent years, sales gradually paid off the production expense and even made profits to fund other instructional projects. Twelve years later, I collaborated with the Arthritis Foundation USA to produce an updated version of the program. The revised version has no testimonials. Over the years I've met countless people whose lives have been transformed by Tai Chi for Arthritis. To include them all, we'd need a video that ran for months—even years! Instead of individuals sharing their own experiences in the new video, medical experts explain the many health benefits backed by the support of scientific evidence. Twelve years after that initial video, Professor Edmonds smiled broadly and said, "Tai Chi for Arthritis is an ideal program for [people with] arthritis and many forms of rheumatism . . . as supported by evidence."

Once we created an excellent Tai Chi for Arthritis video, I thought I'd finished. My old Chinese cultural belief said now that we had created the excellent program, people would find it and want to use it. But my job had only just begun.

I had to tackle the daunting task of getting the Arthritis Foundation on our side. After many phone calls and meetings, I finally met the CEO of the Arthritis Foundation of Australia, Bill Wilcox. Despite his trepidation about the personal testimonials, the minute Bill found out that Professor Edmonds appeared on the video, he threw his full support behind it. All the worry about the professor's final say proved worth it. Once again, hard work paid off. Bill truly cares about people with arthritis. After seeing how tai chi can help them, he introduced me to all of the foundations in Australia and overseas.

Receiving the endorsement from the national body did not mean we'd finished. It took me five attempts to talk to the CEO of Arthritis Victoria, Shirley Caulfield. Around that time, my daughter, Andrea, was scheduled to perform at a concert with the Melbourne Symphony Orchestra. That gave me a perfect opportunity to fly to Melbourne to attend her concert and meet with Shirley personally.

Interacting face-to-face is so different from calling. Magic happened when Shirley and I met. She told me that doctors diagnosed her with rheumatoid arthritis soon after she took up the CEO position. It is a serious form of arthritis that can affect the entire body, including the internal organs. In my medical practice, I watched one patient progress in just six months from the beginning stages of the condition to a wheelchair. Her hands became so badly deformed that she could only move two fingers. Shirley told me that she sought expert advice worldwide for her condition and found alternative treatment helpful, which made her open to the idea of Tai Chi for Arthritis.

Shirley asked an educator named Ann Thomson to take charge of delivering Tai Chi for Arthritis to the community. Ann studied the video and said, "Paul, you can't just give people a video. You have to teach them how to teach the program."

I didn't understand and replied, "Ann, it's easy. The video is full of instructions and anyone can learn it." Like many tai chi instructors, I didn't think about what beginners feel and how much it takes to train instructors to teach safely. I also forgot that not everyone has medical training.

Ann insisted that I train potential instructors of the program about tai chi, the teaching method, and how to take special care of people with arthritis. "You have to train teachers exactly what to do," Ann said. Tai chi helps me to listen to the incoming force and absorb what is said. As a result, I saw the light. Ann was absolutely right.

I gathered the team again and we designed the curriculum, lesson plan, and handbook for the training. Ann coordinated the inaugural instructor-training workshop scheduled for September 26, 1998. We set the fees as low as possible to make the program accessible.

I thought my immense effort in producing tai chi videos might have been wasted, but not so. Once the news got out about my very first workshop, people came out of the woodwork to enroll. They told me how much they learned from my videos and about the many health benefits they gained. As I dreamed they would, the videos had helped many people. They also brought many participants to that first workshop and later ones that I conducted throughout the world. It seemed the videos prepared people for the workshops.

I anxiously awaited that first workshop—especially when Ann told me that some of the participants had taught tai chi for many years. As I prepared for the workshop, I asked myself how to effectively teach a diverse class of people that included everyone from novices to experienced teachers. They also came from a wide range of backgrounds—from health professionals to fitness professionals to tai chi practitioners and students.

The teaching of the tai chi workshop challenged me to new heights. Even though I truly enjoyed being a family physician, teaching is a calling deep within my heart. As I grew up without a father, I adopted teachers as my father figures. I longed to be like my father, the great teacher. On deep reflection, the seed of desire to teach became planted during the Empty Period and its lack of stimulation. Once given the chance to learn, it felt like rain breaking a four-year drought in the desert. When I teach, I am not only sharing my knowledge, I am sharing my pleasure of learning and my hope for the future.

Teaching that first Tai Chi for Health instructor-training workshop presented me with new challenges. The ultimate purpose of empowering people to take control of their lives required a set of different approaches. All of my prior training in tai chi, medicine, and teaching and my life experience prepared me for the task, however. As Tony showed me during the writing of my first instructional book, I worked backward from the purpose, focusing on what I wanted participants to accomplish. Then I prepared the contents and determined how to teach the class to achieve that purpose. I anxiously looked forward to see the outcome.

Finally the big day arrived. The workshop took place at the office of Arthritis Victoria. Twenty-two participants filled up the conference room for three days. Though the workshop attracted people from a wide variety of backgrounds, they all displayed similar traits, including being kind and dedicated to helping and caring for the elderly and disabled individuals. They were also proactive about managing their own lives and medical conditions. Engaged in life, visionary, and inspirational, the workshop participants showed a preference for teaching people how to fish rather than giving them a fish.

During the workshop, I gave the participants a plethora of information. I talked about arthritis and its treatment, as well as how to take care of people with arthritis and other disabilities. I also listened to participants about what they sought and modified the course contents as we went along. Tai Chi for Arthritis is based on Sun style tai chi, and I found that many of the participants didn't know this style. That provided a common ground and helped to keep everyone focused on learning during the workshop.

Near the end of the workshop as we practiced the set together in sync, we all felt a positive energy, as though we knew that the workshop would be a new page in our lives. That became true. All of the participants started teaching Tai Chi for Arthritis and many became the first master trainers who would take over the job of training instructors. Since that first collaboration, more than one thousand instructors from Victoria have received training from my authorized master trainers, and they have in turn empowered hundreds of thousands of people to improve their health and wellness.

CHAPTER 23

RECOGNITION AND CREDIBILITY

If you want happiness for a lifetime,
help someone else.
— Chinese proverb

Two weeks after the first workshop, I conducted another one in my home city, Sydney, collaborating with the Arthritis Foundation of NSW. The foundation's CEO, Phillip Hopkins, supported the project right from the start. He introduced me to Sally Castell, an energetic and proactive physiotherapist and vice president of the National Association for Gentle Exercise, which promotes exercise for health.

Sally challenged me to cut the workshop from three to two days, citing the difficulty of getting participants to come for three days. I thought the timetable for the three-day workshop was already packed, but I understood her reasoning, so I went back to the drawing board, working with my team to make a new schedule for less time without loss of quality. Sally and her colleagues helped me coordinate the event, as well as shared their extensive experience with exercise workshops. The resulting two-day workshop turned out to be a real winner for participants and trainers. Instructional videos and teaching materials helped participants prepare ahead of the event, which gave us sufficient time in the workshop to ensure that participants learned the necessary skills to obtain certification to teach the program.

As we held more workshops, by listening to participants and working with colleagues and experienced teachers, I continued to refine the teaching format. I focused more on stimulating thinking rather than spoon-feeding facts. I provided references where interested class participants could find more information. I learned to keep the objective of each workshop firmly in mind—to train safe and effective instructors of the Tai Chi for Arthritis program. Later on, when I realized that I could share the healing power of tai chi with people experiencing many different types of medical conditions, I created Tai Chi for Health as an overall umbrella for the various programs. In addition to the Tai Chi for Arthritis program, I developed Tai Chi for Diabetes, Osteoporosis, Back Pain and others, all with the same objective and using similar training methods.

Over the years, I have refined the teaching methodology and incorporated modern knowledge of how people learn best, which has allowed me to reach a wide variety of learners and motivate them. Most people know exercise is good for them, but many stop after a few months. Our Tai Chi for Health teaching method includes encouraging learners to feel good about themselves so that they take control of their own health and wellness. We strive to share with teachers how to empower their students and inspire intrinsic enjoyment.

Tai Chi for Health instructors differ from traditional tai chi instructors. We have different goals, methods, and approaches. The most challenging aspect for Tai Chi for Health instructors is not learning tai chi or the teaching methods, but changing people's preconceived idea of tai chi and tai chi instructors. As such, in the early days of developing workshops, we felt like pioneers. Tai chi is a complex art developed in ancient times for elite martial artists. People traditionally believed that tai chi must be practiced full time for ten or more years before the individual could teach. By applying medical and educational knowledge and redefining the purpose, we transformed the art to a universal tool. The twelve-movement set is so easy that just about anyone can learn it in a short period of time.

My most extraordinary and fulfilling experiences teaching tai chi have occurred over the last sixteen years conducting Tai Chi for Health instructor's training workshops. Other master trainers who conduct the workshops relate similar stories of wonder and fulfillment. Why is the experience so phenomenal? The ingredients of the Tai Chi for Health workshop make it "magical." Those ingredients include:

1. Empowering, challenging, and informative content

2. A program that is effective for personal and professional development

3. Extraordinary people attending the workshops

Thanks to the popularity of our initial workshops, arthritis foundations in other states throughout Australia soon joined in. Every workshop proved a unique and uplifting experience, and as I progressed in my skill, I enjoyed conducting the workshops even more. Almost all of the participants became certified instructors of the Tai Chi for Health program, each of them going on to teach hundreds of students, making the workshops' benefit exponential.

As a bonus, teaching and practicing the twelve movements hundreds and thousands of times significantly improved my tai chi. The more I talked about the tai chi principles and how to incorporate them into the forms, the more I deepened my understanding and the more my tai chi progressed. I felt almost as though I gained more from the teaching than my participants learned from me.

Of the many ways to get the message across about the benefits of Tai Chi for Health, I found approaching fellow doctors, especially family physicians, to be especially effective, because they reach many people who respect and heed their advice. A good way to reach health professionals is to present at medical conferences. Large medical conferences are nearly impossible to break into, so I set my sights on meetings held by drug companies. I got to know a drug company sales manager, whose company ran regular five-hour meetings of three hundred to five hundred doctors throughout Sydney. I told him that a five-hour conference is tiring, and the doctors needed something to break up their fatigue so they could stay awake. I offered to act as their wake-up person by conducting five-minute exercise breaks with my Tai Chi for Health. I got lucky and his boss agreed to try me out at one of the conferences.

They gave me a total of five minutes for this once-in-a-lifetime opportunity, for which I spent much time preparing and rehearsing. At the conference, I started worrying when the speakers went past their allocated times, because I knew that my unscheduled minipresentation would be the first thing they cut. My friend arranged for me to sit in the front row, and as luck would have it, the chairperson happened to sit next to me. At one point, I nudged him and remarked how tired and disinterested the attending doctors had become. When he nodded, I offered my service. Despite being behind schedule, he called me up on stage. I taught two simple movements, making it fun and enjoyable for the attending doctors, and let them know about Tai Chi for Health through doing it.

Even though they hadn't listed my presentation on the feedback form, many doctors wrote on top of the form, "I liked the tai chi best." After that the conference, organizers invited me back to more meetings with longer and longer time slots. Later other companies started asking me to present.

I learned that giving presentations is like teaching. The key is to tune into the learners or attendees and discern what they want and need, which I am able to do thanks to my aunt, who taught me how to feel the mood of others. I also found that presentations gave me a good place to share my impromptu humor, which is like a sneeze—I never know when the one-liners will come. When they do, people laugh while receiving information from me.

At a recent national conference of exercise leaders for returned soldiers by the Department of Veterans' Affairs, I gave a talk right after our state premier (governor in the US). The overwhelmingly positive feedback included the following comments:

~ Very informative and fun
~ Dr. Lam was engaging and very informative
~ Having listened to Dr. Lam, I think I am going to take up tai chi
~ Dr. Lam was humorous and very interesting

I felt the most challenged by presenting at an international scientific conference. The American College of Rheumatology Annual Meeting is one the world's largest and most respected conferences, with around eight thousand delegates from all over the world attending. In 1999, they accepted my abstract for a presentation. I felt overwhelmed, as if I'd won the lottery. Presenting at such a prestigious international conference would be a scary experience for me, a suburban family physician. It also proved an expensive affair. I paid for my airfare to Florida, hotels bills, and a substitute doctor to cover my work. When I arrived, I felt lost and threatened in the midst of eight thousand of the world's foremost leaders and experts in the field of rheumatology. Why had I come, and what could I hope to achieve?

On the second day, I sat in the corner during a coffee break feeling bashful when I remembered the fifty-five cold calls in London. Medical experts couldn't be worse than video distributors. Why waste this opportunity? I introduced myself to a couple of ladies having coffee. Nursing professors from Korea, they knew nothing about tai chi. I told them about Tai Chi for Health and its benefits. They smiled politely out of courtesy, bowed, and left. That made me feel even more embarrassed. I didn't realize it then, but as always, no effort is wasted. Years later, Korean colleagues would make a huge impact for the Tai Chi for Health vision. With that mind-set, I did well at my poster presentation during the conferences. While a rare privilege for a family physician, such a small presentation is vastly different from a keynote presenter who addresses the whole conference from a podium. During my presentation, I reached out to the audience, however, and made connections with some delegates.

The launching of the new book, *Arthritis Foundation's Guide to Alternative Therapy*, was a big event at the conference. Alternative therapy had started gaining acceptance in the orthodox medical world, especially for chronic conditions. The AF received five thousand calls every month inquiring about alternative therapy, which led to them commissioning Judith Horstman, a well-known journalist and writer, to write the book. They held the book presentation in the largest hall of the conference center, and it became jam-packed with even standing spaces filled.

I stayed after the lecture and talked to Judith, discovering that she practiced yoga for more than twenty years before she fell off a horse and injured her back. After the accident, her back pain worsened when she did yoga. Ever the opportunist, I told her about

Tai Chi for Arthritis and offered to send her a complimentary copy of my instructional video. Judith took up Tai Chi for Arthritis and gained relief from the exercises. She liked it so much that she traveled from California to Sydney to attend my one-week tai chi workshop the following year. As our friendship grew, Judith coauthored with me on the book, *Overcoming Arthritis.*

With more of our research studies being published and the programs reaching more people, I began to receive invitations to present from the podium. One of my shortest presentations occurred at the American Association of Diabetes Educators (AADE) 31st Annual Meeting in 2004. They invited me to present my Tai Chi for Diabetes program alongside three other speakers: Bob Greene (Oprah Winfrey's personal trainer); Dr. James R. Gavin III, president of Morehouse School of Medicine; and Rita Saltiel-Berzin, manager of diabetes education for BD consumer healthcare. They allocated each speaker fifteen minutes. Located in their largest room and filled to capacity, the presentation was meticulously coordinated.

I found sitting next to Bob Greene rewarding and exciting. One of the most impressive presenters I've ever met, Bob advised me not to ask the audience to join me for tai chi movements. "Don't give people a choice," he suggested. "Just say, everyone please join me." It turned out to be brilliant advice. When he presented, I noted that he was extremely charismatic and well tuned-in to the audience.

They paid me well for that brief presentation, but more often I give free presentations to universities, governments, Diabetes Australia, and many arthritis foundations around the world. With every presentation, I always learn something and enjoy the experience. I find it fulfilling to communicate with people in all kinds of situations.

On a very busy day and with little notice, the NSW State Health Department, which was focusing on fall prevention, called and asked me to give a talk about tai chi to a meeting of health promotion managers from different parts of the state (NSW is the largest state in Australia.) Reluctantly, I found another doctor to cover my patient appointments, and I went to give the talk.

The managers showed so much interest in the information I shared that they asked me to stay after the talk and answer questions about Tai Chi for Health. They became excited about the benefits of the program, especially the affordability of training instructors. This began many years of collaboration with the Health Department, resulting in the training of thousands of instructors, who in turn run classes and reach hundreds of thousands of people. Health departments in other Australian states have also adopted the program.

Best of all, the Tai Chi for Health program exceeded all Health Department expectations as a low-cost health promotion activity. A study by the Australian University found that after eight years of using the program, that for just $76 a year per person (less than the cost of one doctor consultation), the participants experienced many health benefits, including a significant decrease in fall rates. They also found that people enjoyed the Tai Chi for Health program and adhered to it.

As a result of the increasing popularity of the program, the demand for my workshops grew. Many people in the community previously put off by the "traditional" way of tai chi training came for Tai Chi for Health. Many people with disabilities who never thought they could do tai chi changed their minds when they saw the titles "Tai Chi for Arthritis," "Tai Chi for Diabetes," and "Tai Chi for Osteoporosis."

Barely one year after the creation of Tai Chi for Arthritis, enthusiastic learners requested more, so I created Part II—a sequel featuring more challenging movements. Soon people wanted even more. I responded by explaining that tai chi possesses indefinite depth, and it isn't about how many movements you learn. Tai chi is an internal art that integrates mind and body, cultivating internal energy, and promoting health and harmony. The flowing movements of tai chi contain much inner strength, like water flowing in a river. Beneath the tranquil surface there is a current with immense power—the power for healing and wellness. Tai Chi for Arthritis, though a short set, offers all that is needed to develop your internal energy and health and bring your tai chi to as high a level as you wish.

With consistent practice, people will be able to feel the internal energy (*qi*), convert it to internal force (*jing*), and use it to generate more internal energy. This process would greatly enhance tai chi development. After explaining this, I realized the need to show people how to access the *qi* and *jing*, so in 2002 I created my "Exploring the Depth of Tai Chi for Arthritis" workshop. It became my most popular, and I've conducted it hundreds of times around the world, with over ten thousand participants total. This workshop is my personal tour of climbing the tai chi mountain. I am the mountain guide who shows the best path to enjoy the beautiful view as we ascend.

During the workshop, I explain tai chi and its ultimate purpose. No matter what style of forms you do, tai chi consists of movements based on a set of essential principles, and the purpose is to cultivate strong and well-balanced *qi* and convert it to the internal force *jing*; then use that process to generate more *qi*. While these concepts seem esoteric, as if the mountain path is covered with fog, I have worked out varying ways for people to clear the mist and experience them personally. Once you know the direction, these concepts become accessible and the journey of the tai chi mountain becomes more interesting and rewarding. Many participants travel thousands of miles year after year to explore the tai chi mountain with me.

I distill the essential tai chi principles from many years of studies and practice and translate them into plain language that focuses on the body's internal components, structure, and outward movements. *Song* and *jing* are the key internal components. *Song* refers to loosening or gently expanding from within all joints. This loosening then leads to strengthening the joints and relaxation of the mind. *Jing*, when used with tai chi, represents mental quietness or serenity and being mindful of the present. Both *song* and *jing* are most powerful at cultivating *qi*.

The body structure consists of correct alignment and weight transfer. Controlling all tai chi movements to be slow, smooth, and continuous stretches and exercises the entire body and enhances the *jing* and *song*. Moving gently against mild resistance develops internal strength.

Translating the principles into easy-to-understand language and practical movements allows participants to experience them. All principles have many layers of depth, like peeling an onion; there are more layers inside that are shinier and fresher. As we climb the mountain, the air gets fresher and the view more beautiful.

The process of this mountain tour is like discovering the secret of bringing life force to the tai chi movement. I use the Dan Tian Breathing method to tie the concept and technique together. This breathing technique governing each movement is a simpler yet more powerful form of tai chi breathing based on the traditional method, yet modernized with new medical research.

Accessing the *qi* and *jing* reminds me of the ancient Chinese fable, "Dragon's Eyes." A painter named Ch'en Jung, famous for painting subjects that looked alive, drew a dragon on the wall surrounding an ancient community. The dragon had no eyes, and the people kept asking the artist why. Finally, he painted the eyes. On the day he painted on two glaring eyes, they began to slowly blink. Then with a mighty exhalation of fire, the dragon rose into the air, made a graceful aerial circuit, and soared into the mist swathing the mountains.

These workshops bring people of varying backgrounds together, and we share ideas, develop our tai chi and the Tai Chi for Health vision. The workshops represent incubating beds for a growing Tai Chi for Health community. The *qi* is so strong that it keeps attracting new members, generating ideas and enriching and enhancing vision. Along the way, I've met countless people who tell me how much Tai Chi for Health has improved or saved their lives.

While the personal stories are moving, I kept remembering what Professor John Edmonds said to me about needing to scientifically prove the health benefits of Tai Chi for Health. Understanding the importance of scientific studies, I threw the challenge back at Professor Edmonds when I asked him, "John, I am willing to do anything I can for the research studies, but how do we start?" (People often think doctors know about research studies, but it is a different field of expertise.) I soon discovered how challenging scientific studies are when John introduced me to his colleague, Dr. Marlene Fransen, a brilliant researcher on exercise and arthritis. Marlene spent one full week of her own time working on a study protocol. Then we looked for funding.

Most research in Australia is funded by the National Health

and Medical Research Council (NHMRC). Similar governmental bodies exist around the world that fund most medical research. At the time, tai chi research was relatively new and our proposal went nowhere. To get money from anywhere else proved almost an impossible task. I knew that the Tai Chi for Health program would save huge amounts of health dollars. According to an article published in the October 2006 issue of *Injury Prevention* (www.ncbi.nlm.nih.gov/pubmed/17018668), in the year 2000, 2.6 million medically treated non-fatal fall injuries and nearly 10,300 fatal falls occurred. Medical costs totaled $0.2 billion dollars for the fatal injuries and $19 billion dollars for the non-fatal injuries in the US alone.

The financial tolls from falls are expected to increase as the population ages and may reach $54.9 billion dollars by 2020. Tai chi has shown to reduce falls in the elderly by around sixty percent, which would have meant a savings of more than $10 billion dollars in 2000. Arthritis affected 6.1 million Australians in 2005, which is close to a third of the entire population. The cost for arthritis treatment in 2000 in Australia amounted to a staggering $4.6 billion dollars.

Given the cost of billions for arthritis treatment, I thought surely we must be able to find a mere one hundred thousand dollars for a study of a promising treatment that can improve arthritis and reduce falls, plus many other health benefits. One hundred thousand seemed like very little to save billions of dollars and improve the quality of millions of lives. I wondered why no one rushed to fund us.

We tried every avenue to obtain funding. I spent much more time on the fundraising for the study than I ever did selling my videos. I gave countless talks to groups of people, including the Lions Clubs, the Probis Group, the Masonic Lodge, medical associations, and various governmental bodies. I talked to anyone who listened. Selling videos challenged me, but that experience paled in comparison to finding funding for tai chi research.

After three years of tireless work, we won a research grant of twenty thousand dollars from the Arthritis Foundation of Australia, but we still needed eighty thousand dollars. The twenty thousand must be used within two years. Two years went by and

I found another ten thousand, composed of five thousand dollars from the University of New South Wales for a new research initiative and a five thousand dollar research scholarship from the Australian Chinese Medical Association. We became desperate—we had to give the money back to the Arthritis Foundation very soon. Then in a scientific meeting I came across Dr. Klaus Stelter, the CEO of the St. George Division of General Practice. Even though he knew little about tai chi, he opened his mind and listened to the benefits of Tai Chi for Health. He then convinced his division to fund the study with fifteen thousand dollars. Five years down the track, we'd only reached halfway. Well, nearly halfway with forty-five thousand dollars. We needed another fifty-five thousand. Fortunately, the Arthritis Foundation extended its funding for another year, but then one year came and went and by the beginning of 2004, we'd exhausted all of our options. We knew we would have to give all of the money back, and I felt sad after having put in so much work and hope.

Before we gave back the money, however, Dr. Stelter called me one day asking if I knew that the Department of Ageing and Aged Care offered special funding for research projects specifically for people with chronic conditions. The treatment must be a low-cost method, not incur future expenses for the Health Department, be community-based, lead to saving healthcare costs, and be easy to implement. Exactly Tai Chi for Health's mission! I immediately called Professor Edmonds. I could feel the consummate calm as the eminent professor smiled across the phone line and replied, "Yes, Paul we knew about the funding, and we have just about finished the application. Do you have time to look at it now?" I knew the funding would be a godsend for us, but given years of rejections, I did not hold out much hope. After three rounds of reviewing our applications, however, we finally won the grant of fifty-five thousand dollars. Such special funding has never been offered before or since.

The study took one-and-a-half years to complete and another year to get the results published—nearly ten years from the start. Dr. Fransen is a truly dedicated and gifted researcher. The study, "A Randomized Control Trial of 200 Subjects Comparing Tai Chi,

Hydrotherapy and Control, to Measure Improvement In Pain, Physical Function, Muscular Strength and Walking Capacity," published on April 15, 2007 in one of the most prestigious journals, the *Rheumatology Journal.* The largest study using Tai Chi for Arthritis, the study showed tai chi to be effective at relieving arthritis pain and improving people's ability to perform daily tasks. The study proved a milestone that eventually led to the Arthritis Foundation of America partnering with me. Later the study got me into Singapore, where I'd tried for years to introduce Tai Chi for Arthritis.

Since and alongside that first study, I've been involved in many other research studies in different capacities, from the chief investigator to an unknown and unpaid advisor.

In early 2000, I received an invitation to be a consultant on a study using tai chi for fall prevention for the Central Area Health Promotion Unit (of the Health Department NSW) with chief investigator Dr. Alexander Voukelatos. In contrast to artificial experimental settings often used in other research, Alex planned to lead a community-based study. He intended to test tai chi in the community to see if the practice worked for fall prevention in the real world. He invited two tai chi experts and other experts from relevant fields to act as consultants. The excellent group of experts on fall prevention included Professor Stephen Lord, one of the best-known experts on fall preventions, and Professor Bob Cummings, an expert on epidemiology.

The resulting study, "Controlled Trial of Tai Chi for the Prevention of Falls: The Central Sydney Tai Chi Trial," published in August 2007. To date it is the largest community-based fall prevention study with 702 subjects. The vast majority of the participants (seventy-six percent) used the Tai Chi for Arthritis program. The study found tai chi prevents falls by a massive sixty-seven percent less falls. It became one of three studies recognized and listed with the US Centers for Disease Control and Prevention (www.CDC.gov), a most prestigious recognition for any scientific study. The impact of the study reached many national governments and health professionals around the world, and the ripples are still spreading.

I am proud to say that there are more studies published with my name on them than many full-time research academics. The world of scientific studies is fascinating and frustrating. I prefer teaching tai chi rather than working out protocol and hassling with funding, but the scientific validation of Tai Chi for Health is powerful and far-reaching.

CHAPTER 24

SPREADING MY VISION

The wise adapt themselves to circumstances,
as water molds itself to the pitcher.
— Chinese proverb

Thanks to a strong home base in Australia of instructors and participants at Better Health Tai Chi Chuan, we've spread our unique brand of tai chi throughout the world. After thirty years, we've formed a close-knit family dedicated to creating a global Tai Chi for Health community. Key people in locations such as my office, Tai Chi Productions, understand my vision and enthusiastically embrace my ideas and carry them out in innovative ways.

At the core of what we do is empower people to wellness. The story of eighty-year-old Myung Ja Park from South Korea exemplifies the ability of Tai Chi for Health to bring about incredible transformational change. Myung's story also illustrates the constant rewards I experience introducing my program to the world.

I met Myung in 2002 when she reluctantly attended my Tai Chi for Arthritis workshop in Korea. She'd never heard of tai chi, but a nurse friend practically forced her to attend. Too polite to say no, she agreed. Six years later, she wrote about the life-altering experience:

> *I am a retired nurse, high school principal, and researcher at the Korean National Open University. I lived a full life until doctors diagnosed me with brain cancer in 1997. I underwent surgery and since then both my left eye and ear don't function properly, and I used to feel dizzy and tended to fall down. My dear friend, Professor Enok Lee from Seoul National University, pleaded with me to attend*

a tai chi workshop. I went in a wheelchair to the first workshop Dr. Lam held in Korea and there discovered my second life.

Dr. Lam convinced me that I could do the strange movements. At home, I practiced using his video, and after a month I could stand for short periods of time. I volunteered to teach tai chi to elderly people at a nursing home, which started my career as a tai chi instructor. In 2005, while assisting one of the Tai Chi for Arthritis instructors' workshops in Seoul, a nurse from the primary health center in Yangju City asked if I could start a tai chi class in her center. Still using crutches at that time, I met the center's chief doctor, Dr. Soon-Nam Lee, who appeared skeptical of the ability of an old lady on crutches with a hearing problem to teach a class. She let me try, however, and I held a full class with older people who liked doing tai chi and me as their instructor. I still teach at the center and no longer use crutches. People who know me today have no idea that I had brain surgery and became bedridden.

The group Myung teaches won South Korea's annual Silver Exercise contest on three occasions. In 2013, the mayor of Yangju gave her a special award for her contribution to the community.

Even before I came to Australia, my mother, eldest brother Jeng, and sisters Celia and Julia lived in the US with their families, while my second-eldest brother, Andrew, and his family resided in Canada. Later on, my daughter, Andrea, went to the US, too. Back in the '90s, Celia helped me with video distribution in the US. A determined lady, she managed to get me an interview on the US ABC television's *Good Morning America*. Dr. Nancy Snyderman, the show's health correspondent, interviewed me and tried tai chi during filming of the segment. During the short interview, I taught Nancy my Tai Chi for Arthritis program, and she performed tai chi alongside me. After waiting for months for the show to air on television, on December 19, 1998, the day the House impeached President Clinton, my interview aired right after the announcement. Whoever did the programming must have decided the country needed to see something peaceful and relaxing on such an intense day.

While national television exposure helps, nothing works better than word of mouth. Once in the grapevine, Tai Chi for Health spreads quickly. I held my first instructors' training workshop in California with Troyce Thome, a tai chi teacher from Saddleback College. On the first day, Troyce informed me that her teacher, Professor Vincent McCullough, planned to visit the class. I guessed he wanted to evaluate my program. Vince did drop in, but he never left the class. An inspirational and visionary tai chi teacher, Vince pioneered teaching tai chi in the California educational system forty years ago. At that time, hardly anyone taught tai chi, and many mistakenly thought of it as a feminine activity. As the head of the school's Department of Physical Education and a successful football coach, Vince possessed a "manly" reputation, so he could teach tai chi without being regarded as feminine. Vince liked my program so much that he changed his tai chi curriculum at the college from traditional Yang style to Tai Chi for Arthritis.

Vince introduced me to Caroline Demoise, whom he met visiting Durango, Colorado, while practicing tai chi in the park there. At the time, Caroline had done tai chi for fifteen years and headed up continued medical education for the health professionals at Mercy Regional Medical Center. During her first meeting with Vince, he told her about me and the Tai Chi for Health programs. Right then and there Caroline decided to attend my next workshop in California, as well as the annual workshop in Sydney.

I met Caroline at the California workshop, and she surprised me when she said she planned to attend the Sydney workshop, especially since she'd never traveled outside of the US. I love the friendliness and openness of Americans, but I've also learned to be cautious with overenthusiastic people who often don't follow through. Caroline did attend the workshop in Sydney, however, and went on to teach Tai Chi for Health in Durango. We've gotten to know each other well, and I've come to respect her amazing intuition, which she displayed when she chose to attend my workshops the second she heard about them.

I've always been a "left brain" person, which is typical of a medical practitioner. We look at things as black and white and always seek "hard" evidence. The left side of the brain is responsible for conscious control, especially relating to numbers, reasoning, math, lists, categories, and analysis. The right side of the brain sees the whole picture and is responsible for creativity, color, pictures, shapes, emotions, rhythm, music, and motion. Caroline is a tai chi friend who has helped me awaken my hidden right brain.

The fact that tai chi is an art helped me open up my right brain, and the tai chi principle of interacting with others enabled me to better understand spiritual life. Tai chi embraces the mind, body, and spirit. People see spirituality in many different lights. I see it as something bigger than oneself—for example, the desire to contribute to the common good. The positive interaction between people through tai chi principles fosters a stronger community spirit. Another aspect of spirituality involves developing a sense of serenity, as in the *jing* state, being mindful of the inner self without judgment. Tai Chi for Health is a tool that helps us develop an inner sanctuary of strength and harmony in our overstimulated world and has nothing to do with any religion.

When Caroline held instructor-training workshops in Durango, Dr. Kircher also attended. As a family physician and head of the Department of Integrative Medicine at Mercy Medical Center in Durango at the time, Dr. Kircher unsuccessfully tried another form of tai chi prior, so she came to the workshop intending to just support Caroline. Like Vince, Dr. Kircher remained for the entire workshop and ended up learning Tai Chi for Health and eventually teaching her own classes.

Prior to meeting Dr. Kircher and learning about her work regarding near-death experiences, despite my medical background I felt so much apprehension about death that I steered clear of the topic. Most likely because of nearly starving to death during the Great Famine, I always believed I wouldn't live past forty. This belief hit home when my daughter, Andrea, was seven, and I had just turned forty-one. She somehow sensed my fear of aging and said, "Gee, Dad, you're getting old!" I asked her to stop several times, but she knew she hit a nerve, so she continued, "Actually, you're not just old," she said. "You're practically antique." I became furious inside, but held my temper.

That interchange with Andrea prompted me to do some

soul-searching about my fear of death, which I tried to acknowledge and accept. I explored self-psychotherapy and self-growth materials to strengthen myself. Of all the things I learned, I found Socrates's idea the most logical and appealing. He said, "There are only two ways for death—either you have an afterlife, or you don't. If you don't, then imagine having a really beautiful sleep with no pain and no feelings. That is something to look forward to. If you have an afterlife, you get to talk to all of the great philosophers and thinkers over the years. That would be so wonderful."

From then on, when my beautiful daughter talked about my antiquity, I reminded myself of Socrates's words. As my tai chi improved, so did my inner strength. I accepted nature and its cycle of life and death. I also became stronger in terms of my arthritis, hunger pains, and immunity against getting sick. The healthier I became mentally and physically, the less afraid I felt of dying. When I overcame my fear, Andrea stopped teasing me, which illustrated one of the greatest outcomes of personal development. Inner strength leads to the ability to change yourself.

Generally it is extremely difficult to change others. Dr. William Glasser, the guru of choice theory, is a brilliant psychiatrist who firmly believes you cannot change others, but you can change yourself. By changing yourself in a certain way, you help direct the final outcome. For example, if you wish for other people to care more about you, by changing yourself to care more about others you inspire them to care more about you. When you develop better self-esteem, people's discriminative remarks don't affect you as much.

I saw my nephew Stephen, my younger sister Julia's son, develop his physical and mental strength by studying martial arts. A musical genius who plays the cello, Stephen experienced significant bullying in school, so I suggested to Julie he study a martial art that he likes, so he chose tae kwon do. He did so and became very proficient in the art, as well as fit, strong, and confident. Stephen also earned almost a perfect score on his SATs. That and his superior cello skills got him accepted by major US universities like Harvard and Yale. He chose a school in Cleveland with a famous cello teacher. The school welcomed him and gave him a scholarship, but his teacher told him that to improve his playing, he should learn tai chi, so

Stephen came to Australia to learn tai chi from me. As of this writing, he just became a father and is chair of the cello section at the New Jersey Symphony Orchestra.

So that people like Stephen could access Tai Chi for Health training without having to travel across the world, I devised a comprehensive and practical system to train more master trainers. Working with my medical and tai chi team and organizations like the arthritis foundations and health departments, we set comprehensive requirements for instructors to be certified while creating a non-failure policy. We aim to train anyone who wishes to teach.

On April 2002, I conducted the first US master trainers' workshop in Dr. Kircher's mountain ranch in Pagosa Springs. Caroline, Dr. Kircher, Troyce, and Vince were among the first group from outside Australia to become master trainers. Since then they and subsequent master trainers have brought Tai Chi for Health to millions of people around the world through the instructors they've trained.

Dr. Kircher once compared tai chi instructing to practicing family medicine, which got me thinking. She pointed out that rather than spending so much time listening to patient complaints and handing out medication, a tai chi instructor dispenses prescriptions for creating one's own sense of well-being. The more people practice, the healthier they become. This occurred with Daniela, who shared her story at the second international Tai Chi for Health conference:

> After a decade of taking MS meds, my body rejected all forms of medication available at the time. I went from "episodes" to "attacks" to other physical inabilities. One day after coming home from the hospital, I watched Dr. Lam's Tai Chi for Arthritis DVD. I listened to the instructions and visualized the movements, imagining myself performing tai chi in the park with Dr. Lam's group. That became one of my daily inspirations. Physically, I could not do the movements, but the mind is a wonderful tool. When engaged, it takes you far and beyond any physical boundaries. With my eyes closed, I could feel the freedom of each movement.

Exhaustion defined my daily tai chi practice for a long time, but I pushed the disease away and kept trying. No matter how ridiculous the difference between reality and my perception of it, tai chi was there for me. Somehow my internal practice became external, and along the way brought the desire to try again. I became amused by the idea that I resembled a turtle that started and will finish the race. I learned a lot about myself, including the need to be patient and that MS is no longer able to define me. Tai chi made me aware of what balance is all about. Before, my mind worked when my body did not. Grief, frustration, and imbalance were my daily reality for years. It was up to me to fight for restoring harmony between my physical and mental abilities. Instead of dwelling on what I could not do and what I lost, I focused on what I could do and crossing the finish line. That gave me a feeling of accomplishment. Sometimes, through aversion, we discover our future passion.

Experiences like Daniela's remind me of my medical student days when I drove my Mini Moke with the leaking roof. I put Band-Aids on the roof and it worked for a while, but when I stopped at a traffic light, the water dribbled down. Practicing medicine can be like that. We often give people temporary relief with Band-Aid therapy, but the conditions return on rainy days. Teaching Tai Chi for Health, on the other hand, helps you gain physical and mental strength from the inside out. It empowers you to be healthier and more fulfilled. Daniela is a perfect example of this empowerment. When I met her, she walked without aid thanks to her experience with Tai Chi for Health.

The tai chi principles and their magical effects correlate well with new modern medical research findings. In recent years, scientists have discovered a group of muscles located next to the spine known as deep stabilizers or the core muscles. These muscles perform different functions and possess different neuromuscular properties than other muscles. They provide inner strength to support the spine, and the methods for strengthening them are very different from usual muscle building exercise like weight lifting, as they are related to breathing, correct body alignment, and gentle contraction of the pelvic floor muscles. These methods are consistent with the tai chi principles of Dan Tian Breathing, correct alignment, staying upright, and moving slowly and smoothly against gentle resistance. The *song* of spine strengthens these stabilizers and the ligaments around the joints, improving the circulation of the joint fluid and blood and lymphatic systems around the joints. This improves flexibility and strengthens joints. Studies have shown being mindful improves mood, strengthens the mind, and even slows down the aging process.

An upright posture makes you feel better and it will strengthen the deep stabilizer muscles protecting the spine. Medical scientists have also found most major joints have a similar internal system like the deep stabilizer muscles that protect the joints and give them inner strength. This is just like the tai chi concept of internal and external components within the body. For example, the mind is internal to muscles and bones and deep stabilizers are internal to external global muscles. The internal is the most important. When you build stronger internal components like the mind and the spine, it makes the body healthier and more resilient.

Jing and *song* together engage the body and mind fully, leading to a meditative or "flow" state as described by Mihaly Csikszentmihalyi. When you are in flow, you perform above your best and are fully engaged. Studies have shown people in flow are often happier and more fulfilled.

The training of weight transfer improves balance and has been proven to significantly reduce the risks of falling. Studies have shown the close relationship between the body and mind. When you straighten from being hunched over, your mood improves and your thinking becomes more positive. The training of weight transference improves balance; when you are physically better balanced, you tend to be more mentally balanced and vice versa.

All of the tai chi principles integrate with each other. The outward tai chi movements are the outer expression of inner power. Controlling these movements so they consist of slow, smooth, and continuous stretches and exercises enhances the *jing* and *song*. It also improves your body alignment and balance. Moving gently against gentle resistance develops internal strength.

When people experience these principles and the pleasure of moving the body gently and mindfully, they discover these principles take on deeper meaning as they progress. The journey up the tai chi mountain becomes more enjoyable and fulfilling. The depth, the intrinsic substance, and the health benefits of tai chi hold your attention and keep you practicing and exploring tai chi, which leads to a happier and more fulfilling life.

Even though New Zealand is geographically close to Australia, until I held workshops there I didn't know much about the land or its people—despite the fact that Anna Bennett, my workshop and office manager whose dedication and skill helped make the Tai Chi for Health vision a reality, is originally from the country. The more I visited, however, the more I marveled at the nature and beauty of the country and the wonderfully friendly and honest people there.

New Zealand is unique in so many ways. Accident Compensation Corporation (ACC) is a federal governmental body that takes care of all injuries in the entire country, like a huge government-run insurance company. ACC has a no-fault policy, which means that all injuries, whether from a car accident or at home or work, are covered, and no fault is attributed. Even for medical mishaps, ACC sees those as accidents, so no one sues doctors, which makes it more fulfilling to practice medicine when a physician can use sound judgment without fear of litigation.

ACC research shows that prevention is cheaper than a cure. For that reason, the country has injury prevention managers in every region. To prevent the elderly from falling, which is the most expensive medical expenditure of all Western countries, ACC proactively provides free tai chi classes for people over sixty-five (or fifty-five for Maori and Pacific Islanders). The ACC's initial foray into contracting for tai chi instructors met with several challenges. For example, instructors taught different styles of tai chi, making it difficult to assess outcomes and enforce safety standards. One of the major tai chi providers used Chen style, which proved too complex and martial and contained movements with a high risk of injury.

Through the NSW Department of Health in Australia, the ACC found out about my work. The world's largest fall prevention study showed conclusively the effect of Tai Chi for Arthritis for fall prevention. In 2003, the ACC invited me to set up their national training system. I started by training Sue Fry and Toi Walker as master trainers; they went on to train hundreds of instructors throughout New Zealand. By 2009, approximately eighty percent of the seven hundred ACC trained instructors used the Tai Chi for Arthritis program. It has delivered tai chi to more than forty thousand New Zealanders over a decade.

I luckily got to visit New Zealand regularly to do more training. During a workshop in 2010, I met Sophia, who migrated from China in 2003. At a tea break with her during a workshop, our conversation turned to the Cultural Revolution in China—another disastrous era under Mao. The Great Famine caused so much damage that Mao officially resigned and moved from the capital, Beijing, to live in Shanghai. Liu Shaoqi and Deng Xioping took over the administration, and they repaired China. Desperation began to fade and the country started to develop again, but Mao did not retire gracefully. He planned an ingenious comeback using the young students as the Red Guards to take control of the government, which threw China into total chaos for an even longer time than the Great Famine. I am so glad that I had left China by then. My friend De almost died during the decade-long Cultural Revolution, and if I'd been there, I probably wouldn't have survived. During those years, Mao did whatever he could to obtain absolute power over the people. Black label people went through hell, with huge numbers of them killed. Even individuals from privileged backgrounds experienced challenging times. Another indescribable catastrophe, the Cultural Revolution inflicted cruel and inhuman treatment on hundreds of millions and claimed the lives of several million. China also experienced destruction of resources, including cultural traditions, buildings and national treasures. Forty years later, the total number of victims remains a mystery.

I am not sure why I happened to make the comment, but I said to Sophia, "You are too young to have experienced the Cultural Revolution." That caused her disposition to change. Tears filled her eyes, and I realized that I'd said something wrong. Sophia hesitated, but then shared her story. When she was five in the midst of the Cultural Revolution, as she played in front of her house, a tall, skinny man came toward her. "Uncle," she said respectfully, like most Chinese children address an older man. "Who are you looking for?" The man stood there silently as tears ran down his cheeks. That was how Sophia met her father. He'd been a high-level Communist official at a famous university. One day, when the Red Guards prepared to send several professors to jail, he stood up to defend them. This brave act not many Chinese would dare to commit got him thrown in jail right before Sophia's birth.

As Sophia described the pain mixed with happiness of their first meeting, I couldn't stop my tears. Her story brought back memories of meeting my father for the first time when I was sixteen. Both Sophia and I understood our luck. During Mao's Great Famine and the Cultural Revolution, countless millions of children became orphans.

After meeting Sophia, the feeling of abandonment that plagued me all my life reared its head. In true Chinese fashion, I always blamed myself for what happened, wondering again and again what I did to deserve the fate of being left behind in China while my mother and siblings went home to Vietnam. For many years I tried piecing together what I would have become and how I would have felt about myself if I'd grown up with my parents and siblings. This curiosity drove me to grill my family when I finally met them about the details of their lives. I eagerly gathered information about how they lived in an attempt to reconstruct the setting within which I should have grown up. I always imagined that growing up with my natural family would have been wonderful. I definitely wouldn't have undergone the starvation, discrimination, and deprivation that began shortly after Mother left me in China.

In later years, as I developed my inner self and with my medical training, I came to accept and like who I am. If I had gone home with my mother, I wouldn't have experienced being raised by my kind and gentle aunt, whose caring heart loved me more than any mother I've ever known. Aunt's total and unconditional love shaped me into who I am. For many years, I regarded the emotional and caring part of me as my weakness. A man is not supposed to feel too deeply or cry. It took me years of internal growing to reach a maturity where I see these traits as the greatest gifts my aunt bestowed upon me.

I have completely shed the abandoned feeling; now it is quite the reverse. I feel fortunate to have experienced such a challenging life and to have grown up with my aunt, grandmothers, cousins, and friends in China. I've been a part of so many people's lives, and these experiences wouldn't have come about without the China experience. Now rather than focus on the life that wasn't, I embrace the life that is, including my ability to share tai chi with people around the world.

My relationship with my mother was mixed. While she made me feel deeply ashamed when I first met her, it was she who urged me to become a doctor. When I did become a physician, Mother no longer felt ashamed of me. And after I started producing instructional tai chi videos and then DVDs, she surprised me by learning my Tai Chi for Health program. In 2013, at the age of ninety-one, doctors diagnosed her with a terminal condition. Her bone marrow stopped producing blood cells. The doctors discharged her from the hospital after the last transfusion and put her in a home hospice care program.

I visited her several times until her death in January 2013. Toward the end, I visited her every day. She appeared pale, confused, and tired and had her good and bad moments. Sometimes she remembered me and sometimes she didn't. On the fifth day of visiting, one of her caretakers told me she used to do my Seated Tai Chi for Arthritis by following my instructional DVD with my sister when she visited. The caregiver told me that since her illness, she'd been too tired to do the movements but turned on the DVD to show me. To our surprise, Mother started following the exercises. I sat down to do the movements with her, and the caregivers joined in.

Many caregivers have told me that they use my Seated Tai Chi for Arthritis program in aged care, retirement homes, and rehab settings. I've heard of cases where the clients start doing the program and then the staff and relatives join in. The energy and bonding makes everyone feel better. I hadn't experienced this phenomenon personally until that visit with my mother. As we followed the exercises, Mother smiled and became energized. This got the caregiver excited, too. Mother would look at the TV screen, follow the movement, and then smile at me. I looked back at her and followed my own image on the screen and then she would look up as if to question, "Which one is the real you?" We did the tai chi program for an hour. The caregiver told me that prior to that, Mother hadn't been able to stay awake for more than minutes at a time. I felt overwhelmed with a profound sense of bonding with her at this final phase of her life. Something happened at that moment that filled the void in those missing years. By sharing tai chi's power with my mother, I was able to let go of the resentment I'd carried all of those years about being abandoned.

Another region of the globe where Tai Chi for Health has made its mark is the UK. Initially, many traditional tai chi teachers there found it difficult to accept our training methods, which made it challenging to bring them the instructor training workshops. Fortunately, some visionary tai chi teachers in parts of the UK and Europe attended my workshops. Margaret Brade, an international business lawyer turned CEO of Age UK in Stockport, came to one of my workshops. Age UK is a national semigovernmental charity body in the UK. The mission of the organization is to improve the quality of life for people over fifty, which is the same vision as Tai Chi for Health, except we include all ages. Margaret offered to coordinate a workshop, and that proved the turning point in the UK. Passionate about tai chi and helping people, Margaret also possesses great organizational skills.

In September 2006, while coordinating a Tai Chi for Arthritis instructor training workshop in Stockport, Manchester, Margaret e-mailed me: "Paul, I am inundated with participants. Can you stay another two days to run a second workshop?" I told her, "Of course." A few weeks later, she e-mailed me again asking about conducting a third. I ended up changing my itinerary three times in order to teach four two-day workshops in succession. I'd never conducted four consecutive workshops before.

I apply tai chi principles to many of life's challenges. They keep me mentally balanced, focused on the moment, and able to connect with and enjoy the task at hand, such as working with two hundred workshop participants, some of whom attended all four consecutive workshops. The participants ranged from tai chi novices to experienced teachers and high-level tai chi practitioners. Finding a way to share useful techniques and information in a way that's easy for novices to understand and that challenges more advanced participants proved challenging. By using tai chi principles during the workshops, I listened to what people wanted and offered a win-win outcome for everyone. On the eighth day, when I looked at the beaming participants, I felt drained yet at the same time energized, and totally fulfilled.

Another major challenge loomed for me during my years of practicing medicine and teaching tai chi. Patients understandably deserted me when I took too much time off work. Since starting my medical practice, I enjoyed the friendship of thousands of patients. I felt privileged that they entrusted me with their care, so when I began traveling more frequently and they gradually left me, I experienced sadness. It took years to build up my practice and I cared about my patients very much, so it felt like I lost good friends. For me, letting go of personal feelings is always extremely challenging.

Sometimes I make decisions that negatively affect the bottom line. For instance, I couldn't resist holding a workshop in the Philippines. My medical partner, Richard, grew up there and warned me about not getting paid. He was correct about nonpayment, and I had to cover my expenses, but I believe less-developed countries can benefit from tai chi, if not even more so. When life is hard, everyone can use more inner strength and health to work toward a better place. Many came to my workshop in the Philippines, which offered me a chance to make a positive change in people's lives.

I also initially experienced difficulty with the financial aspects of the annual workshops. The second annual workshop I conducted in Monterey, California, proved a financial disaster. I lost so much money that even working double time couldn't compensate for it. The hotel cost too much for us tai chi instructors. As a result, I almost stopped doing the annual workshop in the US, but many people urged me to try one more year, so we held the next workshop in New College of Florida in Sarasota, where things cost less. That year, 2005, I felt overwhelmingly happy to break even. By the next year we had a waiting list of participants and even built up a reserve to offer scholarships and discounts for attendees in need. Even in 2009 during the global economic meltdown that hit the US economy especially hard, while half of the conferences around the country canceled due to lack of attendance, we experienced a full registration at our Memphis, Tennessee, workshop. That told me people do care about their health and wellness and enjoy what we have to offer.

Anyone who loves traveling would think I have a dream job. But the truth is I'd rather stay home and spend time with my family, or in my medical practice or garden. My love for working with tai chi people keeps me going from country to country. In the early days, I arrived at an airport, conducted a workshop the next day, and flew out the following day. With this schedule, I only saw the city from a moving vehicle. Initially I held four workshops during two weeks. After expenses, the remuneration worked out to half of my doctor's earnings. It proved manageable, and I always worked harder once home to make up for any budgetary shortfalls.

Because of my motion sickness and arthritis, the latter of which can become painful when I sit for long periods, traveling challenges me. My luggage is heavy, as I take my computer, cameras, video cameras, and tripods, along with two months' worth of clothing and necessities. One day near the end of a tour, I thought about how living out of a suitcase can be quite freeing. *Why do I need a house full of things,* I thought? Although when important possessions are in a suitcase, losing it can be disastrous.

Airlines often lose luggage, but it usually shows up the next day. One time when I arrived at JFK Airport and my luggage didn't, I remained unworried the first day, but became concerned enough by the second day to call the airline, which proved a frustrating experience. I started with a voice recognition computer that could barely understand my English, so it took ten minutes just to speak to a real person. The customer service representative—who answered from a call center in India—and I experienced trouble understanding one another. The person followed a script and acted polite, but the conversation solved nothing. Day after day I called, only to be told that they found my luggage in Jacksonville, Florida, and it was headed to JFK, but rather than making its way back to New York, it kept returning to Florida, and no one could explain why.

My tai chi training helped me not get too angry and to accept the loss. I could live without the clothes, but losing the all-important files on my hard disk and my favorite teapot really bothered me. I bought replacement clothes and a suitcase, and I went to a martial arts store to purchase a pair of tai chi shoes. The owner recognized me because of my videos and to my pleasant surprise sold me the shoes at cost.

By the eighth day, I thought almost certainly I could forget about getting back my luggage when I saw on TV that a senator became so irate about an airline losing his luggage that he abused the airport staff. I also had to move on to Connecticut for a tai chi workshop. When I arrived in Connecticut, the local workshop coordinator, Marty Kidder, greeted me. He was recently retired from the navy and landed at my Monterey workshop in a naval commander's helicopter. A most resourceful person, he has a solution when you have a problem. When he asked how I was doing, I couldn't help blurting out, "I would feel better if I had my teapot."

When I told Marty what happened, he said, "Jacksonville? Do you know you have a tai chi student there? She lives close to the airport." The student was Maureen Miller, a retired bank manager and a part-time editor. Maureen and her husband, Craig, an artist, are exceptionally nice and resourceful, as I found out when I got to know them later. Craig ended up finding my suitcase at the Jacksonville Airport in lost property right before they incinerated it. It turns out that the luggage tag contained a computer error that made the luggage keep returning to Jacksonville. After all of those trips, the luggage tag eventually fell off, so it went to lost property.

Who says lost luggage is a bad thing? Craig and Maureen became great friends. Maureen is a fabulous editor, who later cowrote and edited my revised version of *Teaching Tai Chi Effectively*. She enhanced the book immeasurably and Craig added a touch of class with his wonderful illustrations.

When I got my luggage, I rejoiced at regaining my little teacups and teapot, which travel with me everywhere. The refined art of making Chinese tea is called kung fu tea. Kung fu became misunderstood in the Western world as meaning a martial art, but in Chinese it means a skill one does well, usually referring to something manual that requires much practice. Kung fu tea refers to the art and skill of making tea.

Before the famine in China, I experienced my most wonderful times there during evenings spent on the top floor of the terraced house where the adults made kung fu tea while my granduncle told fascinating stories. One evening when I felt unwell with a fever, Grandmother told me to lie down in bed to rest and forbade me from going to the top floor. Sneaking upstairs and hiding in the shadows, I took great pleasure in hearing granduncle's "forbidden" stories that night. I've always loved the potential to escape through stories, and kung fu tea and stories make a perfect match.

Once I left China, life became so full I forgot all about kung fu tea until a visit to Malaysia in 1983. After a great meal with friends, I felt full from the sweet, sticky rice pudding, so I took a walk and came across a cart where a pretty lady demonstrated kung fu tea, beautiful carved trays, and delicate teacups. After a satisfying meal, kung fu tea gives a great finish and is one of the nicest moments you can imagine. Making the tea involves an elaborate process that starts with selecting the utensils. The teapots are about the size of a small fist and are made from dark and dense purple clay only found in one region of China. You can tell you have a genuine purple clay teapot if when you gently knock the lid against the body, it sounds metallic. They are highly valued teapots, because the clay keeps the heat and preserves the taste. The cups are refined and resemble tiny sake cups, and the tea is pure and strong, like an authentic Italian espresso.

The tea tasting in Malaysia brought back those happy memories from my childhood, so I bought a teapot, cups, teas, and equipment. The lot cost me two hundred and fifty dollars. Since then I've made kung fu tea almost every day, and I have a travel set. My love of tea brought me to the magnificent Wuyi tea Mountains as I traveled full circle to China in 2014. My tea is a connection between East and West and an integral part of my past and present. I love the art of making tea and the delicate taste. But most of all, I love sharing tea with my tai chi friends.

Barcelona is one of my favorite cities to visit when I travel. One morning while in Hong Kong getting ready to go to the airport for a flight to Spain, I noticed a mole under my left toenail that I hadn't seen before. I recalled a patient I'd treated with a mole under his left fingernail. It turned out to be melanoma, and he only lived two years. For thirty-five percent of Asians who develop a mole under a nail, it is melanoma. I took a photo of the mole and e-mailed it to my dermatologist in Sydney. A classmate who is a pathologist in Hong Kong, Rob Collins, also took a look. He advised me to go home immediately and have a biopsy of the mole at the Sydney melanoma clinic.

Rob's advice scared me enough to abandon flying to Barcelona. I arranged for master trainers Jef and Roberto to take over the workshop and flew straight home. The doctor did a biopsy, and I waited anxiously for the results over the weekend. At that time I realized how my patients must feel waiting for results. Not until it happened to me did I realize how painful the process is. I sat at home sweating about the outcome and wondering what I'd do with my two years if I ended up being one of the thirty-five percent.

The soul-searching led me to appreciate my family and my life much more deeply. It also confirmed and rekindled my desire to bring Tai Chi for Health to the world and to spend more time creating permanent material like videos and books. That weekend of waiting and worrying sowed the seeds for me to write my *Teaching Tai Chi Effectively* book and produce more instructional DVDs.

Happily, my lab results came out fine. While I missed a great workshop, the outcome of the weekend proved significant. Soul-searching when you realize the limitation of life wakes you up to focus on what matters most.

CHAPTER 25

COMING FULL CIRCLE

With time and patience the mulberry leaf
becomes a silk gown.
— Chinese proverb

I've always loved reading. A good book is a priceless treasure and just holding one in my hands fills me with happiness. During my childhood in China, reading materials were precious and scarce. In today's society, it's hard to imagine not being able to afford a book, visit a library, or log on to the Internet, but back then I had access to few written materials. If children ever lingered in bookshops, shop assistants chased them away. The modern café bookshops where you can stay for as long as you like and drink your tea and use free Internet would have been heavenly back then!

Books mean so much to me and have transformed my life in many ways. For a long time, writing one seemed an impossible achievement, but after producing videos, I began to think about the possibility.

In 1999, at the very first annual workshop in Sydney, forty-five participants from all walks of life came to learn about the life-transforming powers of tai chi. One morning as I explained how the *qi* flows from the Bai Hui acupuncture point to Hui Yin, I realized that my audience might not know these names. To avoid being presumptuous, I asked if anyone knew what these terms signified. A middle-aged man who looked like a typical English academic raised his hand and answered, "They are two acupuncture points; one at the top of the head and one at the bottom between the legs." His answer made me realize not to ever underestimate the audience.

Though I thought the workshop attendee might be a tai chi teacher or a holistic health professional, Tony Coyle turned out to be an international business executive, working for a large pharmaceutical company. We took our sandwiches and went to a quiet corner to talk during lunchtime. As it turned out, Tony also has the same passion about writing books. I told him that I wanted to write the book *Tai Chi for Arthritis*.

"I will help you, Paul," said Tony, who asked me to visualize the end product.

"I want the book to be in every bookshop," I told him.

"We need to work backward on each step to see how to get to the end result," said Tony, who devised a step-by-step strategy for my venture and guided me along the way.

Step one, and the greatest challenge, was finding a publisher. During my research about publishing, I read about a famous author who tested how publishers worked by sending manuscript copies of his award-winning book to twenty publishers with a pseudonym. They responded by returning his manuscript, mostly untouched, with a standard "no thank you" letter. Some didn't bother to reply. Even his publisher returned the manuscript with a "no thank you" note. Book publishing seemed worse than the video business. I found it virtually impossible to find an open door. Despite the successful sales of my video around the world and the growing interest in tai chi, no publisher showed any interest.

Keith Anderson, the manager of the video catalogue for *Reader's Digest* who helped me introduce my video to his colleagues around the world, referred me to the managing director of Dorling Kindersley (DK) in Australia, Bob Mansfield. DK was a major global publisher with a big presence in Australia. Enthusiastic about the book, Bob delegated Rosemary McDonald, the chief editor, to work with me. By another stroke of luck, Rosemary was not only very nice, she also had arthritis. DK offered me a contract and asked me to change the title to *Overcoming Arthritis*, which I reluctantly agreed to do.

Soon after, DK teetered on the edge of bankruptcy, so Penguin bought the company. This resulted in dramatic changes. Within six months, only two of the original one hundred-plus employees remained. Prior to the turn of events at DK, I'd found a cowriter, Judith Horstman, the author extraordinaire who wrote *Arthritis Foundation's Guide to Alternative Therapies.*

When the changes occurred at DK, we faced a quandary. We'd written the book, but since we signed a contract and received an advance prior, the project remained suspended. Trying to contact anyone at DK proved impossible, because most of the staff had been laid off. We found the circumstances quite frustrating. Our contract restricted us from seeking another publisher, so we had a wonderful book right in front of us and a contract collecting dust.

One year later out of the blue, Penny from the new DK management team called me. DK's research team had discovered tai chi to be an up-and-coming topic, so they dusted off the contract and gave us an additional advance. Overjoyed, we worked diligently to prepare the material in record time. Judith's experience and magical writing gave the book a platinum finish. DK published the book in 2002, and the next year they produced a Japanese and Dutch translation. Becoming an author meant so much to me—like a dream come true. What a great feeling imagining people around the world reading my book and gaining benefits and knowledge.

In my family practice, I enjoy interacting with my patients face-to-face and found helping them rewarding. Tai Chi for Health empowers people to improve their health, and learners and practitioners get what they put in. The more they practice, the more health benefits and enjoyment they gain. I found over the years that it's more fulfilling empowering people than just helping them. My fulfillment multiplied exponentially when I found that millions of people practiced my Tai Chi for Health program.

It had been twelve years since we made the first instructional Tai Chi for Arthritis video. We'd gathered a lot of feedback regarding the video over the years, so it seemed like the right time to update the instructional DVD. The decision proved a bit challenging, as the DVD sold well around the world and had been dubbed in six different languages. The Arthritis Foundation US offered to collaborate with me, though, and this was the first time the organization wanted to work with any anyone outside the foundation to produce an instructional DVD for an exercise program. The offer was too good to refuse, so I took up the project.

Chief medical officer of the Arthritis Foundation US, Dr. Patience White, spoke first on the DVD. She announced: "We at the AF are excited that you are interested in TCA brought to you by Dr. Paul Lam, a worldwide, renowned expert in tai chi. . . . It is very safe and will relieve your pain as well as increase your mobility and muscle strength," said the rheumatologist. "The program has been shown to reduce the risk of falling, which is a big issue for people as we get older."

The resulting 2009 version of my instructional DVD took advantage of new knowledge and DVD technology and as a result is much more useful for learners. I've met many people who learned solely from this DVD, and I'm impressed with how well they've done. I find no reward more satisfying than seeing the wonderful fruit of my work.

In 2010, I was overjoyed when the president and CEO of the Arthritis Foundation US, Dr. John Klippel, reviewed my book, *Teaching Tai Chi Effectively*, and wrote: "This remarkable book needs to come with a warning. 'Beware, Dr. Lam's extraordinary passion for tai chi and creating teachers will change you and the world.' It could not come at a more opportune time as we search for practical and effective solutions to the epidemic of chronic disease. The role of tai chi to influence the course of most if not all chronic diseases such as arthritis, diabetes, and heart disease has very much come front and center as an important healthcare strategy. Bravo, a new day cometh."

The latest research shows that almost all chronic conditions are caused by unhealthy lifestyles. In the Western world, ninety percent of the population dies directly or indirectly from chronic conditions like arthritis, diabetes, and heart disease. Therefore, a program like Tai Chi for Health is an ideal and important tool for health and wellness of the future. That was why Dr. Klippel, being up-to-date with medical research, said that tai chi is coming to the front and center of health strategy for the future.

My first book with Judith Horstman proved a great experience. I learned I can be a good writer, and I have a burning passion to share. After *Overcoming Arthritis*, I wrote several other books: *Tai Chi for Beginners and the 24 Forms* and *Tai Chi for Diabetes*. Of all the books, *Teaching Tai Chi Effectively* proved the most challenging to write.

Over the last thirty years as I've conducted more than five hundred workshops and taught more than ten thousand instructors, I came to realize that I've most likely taught more tai chi instructors than any other teacher. Often I met instructors who had good tai chi skills but did poorly with their teaching. Good tai chi skills and an enthusiasm to teach are important components to teaching effectively, but aren't enough on their own. Teaching is a skill.

A way to look at this is that a good tai chi program is like quality fresh food and an instructor is like a chef. The learner is the customer in a restaurant. No matter how good the food is, a lousy chef can spoil it, but with a good program and a good instructor, learners enjoy high-quality "food" (tai chi). Today there is a wealth of good research on effective teaching techniques that didn't exist for the ancient Chinese teachers of tai chi.

Like my father, I have always loved teaching, and I thought it would be easy to write a book about teaching tai chi. But writing is another skill. While there are many similar methods for teaching, no matter the topic, there are specific methodologies for each specific field. Traditional tai chi teachers often place low emphasis on the teaching method, because they often assume that good tai chi skill equals good teaching. When I wrote the book on *teaching tai chi effectively*, I once again felt like a pioneer, and I learned a great deal from the challenge. I worked hard to incorporate modern knowledge of teaching, my personal experience, and the tai chi principles to create an effective set of tai chi teaching methodology.

Once I started working on the book, I devoted any time I could find to write, think about the content of the book, and perform research. After five years, four major rewrites—with much help from my editor Diane Cornwell, many friends, tai chi and medical colleagues—Teaching Tai Chi Effectively published in 2006.

There is nothing more effective at crystalizing your thinking than writing a book. Writing helped me to understand tai chi and teach it at a much deeper level. The methodology I present is practical and so effective that if I teach and the outcome isn't as favorable as I like, I ask myself if I've followed my book. When I try to take shortcuts, the resulting outcome isn't as favorable as it could be.

Tai chi is full of long-established traditions from China, but the world has changed. The purpose and focus of learning tai chi has shifted from martial arts to improving health and wellness. Like any art, tai chi can benefit from modernization, which gives it a new and more useful focus. My teaching tai chi book illustrates a major deviation from the "traditional" type of teaching. It shifts from teacher-orientated to learner-orientated methods, the latter of which constitute the coaching style of teaching. Coaching enables the instructor to teach the way that learners learn best. The coach is a friend, a consultant, an advisor, and he or she empowers participants to reach their goals. The learner-orientated method requires more time and effort from the teacher initially, but in the end not only do the students learn more and enjoy themselves, the teacher finds instructing more fulfilling because of the students' achievement and enjoyment. Happy students return to the teacher and bring more friends.

Since 2000, my authorized master trainers and I have trained more than twenty-five thousand instructors in many countries, including the US, UK, New Zealand, Sweden, China, Taiwan, Norway, Canada, Swaziland, Venezuela, Italy, Sri Lanka, Philippines, Vietnam, many Middle East countries, the Netherlands, Belgium, Spain, and South Korea. More than five million people are practicing my program every day. Health-related governmental departments around the world support us and some partner with us. I am especially proud of recognition from the world's foremost disease control and prevention organization—the US Centers for Disease Control and Prevention (www.CDC.gov). I was thrilled when after years of investigation, the CDC recommended my Tai Chi for Arthritis program for fall prevention in 2013. The organization made this decision on the strength of medical evidence, and consistent and high quality support, training, and instructional materials available from the program.

Scientific evidence regarding tai chi continues to accumulate and has increased exponentially during recent years. Between 2000 and April 2012, 544 articles published on the subject compared to just 48 during the prior ten years. Overwhelming evidence now shows that tai chi is a highly effective exercise for health and wellness; including promoting better balance, fall prevention, relief for arthritis pain, improvement in immunity, stress reduction, improvement in blood pressure, as well as overall wellness and health. The majority of medical studies are based on shorter sets of forms like my Tai Chi for Health programs, which were designed for health reasons. Over the years, medical evidence has shown modernized tai chi programs to be effective for health.

We held the first ever Tai Chi for Health International Conference in South Korea on December 4–7, 2006. Medical experts, research scientists, doctors, and tai chi instructors from many countries attended. I had the honor of serving as the opening keynote speaker in recognition of my work for Tai Chi for Health. After presenting my work, I received a standing ovation.

Working in different countries with people of varying cultures enables me to see the differences and similarities among all of us. The essence of human nature remains the same. Everywhere I go, I meet people who once they tried a Tai Chi for Health program, embraced its simplicity and health benefits, and the enjoyment of practicing resonated and motivated them to become a part of the worldwide chain spreading the vision.

As the Tai Chi for Health vision rapidly grew, the need for a structure to support it became evident. Working with me, Dr. Pam Kircher chaired the steering committee to set up the Tai Chi for Health Institute, founded in 2009, to empower people to improve their health and wellness. It is a nonprofit organization focused on educational aspects of the program's purpose. I was elected to direct the institute.

Caroline Demoise, a lady with a deep spiritual understanding of life, often has good ideas. She considered how the Tai Chi for Health programs so effectively helped many people, but pointed out how many other people didn't know of the program's existence. In 2006, she suggested doing a documentary and enlisting the input of experts, tai chi students, and teachers.

I loved the idea, despite being warned about the cost of the undertaking and the challenges of marketing the film. I started by buying a professional portable video camera and learning how to use it with the help of Anton, my video professional. The camera and required tripod proved costly, but I needed high-quality equipment in order to interview tai chi experts and researchers and practitioners around the world. At twenty-two pounds, the tripod weighed quite a bit, but I managed to haul it around along with my luggage and the camera, despite the fact that thirty-two years before I could barely carry my doctor bag to home visits.

The Great Wall of China seemed the perfect place to film the segment "What is tai chi?" for the documentary. Luckily, my friend and tai chi colleague, Rani Hughes, came to help me. We employed a chauffeur to get us to our location. He and Rani helped me carry equipment to the Great Wall, though I took the heaviest load. By the time we reached halfway to the wall, the driver, though much younger than me, appeared terribly strained, as if he might have a heart attack, and Rani looked breathless. I told the driver to rest until he recovered. I took his luggage and some of Rani's and led the way up to the wall. The Great Wall has many steps, but they never seemed so steep and endless as they did on that day.

When we arrived at the top of the Great Wall of China and started to film, I became worried when two Chinese policemen walked into the area. They spoke with the driver, who finally caught up without luggage. He told me that they were curious and offered to help by controlling the crowds of onlookers so we could film without people walking onto our set. Their assistance helped tremendously in keeping people from moving in front of the camera.

Weather conditions that day proved windy and numbingly cold at minus forty-one degrees Fahrenheit (minus five degrees centigrade). Under my heavy jacket, hat, and gloves, I wore my tai chi pajamas (the silk tai chi performance clothing you see in competitions and movies). Thin silk pajamas don't offer much protection against the numbing cold, even when worn with thermal long johns, so I marshaled my all-powerful inner *qi* energy to keep the blood from freezing in my veins. When we had everything ready, I stripped off my protective clothing and rushed to do my tai chi for the camera. After each set (or when my hands and feet became too painful to bear), I rushed to put all of my layers back on to warm up a little before another set. When we thought we'd finished, Rani noticed that I neglected to tuck in the pajama cord on the silk trousers, so it dangled down, which meant filming the whole sequence again.

We filmed different styles of tai chi in other locations, from the rugged Matterhorn in Switzerland to the tranquil botanic gardens in Christchurch, New Zealand, and in front of the Stockholm Palace in Sweden. When it came time to show how tai chi affected the lives of those who practiced the art, many people wished to tell their stories, so I ended up with hundreds of hours of incredible footage about how tai chi empowered people of all ages to wellness. We also interviewed tai chi teachers and medical researchers, including Professor Rhayun Song and Professor John Edmonds. The experts I interviewed were generous with their time, as were charitable organizations like Age UK; the Araptis Foundation; health departments around the world; and various arthritis and diabetes foundations including Arthritis Victoria, whose CEO, Natalie Savin, spoke enthusiastically about the Tai Chi for Arthritis program and the ACC, a national government department in New Zealand that funded the teaching of tai chi classes across the country.

After we completed the interviews, we worked hard to meld all we'd gathered into a cohesive fifty-minute documentary. I employed one of my patients, Deanne Sheerin, who writes and produces national TV episodes, to work on the film while Eunice, who is a brilliant writer, joined me to write the script and thought up the title, "The Road to Health and Harmony."

I tried everything I could to market the film at festivals and to television stations. People showed interest, but no one bought the documentary. Though I felt guilty about inflicting a financial loss on my family, the countless hours I spent during those two years greatly rewarded me. Making the documentary put me in flow so often, and I learned so much about filming, people, and tai chi. Talking to the many people positively impacted by my Tai Chi for Health programs gave me immense satisfaction. How I wish everyone could see the documentary.

Creating the documentary that started at the Great Wall of China and represents my life's work proved a fitting precursor to recent journeys I've made back home to China. I brought close members of my Tai Chi for Health family with me to visit the village where

I grew up and my boarding school in Chaozhou. They saw the little storage room Aunt and I called home and looked out at the recent renovation of Chaozhou and the West Lake. Most importantly, they met my Chinese family—Zheng's children and grandchildren. The harmony and energy created by my two families fusing into one stirred emotions of gratitude and wonder deep in my heart.

I escaped China as a teenager in a journey fraught with danger. If we'd been caught, there would have been no second chance. I never dreamed that I would freely return on my own terms with people from different parts of the world. Yet there I stood, a mature and successful physician, teacher of tai chi and researcher, traveling back in time with my tai chi family from many countries to show them the wonders of China—not only for my own entertainment and edification, but to broaden their perspectives and improve their skill.

Of all the countries where I've spread the Tai Chi for Health vision, Singapore proved one of the most challenging to enter. I have great admiration for Singapore, which is one of the few governments that has an absolutely spotless reputation against corruption. The people are friendly, honest, hardworking, and self-driven, and the government is efficient and caring. Singapore is multicultural and the country demonstrates that different races and cultures can coexist harmoniously and successfully. Most of the people are Chinese, which makes me proud that the Chinese culture could incubate and sustain an exceptional community for all citizens to grow and enjoy. Singapore is a shining example for the world in so many senses of the word. It's little wonder that many Asian countries look up to it and send teams to learn from Singaporeans.

The culture of working hard does bring some negativity. Singaporeans often become highly stressed from the pressure from within and outside themselves. I have great affinity for them, because I am also obsessed with cleanliness and working hard. Self-driven people are often better able to motivate themselves to practice tai chi regularly. Tai chi is an excellent antidote for the pressure brought on by hard work, as it brings balance badly needed at times of extreme challenge.

It did not matter how much I like Singapore or how hard and how many times I tried, nothing happened for many years until April 2, 2007, when I received an e-mail from the country's chairman of the National Arthritis Foundation, Professor P. H. Feng, referring to the Tai Chi for Arthritis study that had been published in *Arthritis Care & Research.* Impressed at how the study showed that practicing tai chi relieves arthritis pain and improves the ability to perform daily activities, Professor Feng invited me to conduct a public talk and an instructors' training workshop.

Events moved quickly from there. Professor Feng introduced me to Professor Raymond Lau, who has a personal interest in tai chi. He became my translator and assisted me with what would be many packed instructor training workshops and public lectures. I'm honored that many of the attendees of my instructor trainings in Singapore are Chinese tai chi teachers who have taught tai chi full time and some have been teaching even longer than me. Working with them truly validates my confidence that the Tai Chi for Health vision has much to offer.

Professor Lau lectures at the National University of Singapore and is a rheumatologist and a visionary person. We became good friends, shared many ideas, and stimulated each other's thinking. One day he said to me, "For just about every important matter in life there is a simple, common truth, that would be universal. Knowing that common truth would give us a clear direction to understand how everything works." I have always thought in a similar way. There is a simple common core truth at the heart of every art and science. I find it in life everywhere. For example, certain core values of human nature like love and the need to be loved apply to anyone from any country and culture. The essential tai chi principles hold true in so many aspects of life.

Singapore is well located in the world's geography. No matter where I begin in my global workshop tour, I find Singapore to be a convenient and great place to start.

For their Wellness Day in May 2010, which is organized by the People's Association, a national department of the Singapore government, they invited me to hold a teaching session at their headquarters. My tai chi colleagues and friends rallied together to help me prepare for the event, which they initially thought would draw four hundred people. To everyone's surprise, so many people wanted to come that they had to cut off attendance at two thousand.

They planned the event for the early morning hours, because Singapore weather is too hot past nine a.m. for older adults to exercise outdoors. Precisely at eight a.m., forty-five buses brought in two thousand participants, who went through security and lined up by eight-thirty a.m., with each twenty persons assigned a Tai Chi for Health instructor. The planning resembled a military operation; I don't think such precision and timing could be accomplished in any other country.

When I walked onstage at precisely eight thirty a.m., the cheers suddenly sounded like jeers and threw me back all those years to the Midnight Terrors. Just as quickly, my tai chi training pulled me into the present. Without missing a step, I embraced the good will and positive energy of the audience and proceeded to share the excitement and power of tai chi.

As I looked out at the sea of smiling faces on that monumental morning, I experienced an overwhelming joy knowing that Aunt would have been so proud of me.

AFTERWORD

I shake my head sometimes and wonder how a deprived, starving child from a little Chinese village ended up empowering millions to improve their health. On deep reflection, one theme stands out. In those difficult early years filled with potentially cataclysmic events, my aunt showered me with unconditional love that saved me from destruction. Love gave my life value and formed a firm foundation from which I developed inner strength. The bond between us gave me the will to fight against all odds to survive the Great Famine.

I experienced an incredible mixture of challenges in my life, with some so overwhelming they could have broken me. No matter how much mistreatment I endured, I knew at home my aunt would always cherish me. The value of this unconditional love grew as I developed.

Challenges that did not crush me made me grow in strength and skill. Rising from "down under" kindled my fighting spirit. The Empty Period taught me to embrace every opportunity. I learned to cope with culture shock in Hong Kong and Australia and appreciate the best each had to offer.

With my training in Western and Chinese medicine, as the Tai Chi for Health vision grew, I realized I possessed the opportunity and skills to bridge the gaps between Eastern and Western culture and modernize traditional tai chi, making it accessible to everyone. My arthritis, though painful, proved a blessing in disguise as it motivated me to practice and develop a program to help others. As if organized by a powerful underlying force, my unique combination of skills enabled me to conceive and lead the Tai Chi for Health vision.

The modern world is a stressful place, and I increasingly realize how much Tai Chi for Health can do—not just for chronic conditions but for everyone. Self-management and prevention is the best, if not the only way for the future. To enable people to proactively pursue health and wellness, we created Tai Chi for Beginners and

Tai Chi for Energy. Later we built yet another bridge, Tai Chi for Rehabilitation, to help everyone from the simply tired and burned out to those with major health challenges to recover and follow a path to better health and wellness.

Reaching millions proved just the beginning. With the Tai Chi for Health Institute, my colleagues can take over. Our instructors and participants can pass on the baton, helping society reconnect with nature and themselves, improve relationships, and maybe even help make the earth more sustainable for the human race.

I embrace every challenge and love finding ways to listen to and redirect the incoming force. When I practice tai chi, I feel strong and serene from within. I relish my increasing strength and flexibility and value the serenity that tai chi gives me. It is wonderful to hear from people whom I have never met that I have changed their lives for the better. Any energy I expend on my mission is returned to me many times over.

In 2013, I retired from my medical practice. I continue to be involved in medical research and regard myself as a doctor, but now I practice preventative medicine full time. The world is my waiting room and my potential patients are everywhere. With the help of my tai chi colleagues, the size of my practice is unlimited.

I wasn't sure if I was ready for "retirement," but now I realize that I haven't retired, simply refocused. My excitement and energy is unbounded as I devote the rest of my life to the Tai Chi for Health vision. I hope you will join me on my journey and that one day our paths will cross.

CONNECT WITH THE AUTHOR

Dr. Lam enjoys interacting with people interested in wellness and tai chi. Here are his social media links and the best ways to connect with him online.

Website: taichiforhealthinstitute.org/bornstrong
Email: service@tchi.org
Twitter: @ taichihealth
Facebook: www.facebook.com/taichihealth

MY RECIPE FOR HEALTH

I enjoy analyzing all of the factors of a problem and devising a formula to solve it. Using this method to understand how the body and mind function, I worked out Tai Chi for Health programs that help people function in more effective and fulfilling ways. I am thrilled when I discover just the right therapy to solve a person's health challenge.

Ultimately, I love to find a solution to empower people to achieve better health and wellness. I talk to my patients, friends, tai chi colleagues, and participants of my workshops about this topic frequently. Here is a recipe for health that works for me and many of the people with whom I've interacted. Most of these are woven into this book.

The Ingredients:

Positivity
Responsibility
Activity
Engagement
Interaction

1. Positivity

Though it's human nature to highlight the negative, I always try to focus on the positive or bright side. Focusing on difficulties may help us work harder during disasters, but in normal times, negativity can adversely affect our health, thinking, and relationships. By looking for the best qualities in people, I enhance my relationships with them. Everyone likes to be recognized, which bolsters their confidence, resulting in more positive attitudes that lead to more win-win situations.

Whenever I feel down, I remind myself to "*song*" my joints—a tai chi state of gently loosening the joints, thus strengthening the body, inducing serenity and reminding me to stand tall. I may not feel great, but that simple change in posture tricks my mind into feeling less stressed and thinking more upright.

Even during really bad times, being sad does not make matters any better. I find psychologists are helpful when they advise that if you can't be happy, pretend to be, and soon you will be. Even if I can't be happy, it's best to avoid focusing on sadness.

2. Responsibility

I realized in my twenties that I needed to take responsibility for my own health. With crippling arthritis, I could have relied entirely on drugs to keep me relatively pain free. It took dedication to establish a major improvement through tai chi, but on the way I learned that keeping physically and mentally balanced in life provides the best way to cope with arthritis, as well as most matters in life.

As I mature, I take more responsibility for my actions. Whenever something goes wrong, I make an effort not to blame the circumstances and other people—not even the weather. Blaming anything or anyone, including myself, when something goes wrong fails to help me get to a better place. Blame might soothe my insecurity for a little while, but it wastes time and prevents healing. I find it more helpful to focus on analyzing a situation rationally and looking at what was done and what can be improved. My best line of defense is developing inner strength, which reduces my insecurity.

I've also learned to be responsible for my reaction to other's actions. For example, when someone makes a racially discriminative remark, I hold my anger and make a great effort to keep my mind balanced. If that person means to upset me and I become angry, he or she controls me. If the person made an innocent mistake, I would have gotten upset for no reason. Worse still, an angry reaction would harm my relationship with that person. It is my responsibility to stay calm and find the most rational way to deal with life events.

3. Activity

Move it or lose it. If "it" equals physical ability, then I certainly have kept moving it, and I'm far from losing it. I'm now fitter, more flexible, and stronger than many people half my age. I truly enjoy gaining more strength and flexibility as I become older, instead of getting weaker and stiffer. I find excuses to be active. For example, if I forget something in my study on the third floor, I don't wait to accumulate all of the things I have forgotten. I immediately walk up to the study to fetch it. I find excuses to practice tai chi whenever I can. If someone asks me to show them some tai chi, that provides an excellent excuse to practice. Being active applies to mental activity as well, if not more so. I find ways to exercise your mind, but more about that in the next two ingredients.

4. Engagement

I fully immerse myself in most things I do—from my morning practice to working in my office to enjoying an excellent meal with friends. By engaging with activities, goals, and relationships, I feel I'm truly living my life. One of my patients told me that he would do a day's work, come home and not remember anything he had done. The work proved too boring to engage him. He responded by changing his job.

If I'm just doing something to kill time, I am wasting life's most precious gift, and I'm not fully living. I would rather be engaging with a venture, like producing a video, even if it turns out not as well as expected. Not venturing is not living my life as fully as I could. We learn from every experience. The same holds true for relationships. By engaging with others, I gain happiness and excitement that I wouldn't experience without being fully present. I love "having a go" at so many things.

5. Interaction

Studies show that interacting with a lot of people increases our immunity. I have friends all over the globe and take an interest in their culture, views, and personal stories. I strive to make my relationships with others as positive as possible. I take the same stance when representing our group to the community. I have an interest in conservation and the future of our planet and have been taking steps to make my workshops and business environmentally friendly. Though apolitical, I have a keen interest in our democratic system. I firmly believe that the tai chi community has a role to play in the health and well-being of our community and the planet.

A Good Way to Cook It Up

Once I make a decision to proactively take control of my health, I feel better immediately. As I proceed with implementing my decision, every step makes me feel more in control and confident. When I overcome the inertia and persist with regular use of these ingredients, I feel even better. Feeling good about myself is the key to mental health.

From my lifelong learning, I've found that the latest medical research correlates well with the ancient art of tai chi. Tai Chi for Health is an effective tool to enhance all of these five ingredients and helps to put them together in a balanced and harmonious way, like a good chef masterfully combining ingredients.

- By maintaining an upright posture, we "*song*" the joints, especially the spine, which facilitates a positive mind-set. Tai chi principles emphasize physical and mental balance with more positivity balancing out the human nature of being negative.

- Tai chi trains us to control our movements, improve our balance, and achieve serenity of mind or *jing*. This controlled training leads to freedom to move better with greater flexibility. More mobility from improved balance and a more balanced mind lead to thinking more freely. In turn that enhances responsibility for our health and actions.

- Tai chi is an ideal activity that not only stretches, exercises, and strengthens all muscles, ligaments, joints, and internal organs, it also exercises the mind.

- Tai chi is meditation in motion; it facilitates engaging your body and mind, and leads to more mental tranquility.

- Tai chi principles teach us how to interact with others more positively and effectively. By listening to the incoming force, we understand others better. By absorbing the incoming force, we can better redirect others to a win-win solution, thus establishing positive person-to person-relationships. The same rationale can improve interaction between one group of people and another. If a country listens to another, there might be no war.

Tai chi is based on nature and provides many natural ways to conserve our environment. To practice and experience health benefits, there is no need for equipment or to burn carbon.

Practicing Tai Chi for Health offers all of these healthful ingredients. So have a go!

Which Tai Chi for Health Program is Right for You?

Millions of people have found that learning tai chi can be an enjoyable and rewarding experience. As you embark on your tai chi journey, take the time to find the most effective and satisfying way for you to enhance your life with this ancient practice.

1. Ask yourself why you want to learn tai chi. Is your purpose to improve health or for physical and spiritual growth? If your purpose is to improve your health and wellness, most of my Tai Chi for Health programs will work for you. (See item 4 for more explanation.)

2. Consider finding a suitable teacher. Tai chi teachers have different ways of teaching. A good way to determine if a teacher is well-suited for you is to talk to his or her students and the teacher, which will help you determine if the class and teacher resonate with you. You can find a list of instructors trained and certified by my Master Trainers or me on the Tai Chi for Health Institute website at www.tchi.org.

3. Use my instructional DVDs alone if you have difficulty finding a suitable teacher or in conjunction with your class. My DVDs are designed to teach you as though you are in my class. I worked with my medical and tai chi colleagues to design special programs that are safe and effective for beginners and beyond and for people with a variety of medical conditions. Read on to find out which program suits you best.

4. If your reason for learning tai chi is to strengthen your body, improve your mental balance and add harmony to your life, I suggest you start with the Beginners series, and as you become more proficient, progress further through my Intermediate series. Tai Chi for Beginners and Tai Chi for Energy are suitable for most people. Tai Chi for Energy is a combination of Chen and Sun style and is more vigorous than Beginners and slightly more challenging to learn.

If you are recovering from an illness or injury, or looking for an antidote to stress, I recommend my Tai Chi for Rehabilitation program.

If you are a person with:

- arthritis, fibromyalgia, MS, stroke or similar conditions, I recommend the Tai Chi for Arthritis program

- back pain, I recommend the Tai Chi for Back Pain program

- osteoporosis, I recommend the Tai Chi for Osteoporosis program

- diabetes, heart-related problems or similar conditions, I recommend the Tai Chi for Diabetes program

- a lung problem such as asthma, chronic pulmonary obstructive conditions, bronchiectasis, or a weakening condition like chronic fatigue syndrome or fibromyalgia, I recommend the Tai Chi for Arthritis program

- excessive stress and/or depression, I recommend the Tai Chi at Work program

If you are looking for a program for young children that will improve health and coordination, I recommend the Tai Chi 4 Kidz program.

An excellent way to determine which program suits you is to try out the first free lesson of each program. To do this, visit my website at www.taichiproductions.com, find the respective program and click on product information where you will find a free introduction and your first lesson on YouTube.

5. Persevere with your practice. Give yourself time to absorb and understand the essential principles of tai chi. Doing this will enable you to enjoy your practice, gain health benefits, and progress steadily. A good way is to set a regular time daily to practice—even ten minutes is a good start.

Whichever program you chose, I would love to hear from you! You are welcome to write to me through my office at service@tchi.org. It may take me some time to reply, as I receive many emails, but I will reply. If you don't hear from me within a month, send your e-mail again, in case it went into the spam folder.

Below is a list of my instructional materials.

Health Series
The following programs were specially designed by Dr. Paul Lam and his team of medical and tai chi experts for better health. These programs are proven by scientific studies to improve health and quality of life.

Tai Chi for Arthritis
12 Lessons with Dr. Lam – 8 Hours (2 Discs)
This program has been designed specifically for people with arthritis. Recommended by the Centers for Disease Control and Prevention (www.CDC.gov) and supported by Arthritis Foundations around the world, this program is safe and proven to be effective. Take the first step on your journey to better health.

Tai Chi for Arthritis II
6 Lessons with Dr. Lam – 4 Hours

Seated Tai Chi for Arthritis – 2 Hours
This easy, safe, and effective program is suitable for people who are unable to walk or prefer practicing sitting down.

Tai Chi for Rehabilitation
6 Lessons with Dr. Lam – 5 Hours
Dr. Lam has combined his medical and tai chi expertise to create an ideal program to aid recovery from ill health. Physical and occupational therapists may find it a useful tool for their patients/clients. Almost anyone can learn this program to help recover from conditions including stroke, heart disease, injury, surgical procedures, or tiredness and stress. Tai Chi for Rehabilitation will improve health and wellness after recovery. This program is also a great introduction to Tai Chi for Energy and Tai Chi for Diabetes.

Tai Chi for Osteoporosis – 90 mins
Designed to build strength and improve balance. This effective and safe program is based on medical evidence on osteoporosis and fall prevention.

Tai Chi for Diabetes – 90 mins
Designed to help prevent diabetes or improve the control of diabetes by gently increasing physical activities, cellular uptake of glucose, and relaxation. This program is supported by Diabetes Australia.

Tai Chi for Back Pain – 90 mins
This program is proven to relieve back pain. It also aims to restore your ability to work and play and improves health and quality of life. The movements are the same as Tai Chi for Arthritis but presented with emphasis on medical information that is relevant to back pain.

Qigong for Health – 60 mins
Qigong is an exercise especially beneficial for achieving relaxation and building inner energy.

Beginners' Series
This series is designed to empower beginners to improve their health and lifestyles.

Tai Chi for Energy
8 Lessons with Dr. Lam – 5 Hours
Dr. Lam has carefully combined movements from Chen and Sun styles to produce a powerful synergy in Tai Chi for Energy. This program will improve your health and wellness, internal energy, and the ability to manage stress. This is a natural sequel to Tai Chi for Rehabilitation.

Tai Chi for Beginners
8 Lessons with Dr. Lam – 5 Hours
Based on Yang style tai chi, in six easy steps, Dr. Lam teaches the forms from different angles, with close ups, repetitions, and diagrams. It is just like being in his class.

Tai Chi for Older Adults – 110 mins
This easy-to-follow, authentic Yang style tai chi form is specifically designed for older adults.

Tai Chi 4 Kidz – 60 mins

This fun program was designed to develop childrens' bodies and minds by improving their concentration and coordination.

Tai Chi @ Work – 90 mins

Learn how the wisdom of ancient tai chi principles can be applied in today's workplace, turning the burden of stress into a source of strength.

Intermediate Series

Designed to improve your skill and knowledge, these programs are recommended for people with approximately one year of tai chi experience.

Tai Chi for Energy II – Twice the Energy

8 Lessons with Dr. Lam – 5 hours

(The sequel to Tai Chi for Energy) Dr. Lam has added new Chen style movements from the 36 and 56 Forms to enrich your Chen style experience with more sophistication. He explores the mysterious spiral force (Chan Suu Jing) and develops the synergy of both styles to deliver unbelievable power and vitality.

24 Forms – 4 Hours

Based on Yang style, this program is suitable for people of almost any level of physical fitness and age. The book Tai Chi for Beginners and the 24 Forms (B24) complements this DVD and makes learning much easier.

32 Sword Forms – 95 mins

The sword is a beautiful extension of the essential principles of tai chi, based on Yang style.

Sun Style 73 Forms – 4 Hours

Sun style is characterized by its powerful Qigong elements, agile steps, and flowing movements that are ideal for developing inner strength and enhancing healing and relaxation.

Advanced Series
Designed to further enhance your tai chi skill, these programs are recommended for people with two or more years of tai chi experience.

The Combined 42 Forms Part 1 & 2 – 95 mins
Combining the essential principles of the four major tai chi styles, these are the official forms used in major international competitions.

42 Sword Forms – 95 mins
Created to complement the Combined 42 forms, the Sword is a beautiful extension of the essential principles of tai chi.

The 36 Forms – 100 mins
This set is the best known expression of the Chen style. It is characterized by inner power, silk reeling energy, and explosive forces.

Yang Style 40 Forms – 106 mins
This features step-by-step instruction of this popular gentle and graceful set.

Other Products

Tai Chi Music CD
Four beautiful and relaxing pieces of music composed to enhance tai chi practice and performance.

Tai Chi Music CD Vol. 2
Music composed exclusively for Tai Chi for Arthritis, Tai Chi 4 Kidz, Tai Chi for Beginners, and for the Chen, Yang, and Sun styles.

Teaching Tai Chi Effectively – Book
As one of the most experienced and respected of tai chi teachers, Dr. Lam shares simple and proven methods to make tai chi accessible to everyone. The book contains useful material for any tai chi teacher and includes instructions for working with people of different ages and conditions, including those with arthritis and Parkinson's, older adults, and even pregnant women. Thousands

of teachers have adopted Dr. Lam's teaching methods, resulting in dramatic reductions in dropout rates and greater student and teacher enjoyment.

Tai Chi for Beginners & the 24 Forms – Book

This book contains step-by-step instructions and photographs of Six Easy Steps for the Beginners and 24 Forms. It also shows how you can progress to higher levels of tai chi.

Overcoming Arthritis – Book

A practical guide for a more active, pain-free life, this book features Dr. Lam's Tai Chi for Arthritis program.

Tai Chi for Diabetes, Living Well with Diabetes – Book

This book provides practical information on diabetes, as well as the Tai Chi for Diabetes program, with step-by-step instructions and photographs of the movement.

Handbooks – Tai Chi for Arthritis, Tai Chi for Diabetes

These handbooks are designed to help you learn the program in conjunction with the relevant DVD.